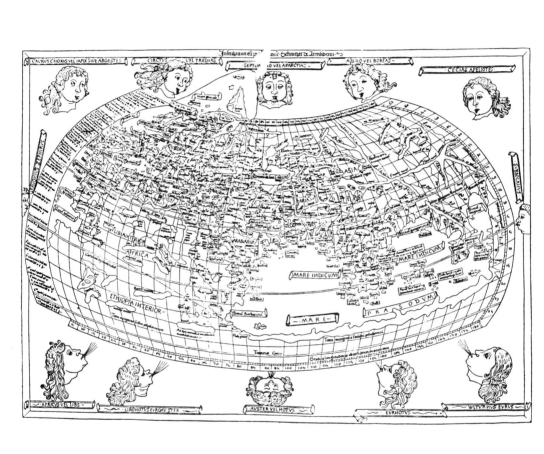

GLOBAL OUTLOOK 2000

An Economic, Social, and Environmental Perspective

by

THE UNITED NATIONS

UNITED NATIONS PUBLICATIONS

United Nations Publications
ST/ ESA /215/Rev 1
Sales No. E. 90. II.C.3
ISBN 92-1-109118-7

CONTENTS

FOREWORD BY
THE SECRETARY-GENERAL

ONE OF THE principal purposes of the United Nations, as defined in Article I of the Charter, is to ". . . achieve international cooperation in solving international problems of an economic, social, cultural, or humanitarian character." To that end, the Charter directs the Organization to promote higher standards of living, full employment and conditions of economic and social progress and development.

Since its inception, the United Nations has accordingly offered a standing machinery and framework for international dialogue on major economic and social problems. It is in no small measure due to this ongoing debate that the international community today gives a high priority to the cause of development in our increasingly interdependent world.

In support of this dialogue, the United Nations provides a wide range of services. These include the collection of economic and social data, research and analysis of current developments, the identification, monitoring and assessment of emerging global social and economic trends and the definition and evaluation of alternative policies.

Global Outlook 2000 is the outgrowth of a study undertaken for the General Assembly of the United Nations. It draws on research and projections prepared in many parts of the United Nations system and represents the Secretariat's most recent effort to review and assess on-going changes in global economic and social conditions and the outlook for the 1990s. Particular attention is devoted to the current and anticipated predicament of developing countries. Many of them have indeed made great strides in improving their economic and social conditions over the last three decades. A large number, however, have experienced a drastically slower pace of progress in the 1980s and, in some, there were dramatic and significant reversals. As a result, absolute poverty has increased in Africa and Latin America.

This work explores some possible policy changes and initiatives which could be taken by individual countries and at the international level in order to reverse this process of stagnation or decline and promote the long-term sustained and sustainable development of all countries. Improved and coordinated policy actions are clearly required to meet the challenges posed by such global concerns as widespread poverty and underdevelopment, the physical environment and related problems in the energy and agricultural sectors; the rapid pace of technological change and its consequent impact on the national and international structures of production, trade and finance; and the continuing rapid growth of population and resulting challenges for continued improvement in education, health and social well-being.

The Charter of the United Nations encourages us to think in terms of common humanity and shared basic human needs. The web of ties which locks all parts of the world together, the urgency of finding solutions to social and economic problems and the increasing salience of such global issues as food security, the environment, energy and international finance, to name but a few, further underline the need for a global approach. It is my sincere hope that *Global Outlook 2000* will reach a large audience and that it will command the attention of concerned policy-makers, non-governmental organizations and members of the academic community. I also trust that its many insights and recommendations will enhance our joint efforts in laying down the foundations of the better societies which we all wish to build for the decades ahead.

JAVIER PÉREZ DE CUÉLLAR
Secretary-General of the United Nations

Global outlook 2000 is a revised version of an earlier study sponsored by the United Nations. The earlier study was chosen for the 1988 Notable Documents List by the American Library Association.

To the Reader:

The tables and most of the explanatory notes are at the end of the chapters in this book.

The figures present selected portions of tables, some not printed in the book, and the tables provide supplementary data underlying the figures. The full set of tables are available free of charge. To obtain a set write to

United Nations Publications
Room DC2-853, Dept. 600
United Nations
New York, N.Y. 10017
Fax No. (212) 963-4116

GLOBAL
OUTLOOK
2000

I.
Introduction

A BASELINE SCENARIO for the 1990s has been prepared for this report to provide a starting point for analyzing the prospects for long-term global economic development. The most likely evolution of the world economy is projected on the assumption that government policies will not change. Since policies in fact will change in response to events, the baseline scenario is not meant to be a prediction of the future. Rather, it is a point of departure for consideration of appropriate policies. Even assuming that no major initiatives will be introduced to deal with the economic imbalances that have arisen during the past decade, significant changes take place under the scenario in the allocation, composition, and distribution of world production and incomes. Populations in many of the poorest developing countries continue to experience acute poverty, however, with little prospect for improvement. In the following chapters alternative policies and their effects are examined. This analysis indicates that substantial improvements in the prospects for world economic growth could be realized through enhanced international cooperation and stronger domestic policies aimed at overcoming structural obstacles.

In a surprise-free scenario, the long-term growth performance in all countries will remain largely unchanged from recent trends. Among the factors that determine the scenario are investment effort, investment efficiency, interest rates, consumption, and saving behaviour, oil prices, employment and productivity trends, and trends in exchange rates and country shares of the world market for exports of different products. The baseline scenario assumes that investment as a share of GDP will remain close to the average of the 1975–1990 period (see table 1.1). The productivity of investment is also based on the same period except in cases where there is strong evidence that the 1975–1990 average is no longer appropriate. Based on these assumptions, and on the continuation of recent trends in the other factors just mentioned, a state of fundamental disequilibrium will continue to prevail in world economic activity in the foreseeable future, but with a gradual reduction of the large internal and external imbalances found in most world regions at the end of the 1980s.

Despite the imbalances and only moderate growth in GDP in most countries, sufficient adjustment takes place to avoid a major economic downturn or financial crisis. The priorities for changes in development policies in the 1990s are already suggested by a number of other disturbing trends. If current patterns were to continue unchanged, the world distribution of income between countries would worsen, that is, the gap between the richest and the poorest countries would continue to widen (see table 1.2). Some social indicators show a slowdown in progress in many developing countries, and even some absolute declines. The risk of serious deterioration of the physical environment will increase unless patterns of production and consumption are radically altered. As assessed under these circumstances, the global economy of the year 2000 would present a picture of both economic advance and decline, of structural change and stagnation, of rapid improvements in levels of living in some countries and rising numbers of people living in absolute poverty in others.

Economic and social conditions are worsening in many countries, but it is important to recognize that a number of positive trends have emerged in recent years. Reduced international political tensions should accelerate international trade and promote investment. The same reduced tensions may lead to a substantial reallocation of military-related investments to more productive civilian use. With an improved political environment the probability of disruptive shocks has diminished. These developments have already contributed to the growth of output and trade in the late 1980s and created a favourable basis for sustainable economic growth throughout the 1990s. The improvement in the political environment will also facilitate economic coordination at the global and regional levels.

Regional diversity in economic growth is expected during the 1990s. For the developed market economies, growth will average 3.1 per cent per year. It will improve to 4.3 per cent annually for developing countries as a whole, but there will be negligible growth or absolute decline in many of the heavily indebted and least developed countries. GDP (gross domestic product) per capita in West Asia and sub-Saharan Africa will be lower at the end of the century than it was in 1985. In contrast, continued rapid growth is expected in some other Asian countries.

Economic growth for Eastern Europe and the USSR will increase to 3.6 per cent in the 1990s. This improvement is due mainly to the reallocation of investment to consumer-oriented sectors. Annual growth in this region could reach 4 to 5 per cent because of recent political changes and related proposals for economic reform.

Sustained development requires a recognition that vigorous economic growth is essential to solve the problems of poverty and underdevelopment and related environmental problems. Current patterns of growth must be changed, however, to make them less resource and energy intensive and more equitable. Inequalities in international economic relations, coupled with inappropriate economic policies in many developed and developing countries, continue to cause environmental degradation and otherwise limit the development process. Growth derived from rapid resource depletion is neither ecologically nor economically sustainable.

Many environmental risks stemming from economic activities

cross national boundaries. Some are global in scope. Although most of the activities that give rise to such risks are concentrated in the industrial countries, they are shared by all countries. These risks include harmful effects from hazardous wastes and from increasing concentrations of carbon dioxide and other greenhouse gases in the atmosphere. The issue of greenhouse gases and climate change has emerged as especially urgent. Global warming and other effects may not reach critical proportions until well into the next century, but their potential magnitude is so great that it would be unwise to postpone efforts to limit their cause. These efforts are discussed in this report, as are the increasingly compelling environmental problems of ozone depletion in the stratosphere and acid rain.

The energy sector has passed through three distinct periods in the past 40 years. After World War II and up to 1973, the energy market was characterized by a rapid growth in energy consumption fueled by cheap and plentiful supplies of energy, especially oil. In the 1970s, the energy market changed decisively when large oil price increases in 1973–1974 and again in 1979–1980 were accompanied by apprehensions about the security of supplies. Higher energy prices resulted in sluggish demand during the first half of the 1980s. This sluggishness reflected energy conservation and improved efficiency in energy use as well as low economic growth rates in developed countries and even negative growth in many developing countries. In the end energy prices were sharply reduced.

The collapse of oil prices in 1986 and their subsequent stabilization, as well as the resumption of higher growth rates in the economies of the developed market economies and several developing countries in Asia, have once again brought about higher than expected increases in energy demand, including oil. Perceptions of energy scarcities have been replaced by widespread expectations of surplus capacities despite several indications that the world energy situation may be on the threshold of new problems of increasing geographic concentration of supplies in the medium term, as well as of environmental problems that were hardly even imagined a few years ago.

The outstanding development in world agriculture since the early 1960s has been the significant improvement in the levels and quality of food consumption. The challenge of feeding some 1,800 million more people, compared with the global population in the early 1960s, has been met, and earlier fears of chronic food shortages over much of the world have proved to be unfounded. In many areas and for many groups of people, however, hunger and malnutrition are rife. According to FAO's Fifth World Food Survey, in the developing countries, excluding China, between 350 and 510 million people are still seriously undernourished, with more than half of them living in Asia. The developing countries will continue to be large and increasing net importers of cereals at about 100 million tons per year. Self sufficiency may not improve, especially in sub-Saharan Africa, but the rapid deterioration of recent years will be checked.

The development of new technologies and their rate of diffusion among industries and countries are the principal forces behind structural change. The process of innovation by which new technologies create new products or production processes and change organizational structures is largely a function of economic variables such as changing patterns of final demand and relative factor prices.

The widening technology gap between the developed and developing countries might threaten future North–South trade much more than disparities in income levels threaten it. One indicator of technological development, the number of scientists and engineers in developing countries, is about one tenth of that of developed countries, and this gap has been increasing. Another indicator is research and development expenditures. They have tripled in developed countries in the last decade (from $60 billion to $195 billion); in developing countries they are slightly above $10 billion, and the gap between the developed and developing countries widened about three times during 1970–1980. Several developing countries have already established programmes to incorporate new technologies in agricultural and industrial activities. Creation of a domestic technological capacity is an important though costly policy pursued by an increasing number of developing countries.

Demographic trends are fairly predictable and provide a good basis for the analysis of structural change and the associated economic and social policy issues of the next decade. Against a background of generally slower population growth resulting in a world population of 6 billion just before the turn of the century, there will be considerable regional diversity. The fastest growth (an annual rate of 3 per cent) will occur in Africa, where the task of economic recovery and restoration of self-sustained growth will be particularly difficult. There will be, however, less diversity in labour force growth rates in the developing world, averaging 2.5 to 3 per cent. In contrast, labour force growth rates in developed countries will be less than 1 per cent. Employment is likely to grow more slowly than the labour force in most countries, and unemployment will be a concern for all groups of countries.

Urban population in the developing countries will continue to grow even faster than total population, as large numbers of people leave rural areas to seek jobs and education. Housing construction and the provision of water and sanitation lag far behind the population increase in both urban and rural areas of the poorer developing countries, and little improvement is expected in the 1990s.

Human resources have long been neglected in development strategies or approached in a piecemeal fashion. Emphasizing the development of human capabilities is an approach to overall development that regards human beings simultaneously as both the means and ends of economic and social policy. It relies on local resource mobilization and participation as agents of constructive change, as indicated in the concluding chapters on education, health, and social policy.

Literacy rates have risen considerably since 1970, but the number of illiterate adults in the world has increased; almost all of them are in the developing countries, and most of them are women. Literacy rates are likely to increase further in the 1990s, but the total number of illiterates is projected to increase between 1985 and the year 2000. School enrollment rates are expected to continue rising, but the number of unenrolled children aged 6 to 11 will remain over 100 million in the developing countries in 2000.

To increase the relevance and efficiency of primary schooling, current understanding suggests the following priorities: improving the availability and use of instructional materials, enhancing teacher effectiveness, improving managerial skills and individual and organizational incentives, and increasing the time actually spent on learning. With little economic growth expected in many of the poorest countries, it also will be important to reduce the total cost per student in these countries, which is high relative to their GDP per capita, and/or to increase the share of GDP devoted to education. In adult education programmes, women deserve highest priority, in view of their history of being educationally underserved and their economic contributions to agriculture and industry, as well as their influential role as mothers and often as head of a single-parent household.

Infant mortality rates decreased in nearly all countries in the past decade, but developing countries with 29 per cent of world population still have rates above 100 per 1,000 live births; it is less than 20 in the developed countries. The goal of reducing infant mortality rates below 50 per 1,000 live births by the year 2000 is projected not to be met in 59 countries, including 41 in sub-Saharan Africa.

In most parts of the world, nutrition has improved during the past 25 years, but some 500 million people are malnourished and no overall reduction in this number is expected by the year 2000. In Africa and Asia, infectious and parasitic diseases account for about half of all deaths, the majority occurring among infants and young children. Many of these diseases can be overcome by improvements in environmental and living conditions and other preventive action. Six major preventable diseases of childhood have been selected as targets for immunization in most countries, but some still have not allocated the relatively modest resources needed to provide this protection. Acquired immuno-deficiency syndrome (AIDS) and the entire spectrum of diseases associated with human immuno-deficiency virus (HIV) infection have rapidly emerged as a major global public health problem. The enormous cost of caring for AIDS patients threatens to divert resources away from other health programmes. In all countries, demand for health services of greater complexity is increasing. The rapidly increasing number of older citizens in all countries will place additional pressure on health systems.

The fuller participation of all elements of society in defining and achieving the common goals of development has the potential to increase people's motivation, innovation, and productivity. There is great potential in further use of co-operative, self-help and community groups, non-governmental organizations, and workers' participation in the management of enterprises. Economic and social development can benefit from greater autonomy for public enterprises, devolution of power to local authorities, and new forms of partnership between governmental and non-governmental organizations. Women make essential contributions to economic and social life, although many of their activities are not formally recognized. This is especially true of their work in households, family farms and enterprises, and in the informal sector. Greater productivity in such activities could be a major source of increased well-being and economic growth. The reorientation of welfare services towards mutual self-help, prevention, rehabilitation, and income-generating activities is of special significance in developing countries. In the developed countries, rapidly rising costs of social welfare programmes have been a cause of concern, as have their alleged inefficiencies and failure to provide for those most in need. Institutionalization is being de-emphasized in favour of community-based and family-based support, prevention, and rehabilitation.

National economies will suffer increasingly from the effects of crime, including the use of legitimate or quasi-legitimate organizational techniques and structures for illegal economic gain. The use of new techniques for non-violent but illegal acquisition and use of money will grow and significantly affect the economy in many countries.

Drug abuse and illicit trafficking have spread throughout the world, a trend that is likely to continue. Drug abuse, primarily among the young, crosses all social, economic, and political boundaries. Its rapid spread reflects expanded illicit demand and production as well as the traffic in drugs, which has become sophisticated and complex, involving organized crime. The cultivation of narcotic plants has grown to enormous proportions in certain areas of the world. While strong law enforcement and advanced technology may improve a nation's ability to destroy illicit crops, production in some areas is likely to continue unless reasonable economic alternatives are offered to those involved.

Education, especially primary schooling for literacy, is both a goal of development and a means for achieving the interrelated goals of better health, labour productivity, and rapid economic growth as well as social integration. More advanced education is increasingly needed to understand and participate in the technological and administrative processes of the modern global economy. But most Governments have not given education top priority as a development objective.

TABLE 1.1 *Population and growth of GDP per capita, by economic region and income groups of developing countries, 1960–1990*[a]

Country group	Population (1980)		Average annual rate of growth of GDP per capita			Per capita GDP			
	Millions	Percentage share	1960–1970	1970–1980	1980–1990	1960	1970	1980	1990
World	4,371[c]	100.0	3.2	1.9	1.3	1,601	2,191	2,647	3,000
Developed market economies	768	17.6	3.9	2.4	2.1	5,501	8,042	10,185	12,490
Eastern Europe & the USSR[b]	378	8.6	6.2	4.2	2.3	1,154	2,101	3,192	4,010
China	996	22.8	2.0	4.1	7.5	169	198	290	600
Developing countries	2,230	51.0	3.3	2.4	0.1	556	763	971	980
By regions:									
North Africa	88	2.0	8.2	1.2	−0.3	590	1,284	1,438	1,400
Sub-Saharan Africa	364	8.3	1.8	−0.4	−2.6	514	606	580	440
Western Asia	88	2.0	4.1	1.0	−4.3	2,478	3,700	4,180	2,730
South and East Asia	1,262	28.9	2.6	4.1	3.7	228	293	435	620
Latin America and the Caribbean	361	8.3	2.7	2.4	−1.1	1,409	1,831	2,320	2,090
Mediterranean	68	1.6	3.7	3.7	1.1	924	1,322	1,936	2,160
By income groups:									
Per capita GDP greater than $700 in 1980	825	18.9	3.6	2.3	−0.6	1,175	1,662	2,105	1,980
Per capita GDP between $300 and $700 in 1980	406	9.3	2.0	3.0	1.6	289	345	463	540
Per capita income less than $300 in 1980	991	22.7	0.8	1.6	2.5	189	203	237	300
Least developed countries	312	7.1	1.1	−0.2	−0.3	227	254	249	240

Source: United Nations Secretariat, Department of International Economic and Social Affairs.

[a] At 1980 dollars and exchange rates.

[b] Based on net material product (NMP).

[c] Excludes a number of countries and territories, with a combined population of 79 million in 1980, for which income data are not available.

TABLE 1.2 *GDP per capita levels and growth rates*[a]

| | Growth rates | | | | GDP per capita | |
| | GDP | | GDP per capita | | | |
	1985–1990	1990–2000	1985–1990	1990–2000	1985	2000
World	3.3	3.5	1.6	1.8	2,770	3,580
Developed market economies	3.0	3.1	2.5	2.6	11,100	16,130
North America	2.9	3.0	2.0	2.3	12,750	17,780
Western Europe	2.9	2.8	2.6	2.6	10,840	15,910
Other developed	4.2	3.9	2.8	3.0	9,150	14,200
Eastern Europe & the USSR[b]	2.7	3.6	1.9	3.0	3,650	5,370
China	8.0	5.6	6.6	4.2	430	900
Developing countries	3.4	4.3	1.0	2.0	920	1,200
By region:						
North Africa	2.7	4.4	−0.6	2.0	1,440	1,710
Sub-Saharan Africa	2.3	3.2	−0.4	−0.1	450	440
Latin America and the Caribbean	1.4	2.9	−0.1	1.0	2,100	2,320
Western Asia	0.3	4.2	−2.6	1.0	3,100	3,020
South and East Asia	6.6	6.1	4.4	3.9	500	920
By export orientation:						
Petroleum-exporting countries	1.3	3.7	−1.3	1.3	1,630	1,930
Major exporters of manufactures	4.9	5.2	3.0	3.6	1,325	1,620
Primary commodity and services exporters	2.0	2.9	−1.1	0.8	640	670
Least developed countries	3.5	3.1	0.7	0.2	240	270
By income level:						
High-income oil exporters	1.5	4.2	−2.5	0.5	7,550	6,200
Other high-income	2.6	3.9	0.0	1.5	3,090	3,560
Middle-income	3.4	4.7	1.0	2.5	1,210	1,720
Low-income	3.5	4.6	1.1	2.3	350	490
Highly indebted	1.9	3.0	−0.8	0.8	1,790	1,860

Source: Ibid.
[a] *At 1980 dollars and exchange rates.*
[b] *Based on NMP.*

2.

Long-Term Trends, 1960 to 1990

AN INTERNATIONAL development strategy for the 1990s will have to take into account the longer-term experience of the world economy as well as the present situation and the immediate prospects.

A. WIDENING DISPARITIES IN PRODUCTION PERFORMANCE

During the last three decades, the gross world product rose at an average rate of 3.9 per cent a year when measured in constant 1980 prices and exchange rates. Accompanying this expanding level of economic activity was an even faster growth in international trade at 6 per cent and significant structural transformation of the world economy. This long-term rise in the capacity of the world economy to supply increasingly diverse kinds of goods and services gave rise to widespread improvements in material standards of living for most of the world's population.

The average pace of world economic growth slowed significantly, however, over the period reviewed here, 1960–1990. Wid-

ening imbalances, beyond what seemed capable of long-term financing, arose in the external accounts of many countries, and
growing disparities could be seen in the production performance
of different areas of the world. In the 14-year period stretching
from 1960 to 1973, total global output increased over 5 per cent
on average each year. All regions shared in this expansion, with
growth in some groups of developing countries in the range of
7 to 9 per cent per annum (table 2.1). Output per economically
active person—a broad measure of the productivity—increased
more than 3.5 per cent per year in three of the four major world
economic regions during this period of extraordinary growth. In
the developing countries productivity rose at a rate of almost 4 per
cent per year.

Following the cyclical upturn from the economic recession of
1974–1975, a slowdown from the average pace of growth registered during the 1960s and early 1970s persisted into the early
1980s. Then another steep recession marked a further slowdown
in the long-term trend in world economic growth. The slowdown
was characterized by volatile price increases, rising unemployment
in North America and Western Europe and widening disparities
in the production performance of different developing country
regions. During this period, the performance of the world economy was also affected by a proliferation of protectionist trade
barriers and by large swings and misalignments of the major world
currencies.

Within the group of developed market economies, rapid and
rising inflation and high and growing unemployment during the
1970s led to a re-assessment of medium-term macroeconomic
policies. This was followed by a sharp tightening of monetary
policies in the 1980s that caused interest rates to rise to record
highs. A number of major industrial economies simultaneously
addressed their widening structural (i.e., cyclically adjusted) budgetary deficits, thereby reducing the net fiscal stimulus on their
economies. The resulting contraction in economic activity that
occurred in 1981–1982 was the deepest recession in the last 50
years. Although the economies of Eastern Europe and the USSR
showed greater stability and continued to grow, the environment

for economic growth in this region after 1979 was also more adverse than it had been previously.

The slowdown in long-term economic growth after the mid-1970s was even deeper in the developing countries. It was especially apparent in sub-Saharan Africa and Western Asia, where labour productivity growth turned negative and average per capita incomes began to fall. Rates of economic growth declined in North Africa and the Mediterranean area. In contrast, the growth of GDP increased in South and East Asia and in China. In 1976–1980, Latin America and the Caribbean experienced a growth rate of 5 per cent per year.

Overshadowing the mild recovery in the long-term pace of world economic growth that has taken place since 1982 is the marked contrast between the productivity performance of different regions. Productivity growth in the developed market economies recovered significantly from its previous slow pace, and inflation and unemployment levels (except in Europe) have tended downward. At the same time, the growth of trade and capital formation have recovered from the slow pace of the previous period. The rise in output has been particularly pronounced in the case of the seven major industrial economies, where growth of GDP per economically active person is expected to average 2.5 per cent a year from 1983 to 1990 compared to the less than 1 per cent recorded for the period from 1974 to 1982. This improvement in production performance followed the adoption of a more expansionary fiscal policy in a number of major industrial economies after mid-1982 and a significant easing of monetary policies in the three largest economies of this group after mid-1985.

Recent years have seen an intensification of efforts directed at economic reforms in Eastern Europe and the USSR. These economies shared in the general deceleration in output growth that has taken place during the 1980s, and the overall growth in their combined net material product is expected to average 3.1 per cent per annum from 1983 to 1990. While their balance of convertible currency trade improved and their net debt and reserve positions were bolstered, a more radical adjustment is now underway and major reforms to improve the functioning of these economies are beginning.

In most developing countries the long-term pace of growth continued to decline in the 1980s. The economic decline in Africa, Western Asia and Latin America and the Caribbean accelerated after 1982 and output levels per economically active person are expected to be lower in 1990 in all of these regions than they were in 1980. In the case of sub-Saharan Africa, average levels of output per economically active person in 1990 are likely to be lower than those that prevailed in 1970. In contrast, labour productivity has risen rapidly in South and East Asia and in China.

During the 30 year period reviewed here per capita GDP of the developed market economies more than doubled, rising from about $5,500 in 1960 to a forecast of almost $12,500 in 1990, when expressed in the prices and at the exchange rates prevailing in 1980 (table 2.2). By comparison, per capita GDP of the developing countries as a whole increased from about $556 in 1960 to $980 by the year 1990, a 75 per cent increase.

The average rate of expansion of GDP per capita in all developing countries income groups was lower than that of the more economically advanced countries. The relative performance of the poorest and most disadvantaged areas of the world has been significantly worse than that of other developing countries. Economic growth in the least developed countries was so poor that given their high rate of population growth, their average GDP per capita in 1990 will be some 5 per cent lower than in 1970. Per capita GDP in the low income countries, representing almost a quarter of the world's population, will have risen only 60 per cent from 1960 to 1990. Per capita GDP in petroleum-exporting countries rose only by about 20 per cent between 1970 and 1990.

Gross domestic product has deficiencies as an indicator of development and economic well-being when assessing the economic performance of different groups of countries. The same is true when measuring the economic distance between them by average incomes. The GDP encompasses the production of marketed goods and services, including both those that enhance welfare and those that detract from it. It measures the services of government and includes subsistence output of farmers only to the extent it is imputed; other household production, in particular that of women, only if it is sold and in practice not even then. Negative aspects of economic growth related to the depletion and degradation of natural resources are not reflected in conventional measures of economic output such as the gross domestic product: in addition, some environmental protection activities are considered as a part of GDP in a positive manner. Informal sector output is not included at all. Aggregate figures for gross domestic product and averages for GDP per capita provide no information about the distribution of income or the economic benefits different groups in society may gain from economic growth. International comparisons of GDP suffer from the failure of the exchange rate to reflect adequately the relative purchasing power of currencies over domestic goods and services. Studies of alternative methods of comparing gross domestic products among countries based on the purchasing power parities of currencies indicate that conventional exchange rate translations may overstate significantly the relative economic distance between high and low income countries. The overstatement is illustrated by the fact that no one could survive in industrial countries on the incomes estimated for survival in poorer countries. Despite these limitations of the statistical measures used to assess world economic performances, it is clear that for a great many of the world's poorest population the years since 1960 have seen at best limited economic progress.

B. STRUCTURAL ADJUSTMENT AND INDUSTRIAL REDEPLOYMENT

Economic growth proceeds by its very nature through continuous changes of economic structure. These changes are induced by factor accumulation as capital and labour enter and exit different sectors, by different rates of technical progress in various sectors, and, of course, by the impact of international trade. Modern economic development magnifies these changes as it transforms essentially rural and traditional small-scale enterprises into more commercially oriented producers of goods and services for market. The pattern of production changes systematically in the process of economic development, with changes in mature economies different in nature from those in developing economies.

The speed and character of structural change varies from region to region, but certain trends stand out: the universal shift out of agriculture; the relative increase in the size of the service sector in mature economies and of industry, particularly manufacturing, in developing economies; and the contrasting trends in the proportion of GDP originating in manufacturing between developed and developing countries. As expected, changes over time in the composition of GDP are more marked in the fast growing developing countries than in other groups of countries (table 2.3).

A main source of structural change in the economically advanced countries was internal economic growth. It caused reallocation of employment and capital from less productive sectors and/or heavy industry to high technology branches of manufacturing and high-value added specialized services. Productivity growth in the manufacturing sector and intensified international competition led to a decline in the share of manufacturing in GDP. In 1960, for example, the manufacturing sector accounted for over 30 per cent of the total value of all goods and services entering the final product of these economies; by 1987 less than 25 per cent of their GDP was generated in this sector (table 2.3). Services, in contrast, grew from just over one half of GDP in 1960 to two thirds in 1987. In Eastern Europe and the USSR, broad patterns of change among agriculture, manufacturing, and services were somewhat similar.

During the three decades since 1960 there has been much structural change in the developing world. Table 2.3 illustrates its pervasiveness and also its limitations. In all developing countries, including the least developed ones, the contribution of the agricultural sector to GDP has dropped sharply for different reasons. Apart from what has happened to the import and export of agricultural raw materials, developing countries range from failure to maintain food production, with the consequent rising imports, to success in raising overall income that reduces the share of agriculture and of related activities in GDP (see figures 2.1 and 2.2). The share of manufactures has grown in all groups of developing countries. In the group of newly industrializing economies, a category of its own, the share of manufacturing in GDP is now higher than in the industrialized countries. The category of services is too heterogeneous to be particularly enlightening: it includes public services, ranging from basic administration, justice, defense, and the like, to transportation, commerce, financial services, and domestic service. The mere fact that it accounts for about half of GDP in developing countries and two thirds of GDP in developed countries makes it obvious that the various elements of the service sector must be considered separately in future studies.

The transformation in patterns of production in the developing countries differed markedly from region to region. Some developing countries underwent large-scale structural change and others very little. The average rate of growth of manufacturing output above that of GDP as a whole was a major source of structural change in a number of Asian economies as well as elsewhere.

In the newly industrializing economies manufacturing accounted for only 17 per cent of GDP in 1960. It rose at an average rate of over 11.0 per cent a year, however, and provided the foundation for a rapid expansion of their international trade. Other sectors of production in these economies also expanded rapidly in a process of mutually supportive growth. Similarly, manufacturing output and exports grew at a fast pace in other manufacturing oriented developing countries and the share of manufacturing rose to over 23 per cent of their GDP in 1987. In the petroleum exporting economies, manufacturing activities associated with the processing of petroleum also rose significantly. On the other hand, the process of structural change was slow or non-existent in many low-income and least developed countries. The share of agriculture in the least developed countries remained

SECTORIAL COMPOSITION OF GDP

DEVELOPED MARKET ECONOMIES
1960

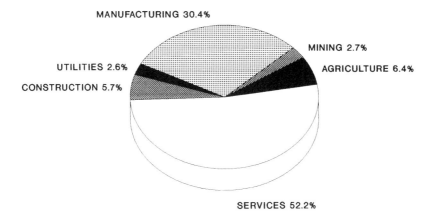

MANUFACTURING 30.4%

MINING 2.7%

UTILITIES 2.6%

AGRICULTURE 6.4%

CONSTRUCTION 5.7%

SERVICES 52.2%

DEVELOPED MARKET ECONOMIES
1987

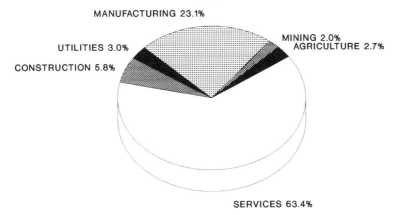

MANUFACTURING 23.1%

MINING 2.0%
AGRICULTURE 2.7%

UTILITIES 3.0%

CONSTRUCTION 5.8%

SERVICES 63.4%

FIGURE 2.1

SHARE OF AGRICULTURE IN GROSS DOMESTIC
PRODUCT, 1960 AND 1987

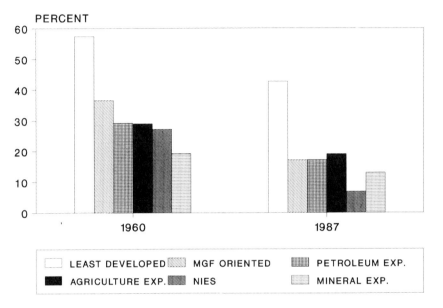

Figure 2.2

at over 40 per cent in 1987, and there was almost no increase in
the share of manufacturing. Moreover, in many countries where
the share of agriculture did fall noticeably, it was a consequence
of deteriorating agricultural performance rather than of successful
development of industry.

The process of world economic development also involves a
continuing shift in the geographical distribution of economic activities. Shifts in the structure of production for market economies
are shown in table 2.4. For the more developed countries, these
changes represent a process of gradual adjustment and adaptation
to technical advance and higher incomes. For the less developed
areas, particularly the low-income and least developed countries,
the process is one of abrupt alteration in the organization and
mode of production, with similar large-scale changes in labour
productivity and export patterns. Given that the elasticity of de-

mand for primary goods is less than 1, and that productivity growth is slowest in the service sector, the rise in the share in industry is inevitable.

The share of the developing countries in world GDP declined by one percentage point over the last 30 years. Except for services, however, the relative weight of the developing countries in world totals in all major sectors has risen. But these changes mask divergent trends. The newly industrializing and petroleum-exporting economies increased their shares in all major sectors of the world GDP. Poorer countries generally reduced their shares in all lines of economic activity. The process of industrial redeployment towards the developing countries is taking place across the entire range of production activities, and the previous pattern of complementarity between developing and developed countries is continually changing.

A significant shift in the origin of income generated in the mining and quarrying sector occurred from the major industrial economies of the North to the petroleum exporting economies of the South. There the petroleum-exporting economies as a group doubled their shares of world manufacturing production by 1987. They accounted for much of the increase in world construction activity. Although the newly industrialized economies make up only a small fraction of gross world product, their share of world manufacturing activity increased significantly. Their growth was not limited to manufacturing but encompassed all lines of activity except mining and quarrying. Similarly, the share of manufacturing oriented developing countries in world industrial product increased, although their share of gross world market output declined.

Negligible shifts occurred in the case of other groups of developing countries. For the low-income and least developed economies agriculture is still the preponderant source of income and employment. The slow growth of this sector led to slow growth in the economy as a whole. In addition, slow growth in agriculture was transmitted to the other sectors and constrained their growth as well. Consequently, the share of those economies in the output of almost all categories of world production also declined. The poorer developing countries have not advanced as rapidly as other economies.

C. RESOURCE ALLOCATION PATTERNS AND INTERNAL IMBALANCES

Capital formation is essential for economic growth and structural change. Countries achieve faster economic growth when they are able to increase their investment and improve the efficiency of capital use.

Table 2.5 assembles historical estimates of shares of domestic investment, national saving, and external resources in GDP by major world economic regions and by groups of developing countries. For the developed market economies as a group, the share of capital formation in GDP, measured in terms of current prices, rose significantly during periods of economic expansion and receded during periods of slowdown. Reflecting this relationship, from 1960 until 1973, when the share of capital formation peaked at 25 per cent of GDP, economic growth in these countries averaged 5 per cent a year. After 1973 the investment share declined by almost 3 percentage points through the early years of the 1980s, and growth fell to 2 per cent. Since 1983 the share of investment has been rising, and rates of economic growth have recovered to about 3 per cent.

In the newly industrializing economies, the increase in investment and the corresponding rise in economic growth were especially marked. Their average share of investment in GDP rose from 16 per cent in 1960 to 26 per cent in 1970, and their growth accelerated from 6 to 7 per cent in the early 1960s to over 10 per cent in the early 1970s. Later, the rate of capital formation in these countries generally remained high, and they continued to record rapid rates of growth.

The experience of the highly indebted countries has been markedly different, but the link between investment and economic growth has been equally close. The proportion of resources channelled into capital formation by these countries was high and rising from 1960 until 1980. During this period, rates of economic growth were generally high, while subject to large fluctuations and a gradual slowdown, particularly in Latin America. Before the onset of the 1981–1982 recession, the level of external debt of almost all of these countries appeared to be within their debt servicing capacity. As the international outlook worsened, however, new loans were extended on an increasingly short-term basis, interest rates rose and export earnings fell. When the foreign debt crises of the 1980s began, a liquidity crisis was averted through a rescheduling of debt and a reduction in imports. The immediate process of domestic adjustment fell heavily on investment. It is expected to be 25 per cent lower in 1990 than it was in 1980. A prolonged period of economic contraction has set in.

In the least developed countries the rate of capital formation has risen from less than 10 percent of GDP in 1960 to about 15 per cent in the 1980s, but investments in these countries still remain significantly below the level in other developing countries taking into account the income per capita gap (see figure 2.3).

During the last few years there were declines in shares of investment in GDP in almost all groups of developing countries. These declines are partly explained by a general deterioration in the international economic environment. Debt financing difficulties and commodity price fluctuations during this period affected investment allocation patterns and further reduced capital efficiency in a number of sectors. In the highly indebted countries the share of national saving in GDP declined by 4 percentage points and that of external resources by 1.7 percentage points in 1980–1987. Raising national saving to finance rising level of capital formation is an essential element in enhancing self-reliance for economic and social progress in developing countries.

In the developing countries the ratio of national saving to GDP increased from 16 per cent in 1960 to 18.5 per cent in 1970. After the mid-1970s, however, there was no increase in their average saving ratios. The decline in the average saving rate during the

SHARES OF SAVING AND INVESTMENT
1960-1987

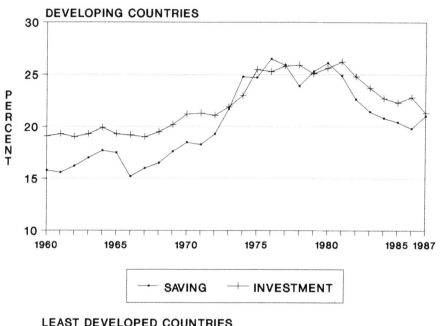

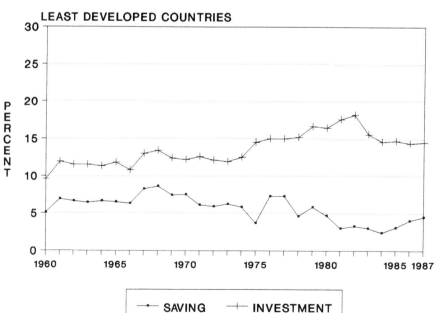

Figure 2.3

1980s may be traced largely to the experience of the petroleum exporting group, where the rates decreased from 39 per cent in 1980 to 22 per cent in 1987; and to the highly indebted group, where the saving ratio fell from 22 per cent in 1982 to 17 per cent in 1987. In the least developed countries already low rates of saving were also reduced during this period. In the newly industrializing economies, on the other hand, over 30 per cent of GDP was made available for accumulation.

Despite the rising saving ratio of many developing countries, domestic saving did not cover investments, and an inflow of external resources occurred. The dependence on external resources has varied over time and among countries (see figure 2.3). During the first two decades surveyed, the share of foreign resources in capital formation was reduced. In the 1980s, however, the savings of most developing countries suffered serious setbacks as per capita output fell in several regions and deteriorating terms of trade further reduced national income.

The dependence of the developing countries on external resources has been greatly influenced by foreign trade. For example, in the petroleum exporting countries, a net inflow of foreign saving equivalent to 2 per cent of their GDP in 1960 was converted to a sustained saving surplus by the early 1980s. Sharp increases in oil prices raised export receipts and led to large increases in income and national saving; conversely, the sustained outflow of domestic resources during the 1970s and early 1980s turned into growing inflow of external resources after 1982 when the value of their exports fell significantly.

In the petroleum-importing countries the link between trade possibilities and trends in external resources was also close. For the entire period studied here, the newly industrializing economies raised exports and production at a rapid rate. This required a substantial rise in capital formation. Because their initial rate of domestic saving was low, inflows of foreign saving equal to almost 10 per cent of GDP were necessary in the 1960s. Although later these countries increased the share of investment in their GDP substantially, their reliance on external resources declined significantly as their exports grew rapidly. Toward the end of the 1980s they became net exporters of saving to the rest of the world.

Most highly indebted countries encountered no serious problems meeting their debt service obligations prior to 1979, even though inflows of foreign saving had averaged 3 to 3.5 per cent of GDP. In the 1970s, however, the exports of different regions expanded at markedly different rates. The purchasing power of these exports changed in response to substantial changes in the terms of trade. Many now heavily indebted countries had borrowed repeatedly on international capital markets in 1974 and 1975 and again in 1979 and 1981 as the price of oil rose and their export markets experienced slowdowns. When the recession of the early 1980s occurred and protectionist measures were introduced in their major export markets, their exports fell, sharply reducing their debt servicing capacity. The combination of higher interest rates and larger obligations from past external borrowings raised in their GDP the share of factor payments to the world. The outflow of foreign exchange diverted saving from investment and imports supporting their growth. Many of these countries eventually adjusted through slower economic growth and greater import substitution, but they were not able to eliminate their reliance of an inflow of external resources.

D. INTERNATIONAL TRADE AND EXTERNAL BALANCES

During the entire period, 1960–1989, international trade grew faster than output. Significant changes occurred in the level and the commodity and geographical composition of world trade. These changes were in response to rising world incomes, technological advances, and changes in the relative prices of traded commodities. As in the case of production and productivity, there has been a long-term tendency for the pace of world trade to slow down and for significant disparities to arise in the trade performance of different groups of countries.

In general, the world trading environment in the 1960s was exceptionally favourable. The decade was one of rapid and widespread growth in economic activity and world trade, of relatively low world inflation and stable commodity prices, and of reduced trade barriers and expanding real resource transfers to the developing countries. The most dynamic component of world trade was the flow of trade among the developed market economies and exports of the newly industrialized economies. During the decade, the total exports of goods and non-factor services of the developed market economies expanded at a rate of more than 8 per cent annually. Significant gains from improvements in the terms of trade of the developed market economies in the 1960s boosted the purchasing power of their exports on world markets. The growth rates of imports and national income exceeded that of their exports and domestic production (see table 2.6). Throughout the decade, the developed market economies recorded a surplus in their foreign trade in goods and services.

In the developing countries the rate of growth of exports was 8 per cent in the 1960s. This average conceals wide variations, of course, in different product groups. Exports of fuels and manufactures grew rapidly, and those of industrial raw materials and foodstuffs increased at a much slower rate (see figure 2.4). World trade prices were generally stable, but there was a steady deterioration in the terms of trade for developing countries: the purchasing power of their exports rose by only 6.3 per cent a year. This had a negative effect on their ability to earn foreign exchange, as did the greater instability of prices for primary commodities that comprised the bulk of their exports. Consequently, the volume of their imports rose by only 6 per cent a year. The balance of payments of these countries recorded increasing deficits in their service trade.

Merchandise exports of the developing countries stood at about $58.3 billion U.S. dollars by 1970, only 18 per cent of the value of world trade. Primary commodities remained the main source of export revenue. They accounted for 70 per cent of all developing country export revenues from merchandise trade. The share of fossil fuels was over 30 per cent of these receipts (see

COMMODITY STRUCTURE OF WORLD TRADE

DEVELOPING COUNTRIES
EXPORTS 1965

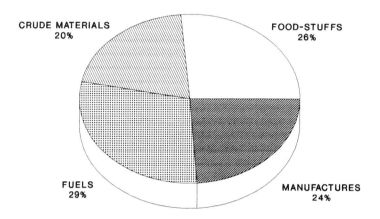

CRUDE MATERIALS
20%

FOOD-STUFFS
26%

FUELS
29%

MANUFACTURES
24%

DEVELOPING COUNTRIES
EXPORTS 1986

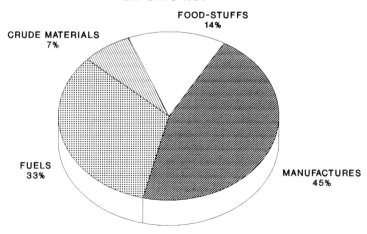

FOOD-STUFFS
14%

CRUDE MATERIALS
7%

FUELS
33%

MANUFACTURES
45%

Figure 2.4

table 2.7). Their exports of manufactured goods (Standard International Trade Classification 5 to 9) accounted for only 8 per cent of world trade in manufactures (see table 2.8). The lagging increase in developing countries' export volume and the deterioration in their terms of trade caused a decline of their share in total world trade. There was also a further erosion in trade among developing countries. Although a substantial surplus was recorded by the developing countries on their merchandise trade in 1970, attributable mainly to low import absorption by the petroleum-exporting developing countries, net payments on service accounts for insurance and freight, property income, and other services resulted in a negative balance on current account in that year.

In the 1970s the pattern of world trade changed dramatically and lowered the pace of its expansion. Fluctuations in economic activity, strong upsurges in prices, and large-scale imbalances in the economies of all groups of countries contributed to the change. The increase in volume of world trade was only about 5.5 per cent a year for the decade as a whole. As in the past, trade between different parts of the world expanded at significantly different rates. By far, the greatest expansion of trade in current prices was recorded in the intra-trade of the developing countries. It also proved to be the most dynamic destination for the exports of the developed economies during the 1970s.

The export volume of the developing countries grew at only 3.2 per cent with wide differences between countries. Petroleum-exporting developing countries, for example, benefited from an almost ten-fold increase in the nominal price of oil, but there was little or no sustained increase in the volume of petroleum sold on world markets. For major developing country exporters of manufactures, their exports rose during the 1970s at 7.5 per cent per annum. Those countries that exchanged non-oil primary products for manufactures and petroleum, however, found themselves with falling terms of trade. These divergent trends caused large-scale changes in the commodity composition of developing country exports and in their trade-balance positions. Reflecting the large increase in unit value, fuels rose substantially as a share of the value of developing country exports and imports. Manufactured products maintained their proportion of total developing country merchandise trade in response to the rapid expansion in the export volume. The rise in export receipts of the major petroleum-exporting countries over the course of the decade more than offset the growing external imbalance of other developing countries.

In the beginning of the 1980s a decline in world economic activity, accelerating technological advance, and shifts in economic policies led to further changes in world trade. As trade in primary commodities declined in importance, trade in services emerged as an increasingly important component of international exchange. New regional trading arrangements in Europe and North America and greater openness on the part of Eastern Europe, the USSR, and China created opportunities for closer international economic integration and rising trade.

The rate of growth of world trade fell at the start of the 1980s. It is expected to average only around 4.5 per cent for the decade as a whole, although the trend rate of growth returned to 5.5 per cent after 1983 and accelerates to about 8 per cent in the late 1980s. Under the impact of the 1982 recession, exports of the developed market economies slowed significantly from 6 per cent in the 1970s. Imports of this group expanded at a slightly higher rate owing to an improvement in their terms of trade. The upturn in the pace of economic activity after 1982, however, has been associated with rates of growth of exports and imports over 5 and 6 per cent respectively in the period 1983 to 1990.

For the developing countries, slower growth in their main export markets led to low prices of their commodities. Mounting debt-service costs have further constrained the growth of their imports. In response to the large oil price rises of the late 1970s and early 1980s and the generally slower pace of world economic growth, the volume of petroleum exports declined. The purchasing power of petroleum exporters has been further reduced by a significant decline in the price of oil in the mid–1980s. As a result their imports fell on average 3 per cent a year from 1980 to 1987.

Lower commodity prices and high interest rates increased the debt-servicing burden of many highly-indebted countries. As their capacity to repay debt was eroded, their imports declined.

Export expansion and import growth remained strong in the 1980s for developing countries in South and East Asia. Manufactured exports from the newly industrializing economies expanded even more rapidly than in the 1970s, and these economies benefited from improvements in their terms of trade. Although the rate of growth of imports exceeded 10 per cent annually during the 1980s, the rapid rate of growth of their exports led to large surpluses on current account. Similarly, other major developing country exporters of manufactured products were able to exploit their comparative advantage in many categories of manufacturing.

TABLE 2.1 *Average annual rate of GDP growth 1960–1990 (measured at constant 1980 prices and exchange rates)*

Country group	Percentage 1961–1973	1974–1982	1983–1990
World	5.3	2.6	3.4
1. Developed market economies	5.0	2.1	3.2
Major industrial economies	4.9	2.2	3.3
North America	4.1	2.0	3.5
Europe	4.5	1.8	2.6
Japan	9.3	3.7	4.2
Other developed economies	5.3	1.9	2.6
2. Eastern Europe & the USSR	7.0	4.1	3.1
Eastern Europe	6.2	3.6	3.4
USSR	7.3	4.3	3.0
3. China	5.4	6.2	9.6
4. Developing countries	6.1	3.4	2.8
North Africa	7.3	4.4	2.7
Sub-Saharan Africa	4.9	1.2	0.4
Western Asia	9.1	0.7	−0.7
South and East Asia	5.6	5.9	6.0
Latin America and the Caribbean	5.6	3.2	1.8
Mediterranean	5.6	4.9	2.7

Source: United Nations Secretariat, Department of International Economic and Social Affairs.

TABLE 2.2 *Population and growth of GDP per capita, by economic region and income groups of developing countries, 1960–1990*

Country group	Population (1980)		Average annual rate of growth of GDP per capita at 1980 prices			Per capita GDP in 1980 US dollars			
	Millions	Percentage share	1960–1970	1970–1980	1980–1990	1960	1970	1980	1990
World	4,334.8	100.0	3.2	1.9	1.3	1,601	2,191	2,647	3,000
Developed market economies	771.6	17.8	3.9	2.4	2.1	5,501	8,042	10,185	12,490
Major industrial economies	596.9	13.8	3.8	2.5	2.3	5,843	8,492	10,870	13,574
North America	251.8	5.8	2.5	2.2	1.9	7,223	9,325	11,636	14,071
Europe	228.3	5.3	4.6	2.7	2.2	5,899	8,554	10,831	13,334
Japan	116.8	2.7	9.2	3.6	3.4	2,683	6,415	9,109	12,697
Other developed economies	174.6	4.0	4.2	1.9	1.3	4,284	6,454	7,845	8,911
Eastern Europe and the USSR[a]	374.9	8.6	6.2	4.2	2.3	1,154	2,101	3,192	4,010
Eastern Europe	109.4	2.5	5.2	4.5	2.4	1,054	1,743	2,776	3,513
USSR	265.5	6.1	6.5	4.0	2.1	1,199	2,253	3,363	4,171
China	996.1	23.0	2.0	4.1	7.5	169	198	290	600
Developing countries	2,192.2	50.6	3.3	2.4	0.1	556	763	971	980
Per capita GDP greater than $700 in 1980	811.2	18.7	3.6	2.3	-0.6	1,175	1,662	2,105	1,980
Per capita GDP between $300 and $700 in 1980	398.8	9.2	2.0	3.0	1.6	289	345	463	540
Per capita income less than $300 in 1980	982.2	22.7	0.8	1.6	2.5	189	203	237	300
Least developed countries	297.5	10.0	1.1	-0.2	-0.3	227	254	249	240

Source: Department of International Economic and Social Affairs of the United Nations Secretariat.
[a] *Based on Net Material Product.*

TABLE 2.3 *Sectoral composition GDP, 1960–1987*ᵃ
(In percentages)

Country group	Agriculture 1960	Agriculture 1987	Mining and quarrying 1960	Mining and quarrying 1987	Manufacturing 1960	Manufacturing 1987	Utilities 1960	Utilities 1987	Construction 1960	Construction 1987	Services 1960	Services 1987
Developed market economies	6.4	2.7	2.7	2.0	30.4	23.1	2.6	3.0	5.7	5.8	52.2	63.3
Major industrial economies	5.6	2.4	2.6	1.8	30.9	23.3	2.6	3.1	5.5	5.7	52.6	63.7
North America	4.2	2.1	2.6	2.6	28.8	19.2	2.6	2.9	4.9	4.8	56.9	68.3
Europe	7.6	2.6	2.8	1.6	35.0	25.3	2.7	3.1	6.9	5.5	44.9	61.9
Japan	13.1	2.8	2.0	0.3	35.1	29.0	2.8	3.2	6.2	7.9	40.9	56.8
Other developed economies	12.5	4.7	2.8	3.3	26.3	21.5	2.3	3.0	7.3	6.6	48.9	60.6
Eastern Europe & the												
USSRᵇ	21.0	18.0			52.9ᶜ	50.5			9.7	9.4	16.4	22.1
Eastern Europeᵇ	22.5	12.4			54.5ᶜ	61.3			8.9	8.7	14.1	17.6
USSRᵇ	20.5	20.0			52.3ᶜ	46.4			10.0	9.7	17.2	23.9
China	38.2	33.8			42.4ᵈ	45.7ᵈ					19.4ᵉ	20.4ᵉ
Developing countries	31.5	16.0	3.9	5.7	16.8	21.0	1.0	2.4	4.9	5.8	42.0	49.1
Petroleum-exporting	29.2	17.2	11.8	15.4	10.7	11.4	0.8	1.2	5.3	6.6	42.3	48.3
Newly industrializing	27.2	6.7	1.9	0.8	17.0	32.4	1.3	3.5	4.4	6.0	48.2	50.6
Manufacturing-oriented	36.5	17.1	1.3	1.7	20.3	23.2	1.0	3.1	5.3	6.3	35.6	48.0
Agricultural-exporting	29.0	19.1	1.6	3.1	18.2	21.9	1.0	2.6	4.9	4.6	45.4	48.5
Mineral-exporting	19.1	12.9	11.1	5.8	16.7	19.8	1.4	2.0	4.9	5.9	46.8	54.0
Least developed	57.4	42.7	0.8	2.4	5.7	8.5	0.7	1.1	3.0	4.4	32.4	41.0

Source: Ibid.

ᵃ *Shares of producing sectors in GDP measured at current prices and exchange rates.*
ᵇ *Composition of net material product produced, data listed under 1987 relate to 1985.*
ᶜ *Data listed under 1960 relate to 1970.*
ᵈ *Includes mining, quarrying and utilities.*
ᵉ *Includes construction.*

TABLE 2.4 *Distribution of economic activity in the world market economy by major regions and countries, 1960–1987[a]*
(In percentages)

Country group	Agriculture 1960	Agriculture 1987	Mining and quarrying 1960	Mining and quarrying 1987	Manufacturing 1960	Manufacturing 1987	Utilities 1960	Utilities 1987	Construction 1960	Construction 1987	Services 1960	Services 1987	GDP 1960	GDP 1987
World market economies	100	100	100	100	100	100	100	100	100	100	100	100	100	100
Developed market economies	50.2	47.3	77.3	64.9	90.0	85.4	93.0	87.2	85.1	84.1	86.0	87.2	83.2	84.1
Major industrial economies	39.3	36.6	68.3	51.1	81.3	75.2	84.1	76.3	73.1	71.9	77.1	76.5	74.0	73.3
North America	19.4	14.7	44.8	34.0	50.2	28.4	54.8	33.7	42.6	27.8	55.3	37.6	49.0	33.6
Europe	15.1	12.5	20.6	14.9	26.3	25.8	24.7	24.5	26.2	21.8	18.7	23.6	21.2	23.3
Japan	4.9	9.4	2.8	2.2	4.9	20.9	4.7	18.0	4.4	22.4	3.2	15.3	3.9	16.4
Other developed economies	10.9	10.7	9.0	13.8	8.6	10.2	8.9	10.9	12.0	12.2	8.9	10.7	9.2	10.8
Developing countries	49.8	52.7	22.7	35.1	10.0	14.6	7.0	12.8	14.9	15.9	14.0	12.8	16.8	15.9
Petroleum-exporting	8.0	14.3	12.0	24.1	1.2	2.0	0.9	1.6	2.8	4.5	2.4	3.2	3.0	4.0
Newly industrializing	1.6	2.9	0.4	0.6	0.4	2.9	0.3	2.5	0.5	2.1	0.6	1.7	0.6	2.1
Manufacturing-oriented	19.1	17.0	2.5	3.2	4.0	5.0	2.4	5.1	5.3	5.2	3.9	3.8	5.6	4.8
Agricultural-exporting	12.3	11.3	2.5	3.4	2.9	2.7	1.9	2.5	3.9	2.3	4.0	2.3	4.5	2.8
Mineral-exporting	3.3	3.0	4.9	3.3	1.3	1.9	1.1	1.9	1.8	1.4	2.3	1.5	2.1	1.7
Least developed countries	5.5	4.2	0.3	0.4	0.2	0.2	0.3	0.2	0.5	0.4	0.7	0.3	1.0	0.5

Source: Ibid.

[a] *Shares of country groups in gross sectoral product of world market economies measured at current prices and exchange rates.*

TABLE 2.5 *Indicators of investment and saving performance in the world economy, 1960–1987[a]*

Country group	Growth of GDP per capita[b]			Share of gross capital formation in GDP				Share of national saving in GDP				Share of external resources in GDP			
	1960–1970	1970–1980	1980–1987	1960	1970	1980	1987	1960	1970	1980	1987	1960	1970	1980	1987
World market economies	3.0	1.5	0.4	21.0	22.8	23.6	21.5	21.1	22.9	23.5	21.4	0.0	−0.1	0.1	0.2
Developed market economies	3.9	2.4	1.9	21.4	23.1	23.1	21.3	22.2	23.6	22.8	21.4	−0.7	−0.7	0.3	−0.1
Major industrial economies	3.8	2.5	2.1	20.9	22.4	22.8	21.2	22.0	23.4	23.1	21.5	−1.0	−1.1	−0.2	−0.3
North America	2.5	2.2	1.9	19.0	18.2	19.3	18.4	19.8	18.9	20.2	16.0	−0.8	−1.0	−0.9	2.4
Europe	3.8	2.4	1.8	23.2	24.7	22.9	19.7	24.5	26.0	22.7	21.4	−1.3	−1.3	0.2	−1.6
Japan	9.2	3.6	3.1	32.9	39.0	32.2	29.1	33.3	40.1	31.3	32.9	−0.4	0.0	0.9	−3.8
Other developed economies	4.2	1.9	1.1	24.7	27.4	24.4	21.7	23.8	25.0	21.6	20.8	−1.0	−2.3	−2.7	−0.8
Developing market economies	3.3	2.4	−0.5	19.1	21.2	25.6	22.8	15.8	18.5	26.1	21.0	3.3	2.8	−0.5	1.8
Petroleum-exporting	4.2	0.8	−3.5	19.3	22.8	25.5	26.6	17.3	22.0	39.2	21.9	2.0	0.8	−13.7	4.7
Newly industrializing	7.0	7.0	6.4	15.5	25.8	34.2	25.7	5.8	20.8	27.2	35.8	9.6	5.0	6.9	−9.3
Highly indebted countries	2.8	2.6	−1.2	23.2	23.4	25.6	19.7	20.5	20.0	21.5	17.4	2.7	3.5	4.0	2.3
Least developed countries	1.1	−0.2	0.3	9.6	12.2	16.5	14.5	5.1	7.5	4.7	4.5	4.5	4.8	11.7	10.0
Other developing countries	1.2	1.6	1.3	16.4	18.3	23.7	21.7	12.8	15.9	18.8	18.6	3.5	2.4	5.0	4.1

Source: Ibid.

[a] *Percentage share of capital formation, gross national saving and external resources in GDP measured at current prices and exchange rates.*
[b] *Measured at 1980 prices and exchange rates.*

TABLE 2.6 *Growth of exports and imports in the world economy, 1961–1987[a]*

Country group	Period	Exports	Exports at import prices	Imports	GDP[b]	Gross national income
World	1961–70	8.1	8.3	8.2	5.2	5.3
	1971–80	5.3	5.4	5.7	3.8	3.8
	1981–87	3.9	4.5	4.3	2.6	2.7
Developed market	1961–70	8.1	8.8	8.9	4.9	5.1
economies	1971–80	6.0	3.9	4.6	3.2	2.9
	1981–87	3.7	5.1	4.5	2.5	2.8
Major industrial	1961–70	8.1	9.0	8.9	4.9	5.0
economies	1971–80	6.4	3.7	4.8	3.3	2.9
	1981–87	3.6	5.3	5.0	2.6	2.9
Other developed	1961–70	8.2	8.4	8.8	5.4	5.4
economies	1971–80	4.9	4.3	4.2	3.0	2.8
	1981–87	4.0	4.5	3.4	1.9	2.1
Eastern Europe & the	1961–70	8.3		6.9	7.2	
USSR	1971–80	7.2		7.7	4.8	
	1981–87	4.2		3.8	2.8	
Eastern Europe	1961–70	7.5		7.3	5.9	
	1971–80	8.4		6.7	4.9	
	1981–87	4.1		3.9	2.2	
USSR	1961–70	9.2		6.3	7.5	
	1971–80	5.7		9.4	4.7	
	1981–87	4.4		3.7	3.1	
China	1961–70	−1.9	−1.3	−2.9		
	1971–80	13.4	12.0	13.0		
	1981–87	16.3	13.3	12.3		
Developing countries	1961–70	8.0	6.3	6.0	5.9	5.3
	1971–80	3.2	9.8	9.2	5.0	6.7
	1981–87	2.4	1.4	1.6	1.7	1.4
Petroleum-exporting	1961–70	8.9	6.0	6.2	7.2	5.0
	1971–80	0.2	14.7	12.7	3.9	10.3
	1981–87	−7.6	−9.1	−3.0	−1.2	−2.0
Newly industrializing	1961–70	13.2	14.4	13.0	9.8	10.2
	1971–80	12.8	11.8	12.0	8.6	8.2
	1981–87	13.5	15.0	10.6	8.3	9.5
Manufacture-exporting	1961–70	6.6	5.5	3.2	5.1	5.0
	1971–80	7.5	4.0	6.0	6.3	5.9
	1981–87	4.0	5.4	−0.8	3.1	3.3

continued

TABLE 2.6 *Growth of exports and imports in the world economy,
1961–1987[a] (continued)*

Country group	Period	Exports	Exports at import prices	Imports	GDP[b]	Gross national income
Agricultural-exporting	1961–70	5.3	5.0	5.3	4.7	4.6
	1971–80	5.8	4.3	6.0	4.8	4.5
	1981–87	6.8	5.3	2.1	1.6	1.3
Mineral-exporting	1961–70	4.2	5.9	5.7	5.2	5.7
	1971–80	3.8	2.6	4.2	3.5	3.2
	1981–87	3.3	0.4	−0.8	1.6	0.7
Least developed	1961–70	4.1	3.7	4.4	3.6	3.5
	1971–80	2.6	1.6	4.9	2.3	2.2
	1981–87	5.6	11.0	7.7	1.8	2.7

Source: Ibid.

[a] *Average annual rates of growth of exports and imports of goods and non-factor services measured at 1980 prices and exchange rates.*

[b] *For Eastern Europe and the USSR, NMP.*

TABLE 2.7 *Commodity structure of world trade 1965–1986*[a]

Region	Year	Composition of Exports				Composition of Imports			
		Food-stuffs	Crude Materials	Fuels	Manufac-tures	Food-stuffs	Crude Materials	Fuels	Manufac-tures
World	1965	16.0	12.6	9.5	61.8	16.0	12.6	9.5	61.8
	1970	13.1	10.5	9.1	67.4	13.1	10.5	9.1	67.4
	1980	9.6	6.6	23.1	60.7	9.6	6.6	23.1	60.7
	1986	9.5	5.7	12.2	72.6	9.5	5.7	12.2	72.6
Developed market economies	1965	13.5	10.5	3.4	72.6	15.8	14.3	10.6	59.3
	1970	10.7	8.7	3.4	77.2	13.0	11.5	10.0	65.5
	1980	10.0	6.4	6.8	76.8	8.9	7.0	26.3	57.3
	1986	8.5	5.2	4.9	81.4	9.7	5.5	11.4	73.4
Eastern Europe and the USSR	1965	10.8	10.5	13.3	65.5	20.6	12.4	6.6	60.4
	1970	10.5	10.9	8.9	69.8	15.7	9.9	6.0	68.4
	1980	5.2	7.5	29.2	58.2	15.0	5.7	10.8	68.4
	1986	4.7	5.2	28.1	62.0	9.5	6.3	19.4	64.8
China	1965	29.4	21.0	1.8	47.8	25.8	14.7	6.0	58.9
	1970	30.6	19.7	0.7	49.0	14.0	10.9	5.0	74.7
	1980	16.1	9.5	20.6	53.8	13.5	16.2	1.0	69.2
	1986	15.8	9.5	12.2	62.5	4.4	8.2	1.1	86.3
Developing countries	1965	26.4	20.4	29.3	23.9	13.9	6.9	8.1	71.2
	1970	22.4	16.5	31.7	29.4	11.9	6.6	8.3	73.2
	1980	9.5	6.7	57.8	26.0	9.8	5.2	18.3	66.7
	1986	14.4	7.2	32.9	45.4	9.5	5.7	12.6	72.3
North Africa	1965	18.6	23.1	46.3	12.1	20.1	8.1	4.7	67.0
	1970	12.8	12.8	63.0	11.4	14.7	8.9	4.4	72.0
	1980	2.3	3.7	85.3	8.7	15.9	5.5	7.5	71.1
	1986	4.9	5.4	75.2	14.4	17.5	6.7	6.5	69.3

continued

TABLE 2.7 *Commodity structure of world trade 1965–1986ᵃ (continued)*

Region	Year	Composition of exports				Composition of imports			
		Food-stuffs	Crude materials	Fuels	Manufac-tures	Food-stuffs	Crude materials	Fuels	Manufac-tures
Sub-Saharan Africa	1965	31.9	33.0	5.2	30.0	10.9	2.4	5.7	80.9
	1970	31.1	23.9	11.6	33.5	10.4	2.2	5.8	81.7
	1980	15.2	10.2	56.7	17.9	11.4	2.3	10.9	75.4
	1986	31.6	12.2	41.3	14.9	13.4	3.7	9.6	73.2
West Asia	1965	3.1	3.3	85.7	8.0	16.8	4.8	2.8	75.6
	1970	2.4	2.4	84.9	10.4	14.5	5.2	3.4	76.9
	1980	0.5	0.3	91.9	7.3	12.4	2.7	5.5	79.5
	1986	1.3	1.2	88.6	9.0	14.4	2.4	5.7	77.4
South and South East Asia	1965	25.4	31.2	6.5	36.9	16.6	9.1	6.4	67.8
	1970	17.6	26.6	6.8	48.9	14.2	9.8	7.6	68.3
	1980	25.8	9.7	36.1	28.4	9.4	4.1	25.6	60.9
	1986	9.7	7.3	10.9	72.0	6.5	7.3	13.9	72.3
Latin America and the Caribbean	1965	37.2	16.0	28.7	18.1	10.3	5.9	13.4	70.3
	1970	37.4	15.2	23.8	23.6	9.6	5.0	10.9	74.5
	1980	25.8	9.7	36.1	28.4	9.4	4.1	25.6	60.9
	1986	32.7	11.3	23.8	32.3	8.3	4.9	18.5	68.3
Mediterranean	1965	33.2	17.5	1.0	48.3	11.6	12.1	6.8	69.6
	1970	26.2	17.4	1.1	55.2	7.4	8.6	5.1	78.9
	1980	20.3	9.9	2.2	67.6	5.5	7.6	29.6	57.3
	1986	17.4	6.0	2.1	74.5	3.9	6.5	14.4	75.2

Source: Department of International Economic and Social Affairs of the United Nations Secretariat.
ᵃ *Percentage share of foodstuffs (SITC 0 and 1), crude materials (SITC 2 and 4), fuels (SITC 3) and manufactures (SITC 5 to 9) in total commodity trade (SITC 0 to 9) measured in current United States dollars.*

TABLE 2.8 *Geographical distribution of world trade, 1965–1986*[a]

Region	Year	Share of world exports					Share of world imports				
		Food-stuffs	Crude materials	Fuels	Manufac-tures	Total trade	Food-stuffs	Crude materials	Fuels	Manufac-tures	Total trade
Developed market economies	1965	57.1	56.2	24.0	79.5	67.6	66.8	77.0	75.3	65.3	68.0
	1970	58.0	58.5	26.7	81.0	70.7	70.6	77.8	77.7	68.8	70.8
	1980	65.2	60.4	18.3	79.3	62.6	63.6	73.0	78.3	65.5	68.8
	1986	63.4	64.4	28.2	79.2	70.6	71.1	68.3	65.0	70.6	69.8
Eastern Europe & the USSR	1965	7.7	9.4	15.9	12.1	11.1	14.9	11.4	8.0	11.3	11.6
	1970	8.2	10.6	9.9	10.5	10.2	12.5	9.7	6.8	10.5	10.3
	1980	4.2	8.8	9.9	7.5	7.8	12.6	7.0	3.8	9.1	8.1
	1986	4.2	8.0	19.8	7.4	8.6	8.5	9.4	13.4	7.5	8.4
China	1965	1.4	1.3	0.1	0.6	0.8	1.3	1.0	0.1	0.8	0.8
	1970	1.4	1.1	0.0	0.4	0.6	0.8	0.7	0.0	0.8	0.7
	1980	1.5	1.3	0.8	0.8	0.9	1.4	2.4	0.0	1.1	1.0
	1986	2.5	2.5	1.5	1.3	1.5	0.7	2.1	0.1	1.8	1.5
Developing countries	1965	32.1	31.6	59.9	7.5	19.5	16.2	10.2	15.8	21.6	18.7
	1970	31.1	28.7	63.3	7.9	18.2	15.6	11.1	14.6	18.9	17.3
	1980	28.0	28.8	71.0	12.2	28.4	22.1	17.1	17.0	23.7	21.5
	1986	28.5	23.9	50.4	11.7	18.7	19.3	19.3	19.8	19.2	19.3
North Africa	1965	1.7	2.7	7.2	0.3	1.5	1.7	0.9	0.7	1.5	1.4
	1970	1.5	1.9	10.8	0.3	1.6	1.3	0.9	0.5	1.2	1.1
	1980	0.6	1.3	8.5	0.3	2.3	2.3	1.2	0.5	1.7	1.4
	1986	0.5	1.0	6.5	0.2	1.1	2.7	1.7	0.8	1.4	1.5
Sub-Saharan Africa	1965	5.2	6.8	1.4	1.3	2.6	1.9	0.5	1.7	3.7	2.8
	1970	5.7	5.5	3.0	1.2	2.4	1.9	0.5	1.5	2.9	2.4

continued

41

TABLE 2.8 *Geographical distribution of world trade, 1965–1986ᵃ (continued)*

Region	Year	Share of world exports					Share of world imports				
		Food-stuffs	Crude materials	Fuels	Manufac-tures	Total trade	Food-stuffs	Crude materials	Fuels	Manufac-tures	Total trade
Sub-Saharan Africa (*cont.*)	1980	3.9	3.8	6.1	0.7	2.5	2.5	0.7	1.0	2.6	2.1
	1986	4.0	2.6	4.0	0.2	1.2	1.9	0.9	1.1	1.4	1.4
Western Asia	1965	0.6	0.8	27.2	0.4	3.0	1.8	0.6	0.5	2.1	1.7
	1970	0.6	0.8	31.1	0.5	3.3	1.8	0.8	0.6	1.9	1.6
	1980	0.5	0.5	41.7	1.3	10.5	5.3	1.7	1.0	5.4	4.1
	1986	0.4	0.7	24.1	0.4	3.3	4.8	1.4	1.5	3.4	3.2
South and East Asia	1965	7.8	12.2	3.4	3.0	4.9	6.4	4.5	4.2	6.8	6.2
	1970	6.3	11.9	3.5	3.4	4.7	6.1	5.3	4.7	5.7	5.6
	1980	7.9	14.7	6.1	6.7	7.2	6.0	8.9	7.6	7.7	7.6
	1986	8.7	11.0	7.6	8.4	8.5	5.7	10.7	9.4	8.3	8.3
Latin America and the Caribbean	1965	15.9	8.7	20.6	2.0	6.9	3.9	2.8	8.5	6.9	6.0
	1970	16.2	8.2	14.8	2.0	5.7	4.1	2.7	6.7	6.2	5.6
	1980	14.6	8.0	8.5	2.6	5.4	5.5	3.5	6.2	5.6	5.6
	1986	14.4	8.3	8.1	1.9	4.2	4.0	4.0	6.9	4.3	4.6
Mediterranean	1965	1.9	1.2	0.1	0.7	0.9	0.8	1.0	0.8	1.2	1.1
	1970	1.6	1.3	0.1	0.6	0.8	0.7	1.0	0.7	1.5	1.3
	1980	1.4	1.0	0.1	0.7	0.6	0.7	1.4	1.5	1.1	1.2
	1986	1.6	1.0	0.2	0.9	0.9	0.5	1.3	1.3	1.2	1.1

Source: Ibid.

ᵃ *Percentage share of foodstuffs (SITC 0 and 1), crude materials (SITC 2 and 4), fuels (SITC 3) and manufactures (SITC 5–9) in total commodity trade (SITC 0–9) measured in current United States dollars.*

3.
The World Economy
to 2000

THE PRINCIPAL macroeconomic variables of the world economy
have been updated to the year 1990 and projected to the year 2000
in the baseline scenario. For the period 1988–1990, preliminary
estimates and project LINK and UN Secretariat assessments were
used. World economic growth beginning in 1991 has been projected using the Global Econometric Model (GEM) of the UN
Secretariat on the assumption that long-term trends in macroeconomic indicators are sustainable. This assumption has been
translated country by country into expected magnitudes for investment and investment efficiency. GDP growth has been derived as the share of investment in GDP divided by the incremental
capital output ratio (ICOR). Given the projections for GDP and
estimated behavioural relationships in constant prices, macroeconomic patterns of resource allocation, trade flows, and output
by industrial origin have been derived separately for each country
included in the model and summarized for regions.

A. THE BASELINE SCENARIO

1. Domestic and foreign resource mobilization

The share of investment in GDP is an indicator of the formation of physical capital such as equipment, buildings, and other physical infrastructure. As discussed in Chapter 2, the long-term experience of many countries, especially of the newly industrializing economies, suggests that sustainable growth calls for strong investment. A high rate of investment facilitates technological change, since adding new equipment to the existing stock or rapidly replacing aging equipment increases the proportion of output produced with improved technologies. However, the investment here does not reflect to the fullest extent the investment in human resources, which is also a major contributor to total factor productivity.

The capacity to invest depends upon the ability of countries to mobilize internal saving and to attract a new inflow of saving from abroad. High rates of growth and favourable external conditions do not necessarily cause strong investment but both help to overcome a scarcity of investment resources. Major changes have occurred in investment trends. Their sources of financing during the period 1975–1990 have been analyzed in Chapter 2. The depressed economic conditions that prevailed in many developing countries in the 1980s and caused a decline in the absolute level of foreign direct investment inflows may improve in the 1990s. The heavy external indebtedness of many developing countries, especially in Latin America, adversely affected investments. Low and even negative rates of economic growth have reduced returns on existing investment in those countries. The factors making for an increase in domestic and foreign investments are quite similar. Since more than one third of foreign direct investment is financed with reinvested earnings, depressed economic conditions and the expectation of lower profitability constrain new capital commitments. If investment is to be restored to a level sufficient to sustain moderate growth in the 1990s, most developing countries will have to increase domestic savings. Which policies will be chosen depends both on the domestic situations and on the international environment. The methods by which many developing countries adjusted previously to the changing external environment in the 1980s often led to a fall in domestic investment, idle capacity, and capital flight.

Given the modest growth expected in the baseline scenario (table 3.1), the percentage share of government and private final consumption expenditure in the GDP of the developed market economies is not expected to change. Similarly, the share of gross national saving in their GDP is projected to change little during the next decade. The share of private consumption in the GDP of developing countries is expected to fall, with sharp differences among developing country regions. In the high income oil-exporting countries and in the least developed countries, the share of government consumption is also projected to fall noticeably. In South and East Asia, domestic policies are expected to be more stimulative partly in response to demands for real wage increases. These increases will also reduce the substantial surpluses in the current account of their balance of payments. For the highly in-debted countries in Latin America the slower growth and reduced consumption shares projected under the baseline illustrate the real costs of adjustment.

Although the adjustment measures already taken in many countries have been incorporated into the baseline scenario, they are expected to yield only limited results in changing prevailing macroeconomic spending patterns in the short term. One key problem requiring a substantial period of adjustment is the elim-ination of the large internal and external imbalances that arose in the last decade. With improved policy co-ordination among all countries and appropriate fiscal and monetary policies, however, the baseline projection assumes that saving-investment imbalances will be progressively reduced during the 1990s. In the developed market economies, this adjustment is accomplished largely through a slowdown in the rate of growth of government ex-penditures. For many countries with current account deficits, rais-ing national saving would be preferable to squeezing investment because the latter would slow the growth of productive capacity.

In the late 1980s this strategy combined with strong consumer demand and increased investment demand in the European Economic Community (EEC) has produced an investment boom that may continue in the beginning of the 1990s.

The U.S. is so prominent in world markets that special mention should be made of the assumptions regarding the "twin deficits". The baseline scenario assumes that the United States will continue to pursue policies aimed at preventing further deterioration of its internal and external deficits. On the internal side, this translates into a declining share of government consumption in GDP and increasing private savings. This will be a consequence of demographic changes and of national policies to encourage private household and corporate saving. The exchange rate of the U.S. dollar is also expected to fall against the currencies of its major trading partners. This together with improved productivity will raise corporate saving. A result of these assumptions is that the import share in GDP for the U.S. may remain relatively constant, at about 15 per cent, throughout the projection period whereas the export share is expected to rise.

In Eastern Europe and the USSR lower investment shares and higher investment efficiencies imply the continuing shift of these economies toward consumer goods sectors. The decreasing investment shares also imply an improvement in their external account situation, because their imports share of capital goods would also be smaller.

Investment is assumed to increase in developing countries, with the adjustment process centered on reducing government consumption expenditures. This is expected to release savings for productive investment, with the result that the pace of growth in these countries will accelerate slightly under the baseline as the year 2000 approaches. Nevertheless, the projected rate of economic growth, particularly in the low income and least developed countries, is expected to remain below its long-term historical trend.

The increases in investment shares before the mid-1980s were facilitated by increased export earnings among the oil-exporting countries. On the expectation of sustained demand for oil in the

1990s, this tendency may be restored. An observed long-term tendency for investment to increase in the fast-growing exporters of manufactures will continue. Assuming improved access to international capital markets in the case of other developing countries seems plausible. In a long-term perspective, countries with buoyant export earnings could raise domestic saving ratios. They have fallen in most of the major borrowing countries. The higher rates of investment during the 1990s will be associated with considerable structural change and GDP growth rates sustained at moderate levels.

The abrupt deterioration of the world economy in the early 1980s depressed export earnings and led to a net transfer of financial resources from the indebted developing countries. Domestic savings ratios first tended to fall but have since risen in response to the implementation of balance-of-payments adjustment programmes. Until now the improved saving performance of these countries has not led to increased investment shares, since the savings have been used to service the external debt.

Falling investment shares were not the only factor affecting economic growth in the developing countries. Measures of productivity, such as incremental capital efficiency, labour productivity, and the net rate of return on fixed capital, have all tended to worsen. The importance of capital efficiency is highlighted by country experiences with policies aimed at attracting foreign private capital inflows, external borrowing, stimulating domestic saving, and cutting government spending. In the long run a failure to increase capital efficiency cannot be compensated by other means. Foreign capital and domestic saving must be efficiently transformed into productive investment.

Official development finance can be expected to grow at an annual average rate of 2–3 per cent in real terms in the medium term. This is suggested by present commitments to increasing the resources available to multilateral development institutions and sustained bilateral official development assistance (ODA). Private capital flows may also continue to grow somewhat in real terms. They are comprised of private direct investment but also international bank lending to countries without debt difficulties and—

in the context of concerted lending—to others. Thus, if current account deficits in the developing countries remain at their present levels as a percentage of GDP, they could probably continue to be financed.

The projected investment shares for the 1990s are close to those observed during the late 1980s, reflecting the internal and external financing constraints impeding investment in many countries. In some economies, the investment projections have been further adjusted to reflect financing constraints associated with debt re-payment obligations. By assuming a return to the 1983–1988 av-erage, the projections are based on investment shares somewhat higher than at present (see figure 3.1). In the case of the developed market economies, the projected average share of investment in GDP is 23.6 per cent. This is slightly higher than the 22.3 per cent registered in the 1980–1985 period (see table 3.2) but roughly the same as the 1986–1990 average. In many developing regions,

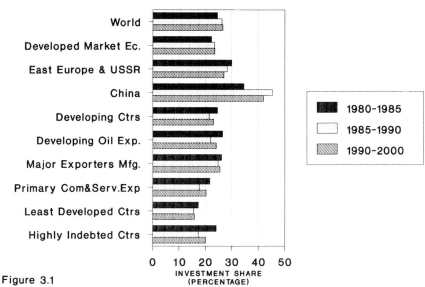

INVESTMENT SHARES: PROJECTED
UNDER A BASELINE SCENARIO

Figure 3.1

INVESTMENT SHARE
(PERCENTAGE)

however, persistent or emerging internal and external constraints are seen as continuing to impede capital formation and productivity growth. This is especially true in the highly indebted countries in Latin America and Africa. In Eastern Europe and the USSR the ratio of gross capital formation to NMP is expected to stabilize, following an expected decline in gross fixed capital formation in the late 1980s. Their allocation will continue to change in favour of the production of consumer goods.

2. Capital efficiency

With the turbulence of the 1980s, when output in many economies has actually fallen in spite of continued investment, it is difficult to assess the contribution of investment to growth. Clearly, however, all cases of rapid growth were associated with high rates of capital formation. And setbacks in output *ex post,* as compared to the expectation when investments were made, have been linked to such factors as an unexpected worsening of conditions in international markets and mismanagement of resources. If it can be achieved, a higher level of capital efficiency is the best recipe for achieving sustainable growth without painful cuts in public and private consumption.

The proxy for capital efficiency in this study is the ratio of investment to changes in output. Changes in this measure, known as the incremental capital-output ratio (ICOR), observed on a year-to-year basis, are the results of several factors. When output expands in the presence of unutilized capacity, the ICORs may be quite low. Investment in modernizing installations may take place, however, even during periods of slack demand. This leads to higher than expected ICORs while underway, but to lower ICORs once the modernization has been completed.

These microeconomic effects may be reinforced by developments in macroeconomic variables. When investment growth rates are high in the economy as a whole, renewal of the capital stock may occur more rapidly, speeding the diffusion of new technologies and leading to more rapid improvement in capital efficiency. Also, when structural change occurs in response to trade liberalization or other policy measures, factors of production may be shifted from less efficient to more efficient economic sectors. Shifts of this sort may also occur when countries pass from one stage of economic development to another. For example, a period of infrastructure development entailing high capital-output ratios may be followed by one where small and medium size enterprises, with much smaller capital-output ratios, dominate the investment process.

During the projection period the assumption is that capacity utilization will remain at the same average levels in the developed market economies and that rates of investment and the pace of structural adjustment will be high. This will lead to the rapid diffusion of new technologies as occurred in the last decade. These assumptions are expected to lead to some improvement in ICORs. The assumption of a better external economic environment for developing countries may lead to stronger investment. The re-orientation of policies to encourage exports and allow more competition for domestic import-substituting industries expected to improve allocation of investments and their efficiency. This effect is not expected to be noticeable, however, until late in the 1990s.

The assumption made in the baseline scenario is that the efficiency of capital in most countries will improve from the historically low levels registered during the early 1980s. Nonetheless, it will remain below those observed during the 1970s. Thus, for the developed market economies, it is assumed that about $7.6 of investment must be made to increase the productive capacity of these economies by $1 in the 1990s, as compared to an average of $6.9 in the 1970s and more than $8 in the period 1980–1990. Capital efficiency in the case of the developing countries is assumed to be close to that of the 1970s and late 1980s, but with significant variations in performance expected among individual countries.

Among major exporters of manufactures, capital efficiency is expected to be almost the same as in 1986–1990, about $5 of investment for $1 increase in GDP. This is about 30 per cent lower than in the 1970s. In the highly indebted countries, capital efficiency is expected to improve in the 1990s to the level of $6.7 per $1 increase in GDP. However, it is about 40 per cent below their standard in the 1970s. Capital efficiency in primary commodities and services exporting countries is expected to be about 20 per cent lower in the 1990s than its level in the 1970s, but this means a significant improvement compared to the 1980s level of $11.4 for 1985–1990 and $8.9 for 1986–1990.

Investment efficiency in Africa is expected to be generally better than in the 1980s. This implies some improvement in agriculture, as indicated in the projections presented in Chapter 6.

The low investment levels in these countries in the 1980s was itself a major constraint to improving capital efficiency. An analysis of the situation by sectors suggests that scarcity of investment combined with minimum requirements for infrastructure development and other capital-intensive sectors limits the scope for efficient re-allocation of investment. The projections presented in table 3.2 are nonetheless based on the assumption of modest improvements in capital efficiency but not exceeding standards of performance occasionally achieved in the 1975–1990 period.

Debt indicators such as the ratio of debt service to exports and of debt to GDP would slowly improve in the highly-indebted developing countries. The sustained growth expected of developed market economies plus China, Eastern Europe and the USSR, together with an expectation of stable oil prices, should promote export growth in developing countries. Debt reduction schemes are expected to have positive implications for an increase in investment in debtor countries. GDP growth would still be modest, however, and in many developing countries it would not permit meaningful increases in income per capita.

3. World GDP growth and the distribution of income

World economic growth is expected to be significantly below its longer-term trend but higher than recent experience. Aggregate gross world GDP has grown at an annual rate of 2.8 per cent during the 1980s, and in the developing countries by not more than 2.5 per cent. The world-wide recession of the early 1980s reduced economic growth in all major world regions. In the developing countries it fell precipitously to less than 2 per cent a year in the period 1980–1985. A recovery in world economic growth is forecast for the period 1985–1990, but it is expected to be highly uneven, below population growth in many African developing countries and barely matching it in Latin American developing countries.[1]

For the developed market economies, the baseline projection is for a growth rate of 3.1 per cent on average during the 1990s.[2] This will be following an expected recovery to an average rate of growth of GDP of 3 per cent a year in the late 1980s. The main reason for this is primarily the increased investment demand and capital efficiency induced by integration in Europe during the 1990s. Although the growth in these countries will be uneven, however, it will lead to further convergence in per capita income among developed market economies. The economies of Eastern Europe and the USSR are expected to recover from their present low rates of growth to a rate of GDP growth of 3.6 per cent over the same period. On a per capita basis, both of these figures (about 2.5 per cent for developed market economies and 3 per cent for Eastern Europe and the USSR) imply steady improvement in average living standards (see figure 3.2).

In the developing countries, on the other hand, the average growth rate of GDP is expected to be 4.3 per cent a year. Although this represents an improvement over recent trends, it is well below the growth rate of 5.1 per cent recorded during the 1970s. Given the marked diversity of expected performance in different developing country regions, it implies negligible growth or an absolute decline in per capita income in some of the heavily indebted and least developed countries. It also implies very moderate increases in most other groups of developing countries except South and East Asia (see tables 3.2 and 3.3).

The average per capita income of the developing countries in the Latin America & the Caribbean region is projected to be $2,320

GROWTH RATES OF GDP PER CAPITA
UNDER A BASE LINE SCENARIO

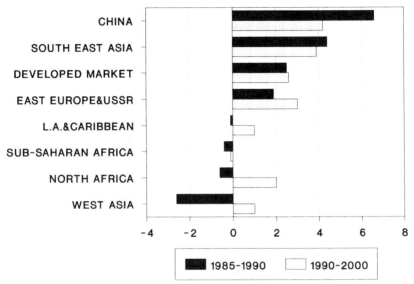

Figure 3.2

in the year 2000; the average for 49 countries in Africa is expected
to be only $670. Within Africa, per capita income is projected to
vary widely among countries. In many of them it will be lower
than in the mid-1980s. The least developed countries are expected
to increase their average per capita income from $240 in 1985 to
only $270 in 2000 (see table 3.3 and figure 3.3).

Swift progress in raising labour productivity and per capita
income levels is an essential prerequisite for full economic and
social development. This is true although the process of world
development involves much more than economic growth and
structural transformation in the developing countries. The alleviation of poverty, greater employment opportunities, good nutrition and health, and better living conditions all contribute to
increasing the level of productivity of the labour force. There are
many aspects of the income distribution process: the allocation of
world income over countries, the proportion of income received

PROJECTIONS OF GDP PER CAPITA
TO THE YEAR 2000

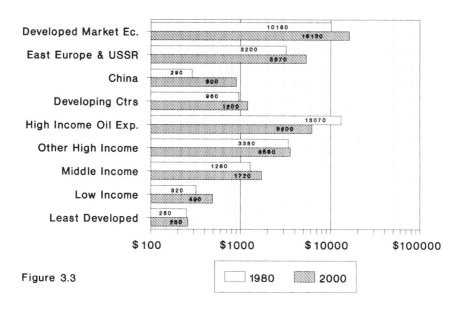

Figure 3.3

by different income groups within any one national economy, and the division of income among factors of production. All are affected by changing production technologies and changes in the patterns of final expenditure and international trade.

Despite the growth of the world economy in the last decades and the expected moderate growth of the developing countries in the 1990s, per capita GDP in the least developed and/or primary commodities exporters will remain at a very low level (figure 3.3).

Measured at constant 1980 prices and exchange rates, the ratio of GDP per capita between the developed and developing areas of the world has worsened significantly during the last decade and a half. Under the baseline scenario it would continue to do so. The ratio of GDP per capita between the developed and developing countries was more than 10 to 1 in 1970, became 12 to 1 by 1985, and is expected to exceed 13 to 1 by the year 2000.

Because population is growing faster than income for most of the African countries in this group, the gap is widening, whereas in some of the Asian countries the gap has stabilized or is slightly shrinking. Although West Asia and Latin America & the Caribbean have the highest per capita incomes of the developing regions, their projected gaps are widening. In the case of West Asia, the gap in 2000 is estimated to be 5.3 as compared to 3.5 in 1985. This is primarily due to a very high projected population growth rate of 3.2 per cent for the region. In Latin America & the Caribbean, where the gap is estimated at 5.3 in 1985, it is projected to grow to 7 in 2000. Although population growth in Latin America is projected to be lower than the average for the developing countries as a whole (1.9 per cent as compared to 2.3 per cent), it is still high as compared to the projected population growth rate of the developed market economies, where it is expected to be only about 0.5 per cent during the 1990s. Another contributing factor to the widening gap in Latin America & the Caribbean is the relatively modest growth rate of GDP (2.9 per cent) projected for this region for the 1990s. There is also considerable variation among countries within groups. For a dozen of the least developed countries, for example, projected income per capita (in 1980 U.S. dollars) for the year 2000 will be about $160, but it will exceed $300 for Bangladesh, and will be close to $400 for some other countries in this group.

When the countries are grouped by export orientation, as in the left hand column of table 3.3, one clear pattern emerges: the major manufacturing exporters are the only group that shows an improvement in its relative GDP per capita gap with the developed market economies. However, not all countries in this group have projected declining gaps; it is only the faster growing countries in Asia. For the group of other manufacturing oriented countries with the highest income per capita of the non-petroleum exporting developing market economies, the projected gap in the year 2000 varies between 21.4 and 3.2, and has a median of 7.

The average figures for per capita GDP for various developing country groupings in tables 3.1 and 3.3 do not fully reflect the widespread incidence of poverty. Using estimates and patterns of

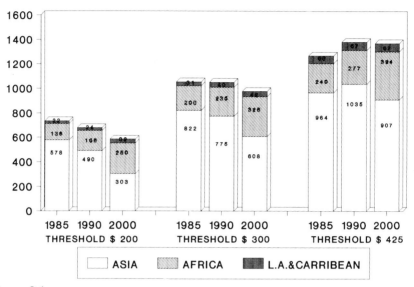

POPULATION WITH PER CAPITA INCOME BELOW
THRESHOLD OF $200, $300, $425 IN 1985,
1990 AND 2000, BASELINE SCENARIO

Figure 3.4

income distribution in countries accounting for about 80 per cent of the population of the developing countries, almost 1 billion people would still have a per capita income of less than $300 per year (in 1980 dollars) by the year 2000. In 1985 this income group represented about one quarter of the world's population, and in the year 2000 it would be about one fifth. Furthermore, all the improvement is expected to be in Asian countries. In Africa and Latin America & the Caribbean, the number of people in this category is projected to increase (see figure 3.4).

If the per capita income threshold is raised to $425, the level used by the World Bank to divide the low and middle income countries, then the number of people below this threshold is estimated to be 1.4 billion by the year 2000. On the other hand, if a lower per capita income threshold is used, say $200, based upon the official estimate of a low income person in Kenya for the year 1980, the corresponding numbers of people below this threshold would be 736 million in 1985 and 585 million in 2000.[3] Regardless of the income threshold chosen, little reduction in the number of people below the threshold is expected by the year 2000.

Even in countries with a better historical performance and with better prospects, a great part of the population will have a per capita income of less than $300 per year. The group of major manufacturing exporters is projected to have at least 400 million people with a per capita income of less than $300 in the year 2000. The group of other manufacturing oriented countries is projected to have more than 31 million people under the $300 threshold in that year. The World Bank has estimated that some 800 million people now lack enough food. They survive on less than the minimum nutritional requirements as defined by the Food & Agriculture Organization of the UN (FAO) and the World Health Organization (WHO). The number of people running serious health risks because of caloric deficiency reached about 340 million in 1980. The number of absolute poor did not change much between 1980 and 1990.

The worrisome trends in some developing country regions are due to two factors: low rates of GDP growth for reasons explained earlier, and high rates of population growth (see Chapter 8). Measures that might improve GDP growth performance are discussed in the present chapter, but they will not have much importance for the incidence of poverty without complementary policies for income distribution and slowing population growth.

4. World Trade

World trade is expected to expand by 4.5 per cent per year during the 1990s. Some degree of policy co-ordination should take place among the major industrial countries, but the baseline scenario assumes that a principal concern will be to make their economies less vulnerable to competition from abroad. Developing countries are assumed to take strong measures to deal with a heavy debt burden leading to greater efforts to increase exports. An unfavourable external environment, however, may cause other countries to limit imports by adopting more inward-oriented growth strategies. The assumption of relatively stable oil prices is associated with the increase in trade in energy products.

For the developed market economies competition from abroad will continue to be a potential source of income loss and labour displacement as well as a source of imbalance in the external accounts. Consequently, the thrust of domestic policy in some countries is to limit import absorption, and in others to rely on domestic demand rather than exports as the main source of growth. Major exporters of manufactured products, among the developing countries, have been increasing their share in all developed country markets, especially in the North American and Japanese markets. They account for about 15 per cent of manufactured imports in both of the markets. Another significant change in trade shares was related to oil-exporting countries. Their shares were falling in the period of declining real oil prices and fast growth of world trade in manufactured goods and services.

The expansion of exports and imports in the 1990s is expected to remain faster than the growth in domestic economic activity in most regions, but the difference will be less than in the most recent five-year period (table 3.4 and figure 3.5). Efforts in developing countries have been directed at restoring external balance by limiting the growth of import demand while attempting to ensure that exports increase faster than imports. In most groups of developing countries imports are expected to grow faster than GDP.

The import content of investment is high in developing countries. Recent import cuts have reduced directly or indirectly the degree of utilization and expansion of productive capacities in these countries. Under baseline assumptions, merchandise trade deficits are expected to decline thanks to strong growth in exports of manufactured goods over the course of the 1990s. Consequently, the balance of payments on current account is expected to improve somewhat. Economic growth and welfare enhancement stemming from specialization in production and diversification in consumption, however, remain less than they would be

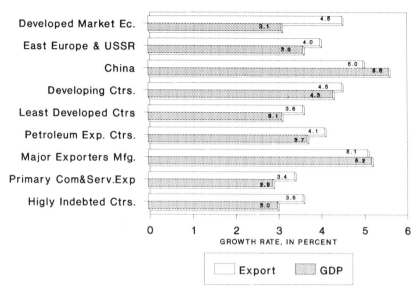

GROWTH RATES OF EXPORTS AND GDP
FOR 1990-2000

Figure 3.5

under more expansive policies. Moreover, continued policies to restrain domestic demand may contribute to a slower pace of capital formation, whereas simultaneous efforts on the part of many countries to increase exports of primary commodities may lead to persistently low commodity prices.

The baseline scenario assumes that world trade will continue to increase at a more rapid rate than GDP, 4.5 per cent as compared to 3.5 per cent per annum. But slower growth in world import demand necessarily implies dampened export possibilities. Considerable changes are envisioned in the source of world exports. There will be a relative slowdown in the rate of increase of exports from the developed market economies, except for intraregional trade in Western Europe. A relative increase in that of the developing countries is expected. These projections also assume increased export shares for heavily indebted developing countries as they continue to pursue efforts towards structural adjustment.

Further, the two-digit rates of export growth of major developing country exporters of manufactures recorded in the past will not be sustained over the next decade.

The internal balances shown in table 3.1 are measured in constant 1980 prices and consequently do not take into account changes in relative prices. Were these balances to be measured in nominal terms, their magnitude and perhaps even their sign would be different; indeed, real internal balances (and identical external balances) shown in table 3.1 for 1985 for some groups of developing countries, notably, the highly indebted countries, differ significantly from the nominal balance computed at current relative prices.

If the terms of trade of the period 1985–1986 were to prevail to the year 2000, the balance of payments in nominal terms for the developed countries would be positive at about 0.5 per cent of their GDP instead of being slightly negative. By contrast, the balance for the developing countries would be negative. The highly indebted countries would have a deficit of about 2 per cent of GDP, and the primary commodity and service exporters would have a deficit of over 5 per cent of GDP.

These deficits would be correspondingly larger if the terms of trade worsened for the indebted developing countries. A sharp deterioration of the terms of trade for these countries forced them to export larger quantities in order to service their debt. When preparing the projections of world trade, it was assumed there would be no further changes in the terms of trade. That is, future movements in export prices would be the same as import prices. On these assumptions, movements in the real balances projected here indicate the direction and movement in nominal balances.

B. ALTERNATIVE SCENARIOS

Long-term projections of the world economy made available by various international agencies show close agreement on the expected'rates of GDP growth at the global level. However, their projections for the developed market economies, China, and Eastern Europe fall within a narrower range than those for developing countries.

The generally low GDP growth rates projected for developing countries are unlikely to be exceeded unless significant policy changes are made by developed and developing countries alike. Some of the premises of the baseline scenario may be modified by policy changes. These may be grouped into four different categories:

1. Accelerated structural change in the developed market economies may ensue from the following: widespread concern with productivity, including more efficient use of energy; the effort to create a European internal market by 1992; and from the implementation of the free trade agreement between the United States and Canada. These three changes might raise annual GDP growth rates by one-half percentage point or more;

2. Improved co-ordination of macroeconomic policies among major developed market economies could result in lower world real interest rates. New arrangements for the channelling of surplus savings towards developing countries could substantially enhance the import and investment capacity of developing countries. The lowering of protectionist barriers against new and competitive producers would also be an essential boost to growth in the world economy;

3. In view of the recent political changes and ongoing economic reforms in Eastern Europe and the USSR, annual growth in this region could reach 4 to 5 per cent;

4. Developing countries have a large agenda for improving their own economic performance and also have much to gain from reducing trade barriers among themselves.

In these more favourable circumstances, the baseline scenario, which holds little hope for the most disadvantaged parts of the world economy, could be modified quite substantially. Instead of a rate of growth of GDP for developing countries of 4.3 per cent, one might expect GDP growth in the range of 5 to 6 per cent, enough to allow a significant reduction in world poverty.

In analyzing the sensitivity of the baseline scenario to changes in policy assumptions, the Secretariat made use of three global models: GEM and the System for Interlinked Global Modelling and Analysis (SIGMA)[4], developed and maintained by the Department of International Economic and Social Affairs of the UN Secretariat (DIESA) and UNCTAD respectively, and the Future of Global Interdependence (FUGI), developed and maintained by Professor Akira Onishi and associates at Soka University, Japan.[5]

These models differ in the numbers of regions or countries identified separately, the types of production functions used, the level of sectoral detail, the extent to which money, prices, and exchange rates are incorporated, and the level of detail on external transactions. Nonetheless, the economic logic underlying the models' specifications is similar, especially in the modelling of the developing countries. Production in developing countries is heavily dependent on fixed capital formation but may also depend on labour force (SIGMA, FUGI), import of intermediate goods (SIGMA), or cumulative government expenditures on education (FUGI). Each model incorporates import capacity as a constraining influence in one form or another: directly in the aggregate full-capacity production function (SIGMA), in the investment equation (FUGI), or indirectly as a determinant of the trade gap (GEM). Ultimately, import capacity depends upon real exports, the commodity terms of trade, and the composition and terms of capital flows (FUGI, SIGMA). In all three modelling systems the exports of developing countries are determined by the demand for imports of goods and services of partner countries (dominated by developed market economies). Export destination is forecast on the basis of country shares computed from available trade data in constant prices.

As this sketchy description implies, several different types of policy simulations can be implemented with any of these models.

The degree of sophistication of the proxies for policy instruments varies quite considerably among the models, however, as does the strength of the transmission effects from one country or group of countries to others.

Nonetheless, as table 3.5 shows, experiments with these three models produced results suggesting a significant impact on GDP growth in developing countries of feasible improvements in policies for international economic co-operation, but only if several of them were to be implemented simultaneously. In order to facilitate the comparison of results among the various scenarios, the baseline scenario is treated as a reference run, and the effects of policy changes are expressed as deviations from the baseline figures.

In scenario A it is assumed that growth in the developed market economies could be accelerated by 0.5 per cent per year (i.e., from 2.9 per cent per annum in the baseline to 3.4 per cent). This acceleration might be brought about by greater policy coordination and more emphasis on expanding demand in surplus developed market economies rather than on demand contraction in deficit countries; or by higher investment rates in response to market integration in the European Economic Community, the trade agreement between the United States and Canada, or the outcome of the General Agreement on Tariffs and Trade (GATT) Uruguay round. It is also assumed that growth in Eastern Europe and the USSR could be accelerated by 1 per cent per year as a result of greater investment efficiency when the share of investments allocated to consumer-oriented sectors, with a shorter investment cycle, will increase significantly. The impact on developing countries would come about by increased import demand on the assumption of no loss in developing country shares in developed economies' imports.

In scenario B further improvement in developing countries' trade shares is assumed to allow their exports to increase by about 0.5 per cent per year more than would otherwise be the case (GEM), or by increasing trade flows in the imports of purchaser countries by 1 per cent (SIGMA), or by a 5 per cent reduction of tariff on manufacturing goods (FUGI). The scenario assumes no deterioration in the terms of trade and therefore should be assumed to involve mainly manufactured exports.

Scenario C assumes a 10 per cent increase in investment by developing countries through increased mobilization of their domestic saving (FUGI and GEM), roughly equivalent to a 5 per cent reduction in both private and government consumption (SIGMA).

Scenario D shows the effect of writing off 30 per cent of the commercial debt of the seven heavily indebted countries and least developed countries in Latin America, namely Argentina, Brazil, Chile, Colombia, Mexico, Peru, and Venezuela, and a 2 percentage point reduction in international interest rates, as represented by the London Inter-bank Offer Rate (LIBOR). The impact on the GDP growth of developing countries in the aggregate and over the 10 year horizon is small because the effect of lower interest rates would be felt primarily by those developing countries with large debts contracted at floating interest rates. For these countries, the effect would be to increase GDP growth by about 0.3 per cent per year in the first five years. This is only an estimate, however, of the impact on the external debt service of developing countries. Lower real interest rates also would be expected to accelerate growth in all regions of the world beginning with the developed market economies. They would probably be a necessary ingredient in the acceleration of GDP growth in the developed market economies (scenario A).

Scenario E is devoted to increasing capital flows. The FUGI results include an increase in capital flows from Japan of $30 billion, one-half on highly concessional terms (ODA) and the other half on commercial terms; full funding of the World Bank's recently agreed capital increase leading to an additional $75 billion of lending; an increase of $6 billion in the structural adjustment facility (SAF) of the International Monetary Fund (IMF), and a doubling of its compensatory finance facility. In the SIGMA Scenario ODA to developing countries is doubled to reach 0.70 per cent of the GDP of the developed market economies.

Scenario F shows the effect of a 5 per cent reduction in military expenditures and the transfer of half of the resulting budgetary savings from developed countries to developing countries as ODA. Also, a 5 per cent cut in military expenditure of developing countries and the use of these resources to increase domestic capital investment has been assumed. Events in late 1989 suggest that in this scenario one might meaningfully have discussed a considerably greater reduction of military spending in the 1990s and evaluate more opportunities for accelerated world growth and development than is assumed here.

The effects of different scenarios vary from region to region. The effects of changes in assumptions of a financial or monetary nature are more localized than those affecting investment and trade patterns. The latter are more widespread in terms of both geographical regions and key macroeconomic variables within a region.

The scenarios show that the prospects for the global economy to the year 2000 depend upon international co-ordination of national economic policies and are not immutably determined. They show that, in the absence of appropriate policies to mobilize savings, to stimulate investment, and to liberalize trade even a substantial reduction in debt cannot be expected to have a significant impact on income growth in the long run. However, a feasible combination of alternative policies may accelerate the growth of developing countries by one percentage point or more.

NOTES

1.   For an analysis of the prospects of developing countries in Latin America and the Caribbean through 1992, see Economic Commission for Latin America and the Caribbean (ECLAC), "Restrictions on sustained development in Latin America and the Caribbean and the requisites for overcoming them". LC/G.1488 (SESS.22(3) Rev. 1), 9 Feb. 1988. For the five year period 1988–1992, ECLAC estimated that GDP growth in the region would be only 2.9 per cent per year in the absence of an easing of the internal and external obstacles to growth.

2.   For an evaluation of the prospects for countries in the Economic Commission

for Europe (ECE) region to the year 2000, ECE, "Overall Economic Perspective to the Year 2000", (United Nations publication, Sales No. E.88.II.E.4). The baseline projections for developed market economies for the periods 1991–2000 prepared by ECE were very close to those presented in table 2.3: North America, 2.6; Western Europe, 2.5; USSR and Eastern Europe, 4.0 (in terms of NMP).

3.   The official estimate of a low family income is 456 shillings per month. This yields a yearly family income of 5,472 shillings, which, when divided by the 1980 purchasing power parity exchange rate for Kenya of 4.918 shillings to a dollar, gives a family yearly income of $1,112.65. The average size family in Kenya with this income was 5.5 in 1980. Hence, the per capita income for this group is $202.30.

4.   Systems for interlinked global modelling and analysis; for a description, see UNCTAD/ST/MFD/5, 19 June 1987, mimeograph.

5.   Future of global interdependence; for a description, see Akira Onishi, "Economics of global interdependence: A report to the United Nations", mimeograph, September 1986.

TABLE 3.1 *World resource allocation and saving: historical and projected under a baseline scenario*[a]

Country group	Government consumption	Private consumption	Shares in GDP in percentage Saving	Invest- ment	Internal balance	Per capita GDP in 1980 U.S. dollars
1970						
World	14.9	58.2	26.5	26.3	0.2	2,210
Developed market economies	17.8	59.1	23.3	25.7	-2.4	8,040
Eastern Europe & the USSR[b]	4.0	70.0	—	25.0	—	2,100
China	12.0	57.9	30.1	30.0	0.1	200
Developing countries	9.8	56.6	30.3	18.6	11.7	760
High income oil exporters	4.9	9.1	74.0	4.0	70.0	14,120
Other high income	9.8	49.6	36.6	19.9	16.7	2,940
Middle income	10.1	69.5	18.7	19.9	-1.1	870
Low income	10.3	73.6	14.9	18.7	-3.8	260
Least developed	11.9	78.1	10.2	14.8	-4.6	250
1980						
World	14.6	59.6	26.0	25.9	0.0	2,650
Developed market	17.1	60.5	22.9	23.1	-0.2	10,180
Eastern Europe & the USSR[b]	4.6	709.2	—	25.3	—	3,200
China	14.4	54.0	33.6	32.2	0.1	290
Developing countries	12.9	59.7	26.5	25.6	0.9	960
High income oil exporters	19.1	26.3	57.8	20.2	37.6	13,070
Other high income	13.6	57.5	28.0	28.2	-0.3	3,380
Middle income	10.8	65.5	20.7	25.0	-4.3	1,280
Low income	11.8	70.2	17.8	22.0	-4.2	320
Least developed	12.7	82.8	3.5	15.3	-11.5	250

continued

67

TABLE 3.1 *World resource allocation and saving: historical and projected under a baseline scenario*[a] *(continued)*

| Country group | Government consumption | Shares in GDP in percentage | | | | Per capita GDP in 1980 U.S. dollars |
		Private consumption	Saving	Investment	Internal balance	
1985						
World	14.8	60.2	24.6	24.9	-0.3	2,770
Developed market	17.2	60.6	22.4	22.4	0.0	11,100
Eastern Europe & the USSR[b]	4.9	72.0	—	23.8	—	3,650
China	12.7	47.0	40.7	43.5	-2.9	430
Developing countries	14.0	61.6	22.1	22.4	-0.3	920
High income oil exporters	36.3	46.6	17.3	27.4	-10.2	7,550
Other high income	13.8	57.7	25.9	22.2	3.7	3,090
Middle income	11.1	64.9	20.0	19.6	0.3	1,210
Low income	12.5	69.8	16.5	21.4	-4.9	350
Least developed	12.7	87.7	-4.2	17.1	-21.2	240
1990						
World	14.3	60.1	25.1	26.5	-1.4	1,800
Developed market economies	16.4	61.1	22.4	24.4	-2.0	7,640
Eastern Europe & the USSR[b]	4.6	70.6	—	24.8	—	2,240
China	11.1	42.7	46.2	45.0	-1.2	290
Developing countries	13.2	62.4	21.8	21.7	0.1	610
High income oil exporters	33.8	45.1	26.0	21.7	4.3	2,660
Other high income	13.2	57.9	25.5	22.9	-3.4	1,790
Middle income	10.3	65.4	20.5	20.6	-0.2	870
Low income	12.9	70.4	14.9	19.3	-4.3	270
Least developed	14.5	88.0	-9.9	15.9	-25.8	210

2000[c]

World	14.0	59.0	26.0	26.0	−0.1	2,110	3,580
Developed market	16.0	60.0	23.0	24.0	−0.6	9,680	16,130
Eastern Europe & the USSR[b]	4.0	73.0	—	23.0	—	3,920	5,370
China	11.0	48.0	41.0	40.0	0.2	430	900
Developing countries	13.0	60.0	25.0	24.0	1.0	720	1,200
High income oil exporters	26.0	47.0	28.0	20.0	7.5	2,900	6,200
Other high income	14.0	57.0	30.0	26.0	3.8	2,030	3,560
Middle income	11.0	62.0	24.0	25.0	1.2	1,070	1,720
Low income	12.0	70.0	16.0	21.0	−4.5	330	490
Least developed	13.0	83.0	−6.0	16.0	−12.1	220	260

Source: Department of International Economic and Social Affairs of the United Nations Secretariat.

[a] Measured in 1980 prices and exchange rates.

[b] Based on data for net material product for all years.

[c] Figures are rounded up so that internal balance may not exactly correspond to investment and savings percentages.

TABLE 3.2 *Investment trends and world economic growth: historical and projected under a baseline scenario*[a]

Period	Investment share	ICOR	Growth rate of GDP	Investment share	ICOR	Growth rate of GDP
	World			*Developing petroleum-exporting countries*		
Historical						
1970–1980	25.9	6.9	3.8	20.0	4.2	4.7
1980–1985	24.6	10.2	2.4	26.5	−37.9	−0.7
Preliminary and forecast						
1985–1990	26.3	8.0	3.3	22.0	17.0	1.3
Projected						
1990–2000	26.6	7.6	3.5	24.1	6.5	3.7
	Developed market economies			*Major exporters of manufactures*		
Historical						
1970–1980	23.9	7.5	3.2	26.2	3.8	6.9
1980–1985	22.3	9.3	2.4	26.1	6.7	3.9
Preliminary and forecast						
1985–1990	23.5	7.6	3.1	24.8	5.1	4.9
Projected						
1990–2000	23.6	7.6	3.1	25.5	4.9	5.2
	Eastern Europe & the USSR[b]			*Primary commodity and services exporters*		
Historical						
1970–1980	31.5	6.3	5.0	22.2	5.7	3.9
1980–1985	30.0	8.6	3.5	21.7	11.4	1.9
Preliminary and forecast						
1985–1990	28.3	10.5	2.7	17.7	8.9	2.0
Projected						
1990–2000	27.0	7.5	3.6	20.3	7.0	2.9
	China			*Least developed countries*		
Historical						
1970–1980	30.8	4.3	7.4	13.8	5.3	2.6
1980–1985	34.6	3.7	9.4	17.3	7.2	2.4
Preliminary and forecast						
1985–1990	45.3	5.6	8.0	15.6	4.5	3.5
Projected						
1990–2000	42.0	7.5	5.6	15.9	5.1	3.5

continued

TABLE 3.2 *Investment trends and world economic growth: historical and projected under a baseline scenario[a] (continued)*

Period	Investment share	ICOR	Growth rate of GDP	Investment share	ICOR	Growth rate of GDP
	Developing countries			*Highly indebted developing countries*		
Historical						
1970–1980	22.0	4.3	5.1	22.7	4.7	4.8
1980–1985	24.6	17.6	1.4	24.1	− 40.1	− 0.6
Preliminary and forecast						
1985–1990	21.5	6.5	3.3	17.3	10.8	1.6
Projected						
1990–2000	23.1	5.4	4.3	20.1	6.7	3.0

Source: Ibid.

[a] *Measured at 1980 prices and exchange rates. Growth rates in this table and all tables that follow in chapter are computed taking into account the growth rate of each year in the period. Hence, they may differ from cor growth rates which are computed using only the beginning and end year of each period.*

[b] *Based on data for NMP and gross fixed capital formation.*

TABLE 3.3 *GDP per capita levels and growth rates*

| | Growth rates | | | | GDP per capita in 1980 dollars | |
| | GDP | | GDP per capita | | | |
	1985–1990	1990–2000	1985–1990	1990–2000	1985	2000
World	3.3	3.5	1.6	1.8	2,770	3,580
Developed market economies	3.0	3.1	2.5	2.6	11,100	16,130
North America	2.9	3.0	2.0	2.3	12,750	17,780
Europe	2.9	2.8	2.6	2.6	10,840	15,910
Other	4.2	3.9	2.8	3.0	9,150	14,200
Eastern Europe & the USSR[a]	2.7	3.6	1.9	3.0	3,650	5,370
China	8.0	5.6	6.6	4.2	430	900
Developing countries	3.4	4.3	1.0	2.0	920	1,200
By geographical region:						
North Africa	2.7	4.4	−0.6	2.0	1,440	1,710
Sub-Saharan Africa	2.3	3.2	−0.4	−0.1	450	440
Latin America and the Caribbean	1.4	2.9	−0.1	1.0	2,100	2,320
Western Asia	0.3	4.2	−2.6	1.0	3,100	3,020
South and East Asia	6.6	6.1	4.4	3.9	500	920
By export orientation:						
Petroleum-exporting countries	1.3	3.7	−1.3	1.3	1,630	1,930
Major exporters of manufactures	4.9	5.2	3.0	3.6	1,325	1,620
Primary commodity and services exporters	2.0	2.9	−1.1	0.8	640	670
By income level:						
High income oil exporters	1.5	4.2	−2.5	0.5	7,550	6,200
Other high-income	2.6	3.9	0.0	1.5	3,090	3,560
Middle-income	3.4	4.7	1.0	2.5	1,210	1,720
Low-income	3.5	4.6	1.1	2.3	350	490
Least developed countries	3.5	3.1	0.7	0.2	240	270
Highly indebted countries	1.9	3.0	−0.8	0.8	1,790	1,860

Source: Ibid.
[a] *Based on NMP.*

TABLE 3.4 *Growth of world import demand and export possibilities: historical and projected under a baseline scenario[a]*

| Period | Average annual rate of growth and percentage share of GDP (in parentheses[b]) | | | |
	Exports	Imports	Exports	Imports
	Developed market economies		*Petroleum-exporting countries*	
Historical				
1970–1980	6.0 (15.2)	4.7 (17.8)	1.0 (50.0)	16.8 (8.6)
1980–1985	3.7 (21.4)	3.5 (21.6)	−6.3 (24.9)	−3.1 (21.8)
Preliminary and forecast				
1985–1990	5.1 (23.3)	6.7 (24.1)	2.8 (25.9)	0.2 (20.1)
Projected				
1990–2000	4.5 (26.7)	3.9 (27.3)	4.1 (26.9)	5.2 (23.2)
	Eastern Europe & the USSR[c]		*Major exporters of manufactures*	
Historical				
1970–1980	8.0 (11.7)	8.5 (10.7)	10.5 (15.4)	8.7 (21.1)
1980–1985	5.4 (17.3)	6.6 (17.2)	8.0 (26.4)	2.7 (24.3)
Preliminary and forecast				
1985–1990	2.5 (17.1)	2.9 (17.0)	12.1 (36.2)	12.8 (34.7)
Projected				
1990–2000	4.0 (18.1)	4.5 (18.9)	5.1 (35.5)	5.6 (36.6)
	China		*Primary commodity and services exporters*	
Historical				
1970–1980	16.0 (3.3)	14.8 (3.3)	2.2 (35.5)	4.0 (38.2)
1980–1985	17.6 (9.0)	24.2 (12.3)	1.3 (29.8)	−2.1 (31.6)
Preliminary and forecast				
1985–1990	10.3 (9.8)	1.6 (8.8)	4.7 (33.7)	2.4 (32.2)
Projected				
1990–2000	5.0 (9.3)	6.0 (9.1)	3.4 (35.4)	3.0 (32.6)
	Developing countries		*Highly indebted countries*	
Historical				
1970–1980	3.4 (31.0)	10.0 (16.0)	2.4 (18.6)	8.1 (11.6)
1980–1985	0.9 (25.2)	−0.4 (23.2)	3.4 (16.8)	4.1 (11.0)
Preliminary and forecast				
1985–1990	7.6 (29.8)	7.3 (27.3)	2.9 (17.2)	4.2 (12.2)
Projected				
1990–2000	4.5 (30.8)	4.7 (27.8)	3.6 (20.5)	4.0 (13.5)

continued

TABLE 3.4 *Growth of world import demand and export possibilities: historical and projected under a baseline scenario[a] (continued)*

Period	Average annual rate of growth and percentage share of GDP (in parentheses[b])			
	Exports	Imports	Exports	Imports
	Least developed countries			
Historical				
1970–1980	0.9 (11.3)	5.6 (16.1)		
1980–1985	6.2 (13.8)	9.8 (31.3)		
Preliminary and forecast				
1985–1990	7.2 (16.0)	5.8 (34.4)		
Projected				
1990–2000	3.4 (16.5)	3.8 (26.9)		

Source: Ibid.

[a] *Average annual rates of growth and percentage shares in GDP measured at 1980 prices and exchange rates.*

[b] *Percentage shares are shown for the years 1970, 1985, 1990 and 2000.*

[c] *Based on NMP.*

TABLE 3.5 *Additional average annual growth in GDP of developing countries associated with different policy initiatives, 1990–2000*

	GEM	SIGMA	FUGI
A. Accelerated growth in developed economies	0.4	0.3	
B. Increased trade shares of developing countries	0.3	0.2	0.3
C. Improved savings performance in developing countries	0.5		0.5
D. Debt relief combined with reduced interest rates		0.1	
E. Increased ODA (selected donors)		0.2	0.1
F. World disarmament scenario			0.2

4.
Environmental Issues

A. SUSTAINABLE DEVELOPMENT[1]

The impact of growing population and economic activity has already weakened the natural resource base of many countries and poses increasing risks to the prospects for sustainable development. But the ability to make development meet the needs of the present and the future increases with scientific knowledge and the development of ecologically sound technologies. Sustainable development does not imply cessation of economic growth. Rather, it requires a recognition that the problems of poverty and under-development and related environmental problems cannot be solved without vigorous economic growth. Sustainable development will require changes in current patterns of growth, however, to make them less resource and energy intensive and more equitable. Inequalities in international economic relations, coupled with inappropriate economic policies in many developed and developing countries alike, continue to cause environmental degradation and otherwise limit the sustainability of the development process. Growth derived from rapid resource depletion is neither ecologically nor economically sustainable.

Many environmental risks stemming from economic activities cross national boundaries. Some are global in scope. Although most of the activities that give rise to such risks are concentrated in the industrial countries, the risks are shared by all countries whether they benefit from these activities or not. And most countries have little influence on the decisions that affect these activities. These risks include harmful effects from hazardous waste and from increasing concentrations of carbon dioxide and other greenhouse gases in the atmosphere. The issue of greenhouse gases and climate change has emerged as particularly urgent, with scientific observations and analysis indicating that significant global warming and climate change are likely over the next few decades. Although the effects may not reach critical proportions until the next century, their potential magnitude is so great that it would be unwise to postpone efforts to limit their causes. In addition, there has been a transfer of environmental costs from industrial to developing countries, as some of the "dirty" manufacturing processes have relocated away from the developed countries.[2]

Environmental stress has long been seen as a result of the demand for scarce natural resources and the related pollution of the air, water, and land generated by rising living standards. But poverty also creates environmental stress. In order to survive, the rural poor often degrade and destroy their immediate environment as they cut down forests for fuelwood, overuse marginal agricultural land, and eventually migrate to the shrinking areas of vacant land or to urban areas. Severe air and water pollution is tolerated in many cities because it permits other gains deemed more valuable than the immediate benefits of pollution abatement and because the long-term benefits of abatement are heavily discounted.

Proper management of the natural resource base is actually especially important in poor countries that cannot afford the consequences of rapid soil degradation and other irreversible losses of potentially renewable resources. Nor can they afford high-cost efforts to remedy environmental damage. Efforts to develop sustainable agriculture, forestry, and fisheries may fail unless population growth slows down. Appropriate technologies do not exist in many resource-poor areas to sustain the present and projected population; even some resource-rich areas are reaching their maximum output.

As FAO noted, "The objective is to create an economic environment in which it is more profitable to conserve resources than destroy them. Soil and water conservation measures, for example, should, where possible, be designed to show an economic return to the farmer in the year of application, because otherwise they are unlikely to be widely adopted. Similarly, habitat conservation and game cropping for tourism should be seen as a socially and economically profitable alternative to forest and savannah destruction."[3] Sustainable agriculture will thus require changes in the ways the rural poor live, increasing their income-earning capacity and helping them to withstand shocks and stresses in their life support systems.

International economic relations pose a particular problem for developing countries' efforts to manage their environment, since the export of natural resources is a large factor in their economies.

B. CLIMATE CHANGES AND THEIR IMPACTS

1. Greenhouse gases and global warming★

Increasing concentrations of carbon dioxide and other trace gases in the atmosphere, largely as a result of human activities, are expected to cause a significant increase in the earth's temperature over the next several decades. The increase would entail major ecological, economic, and social consequences.[4] The likelihood of such global warming is high, and its causes seem to be fairly well understood. The emission of these gases into the atmosphere,

★ Except as otherwise noted, this section is based largely on UNEP, *The State of the World Environment 1989* (UNEP/GC.15 /7/Add.2), April 1989, Chapter 3.

therefore, should be monitored carefully and probably should be reduced considerably in order to prevent serious harm to human welfare. While the harmful effects would not be great in the short run, it would be extremely unwise to postpone serious efforts to limit the build-up of most of these gases. While "it may be too soon to start implementing drastic measures for either limitation or adaptation, . . . there is an immediate need for adoption of measures that ensure that the world is better prepared to respond to climatic change."[5]

The concentration of carbon dioxide in the atmosphere by 1985 had increased by about 25 per cent since pre-industrial times. It is likely to increase by a further 40 per cent by the year 2050 if present trends in energy use continue; by 80 per cent if energy use accelerates.[6] The additional warming effect of other trace gases, especially methane, nitrous oxide, and the so-called chlorofluorocarbons, is expected to be about equal to that caused by carbon dioxide. (The chlorofluorocarbons are also a principal cause of the depletion of stratospheric ozone, discussed below.) The expected climatic change would exacerbate the problems of drought, desertification, deforestation, and soil erosion and worsen the prospects for sustainable agriculture. Another consequence of global warming would be a higher sea level, which would profoundly influence habitation patterns, agriculture, and industry, particularly in river deltas, flood plains, and other low-lying coastal areas.

While most of these effects are expected in later decades, already in the 1990s the increased climatic variability will require a greater buffer capacity in food supplies than has been considered necessary in the past, at both national and international levels. In later decades adjustments of rainfed cropping patterns, extension or modification of irrigation systems, or changes between major land uses (e.g., arable use versus grazing or forestry) may be necessary.[7]

Although the forces driving global warming are now broadly understood, its precise regional distribution and environmental impacts are not. Concerted efforts by the international scientific community will be necessary to clarify the prospects. If things are allowed to go on as at present, the world might in a few decades have to adapt very rapidly in the face of catastrophic change. But immediate measures to slow down the buildup of greenhouse gases would reduce the warming and its undesirable consequences. The 1987 Montreal Protocol on Substances That Deplete the Ozone Layer and the 1989 Helsinki Declaration on the Protection of the Ozone Layer[8] are steps in that direction. They call for drastic cuts in production of fully halogenated chlorofluorocarbons (CFCs), which are greenhouse gases, by 1999.

Carbon dioxide is responsible for about 50 per cent of the greenhouse effect, so major attention should be given to strategies that would limit or even reduce its emission. The strategies include increased energy efficiency and modification of technologies in ways that lead to reduction in the use of fossil fuels. The preservation of forests, especially the tropical forests, is also essential.

About two thirds of the global carbon dioxide released by human activities arises from the combustion of fossil fuels. They released about 5.3 billion tons of carbon in 1986.[9] In addition, deforestation, land exploitation, and burning of other components of the world's biomass currently release 2 to 3 billion tons of carbon annually, nearly 80 per cent due to deforestation.[10,11] Annual emissions of carbon dioxide from fossil fuel are projected to contain about 7 billion tons of carbon in the year 2000, between 10 and 14 billion tons in 2030, and between 13 and 23 billion tons in 2050, depending on the rate of growth in the demand and supply of fossil fuel energy.[12]

The developed market economies of North America, Western Europe, and Japan produce 49 per cent of global carbon dioxide emissions, the economies of Eastern Europe 25 per cent, and the developing countries 26 per cent.[13] In addition to the enormous use of fossil fuels in the industrialized countries, virtually all production of chlorofluorocarbons takes place in these countries.[14] They have the major responsibility, therefore, for devising ways to limit the output of the greenhouse gases. Although they have reached initial agreements to reduce the production of chlorofluorocarbons in order to preserve stratospheric ozone, very little has been done to reduce or even to slow the growth of CO_2 emissions.

In view of the opposition to nuclear power, adjusting the world energy mix to environmental concerns will be difficult unless technological breakthroughs can provide benign, economically competitive alternative energy sources and/or radically improve energy efficiency. Such developments can be expected in the long term at best, and adjustments in the medium term will by necessity be limited to greater reliance on the less malignant energy sources.[15]

Vigorous application of the following policies to reduce carbon dioxide emissions could limit global warming to a rate that would make the necessary adaptation of global economic activity relatively manageable:

(a) Reduce fossil fuel use through increases in end-use energy efficiency;

(b) Shift the fossil fuel mix toward natural gas. For the same energy output the combustion of natural gas produces about 57 per cent of the amount of carbon dioxide produced from coal, and the combustion of oil produces about 83 per cent. Available technologies and reserves favour such an adjustment, particularly in the electric power sector;[16]

(c) Replace fossil fuel combustion with alternative energy technologies;

(d) Eliminate net forest loss by more careful management of development in forest areas and by large scale reforestation;

(e) Remove carbon dioxide from the flue gas of thermal power plants for disposal in the deep ocean. They account for 15 per cent of carbon dioxide emissions.

The first four of these measures can serve more than one environmental and economic purpose. Even if the worst scenario does not come about, the world would benefit in other respects by taking these measures now. Other greenhouse gases that could be controlled to varying degrees, based on present technical knowledge, are methane, nitrous oxides, and tropospheric ozone. Priority should be given to detailed studies of the sources of these gases, their interactions in the atmosphere, and technologies that would reduce their emissions.[17]

2. Stratospheric ozone and ultraviolet radiation

The global average level of stratospheric ozone fell by about 5 per cent during the eight years from 1979 to 1986. In the tropics the trend is nearly independent of the season, between −0.5 and −1.0 per cent per year. Outside them the losses vary seasonally and increase with the latitude, becoming greatest at the poles. Since 1969 ozone levels have fallen by about 2 per cent in temperate latitudes in summer, and around 5 to 6 per cent in winter. There have been especially sharp seasonal drops in Antarctica and recently over the Arctic.[18]

Stratospheric ozone is a form of oxygen that acts as a filter for harmful ultraviolet radiation (UV-B) emitted by the sun. It also is one of the minor greenhouse gases, but its effect on ultraviolet radiation is far more important. Several manufactured chemicals, especially some of the chlorofluorocarbons (CFCs) and halons, accelerate the breakdown of stratospheric ozone. The consequent increased exposure of people to UV-B will lead to increased incidence of skin cancer, sunburns, eye damage, and the aging and wrinkling of skin. In addition there will be harmful effects on other species, including some important agricultural crops.[19] Increased UV-B also has a tendency to suppress the efficiency of the body's immune system and to increase the incidence of skin infections. UV-B can also damage plant hormones and chlorophyl and reduce the rate of photosynthesis. Plant species sensitive to UV-B, such as cotton, peas, beans, melons, and cabbage, would grow more slowly, and in some cases pollen would fail to germinate. Increased UV-B levels would also damage algae and aquatic ecosystems, perhaps leading to declines in fish stocks.

The 1987 Montreal Protocol on Substances That Deplete the Ozone Layer entered into force on 1 January 1989. It calls on the signatories to reduce production and consumption of harmful chlorofluorocarbons (CFCs) by 50 per cent from 1986 to 1999; a ten-year delay is allowed for developing countries whose consumption is less than 0.3 kilograms per capita. Measures have already been taken in some countries to reduce or ban the use of the controlled CFCs in all or some products, non-essential aerosols, for example. Some recent studies point to the necessity of amending the Montreal Protocol to ban the production of CFCs and halons altogether and to freeze the production of methyl chloroform. In May 1989 in the Helsinki Declaration on the Protection of the Ozone Layer, ministers and senior officials of 81 countries and the European Community agreed to a total phase-out of ozone-depleting CFCs by the year 2000 or sooner if possible. They also agreed both to phase out halons and to control and reduce other ozone-depleting substances that contribute significantly to ozone depletion as soon as feasible. In addition, they agreed to "facilitate the access of developing countries to relevant scientific information, research results and training and to seek to develop appropriate funding mechanisms to facilitate the transfer of technology and replacement of equipment at minimum cost to developing countries". They committed themselves, "in proportion to their means and resources, to accelerate the development of environmentally acceptable substituting [sic] chemicals, products and technologies". Major producers and users of CFCs are seeking alternatives to CFCs for use in foam blowing, refrigeration, air-conditioning, solvents and other uses.[20] Several major companies that use CFCs and halons recently agreed to eliminate these chemicals in their world-wide operations.[21] One of the major producing companies (the DuPont Corporation) has indicated that it will phase out its production of CFCs entirely over the next few years.

3. Acid rain★

Research on the effects of acid rain has shown that it is damaging to aquatic life in lakes and streams, diminishes the productivity

---

★ Based on *World Economic Survey 1989, op. cit.*, pp. 108–111.

of forests and crops, accelerates the deterioration of buildings and other exposed structures, and contributes to human health hazards. It is the result of acid precipitation in the atmosphere through chemical transformation of sulphur dioxide (SO_2) and several nitrogen oxides (NO_x). In the air they become oxidized to form acid sulphate (SO_4) and acid nitrate (NO_3), respectively. These acids return to the earth in rain, snow, and hail, and as dry microscopic particles, sometimes after travelling hundreds or even thousands of miles.

Man-made sources of these air pollutants include electric generating plants, smelting of ores, industrial installations, motor vehicles, and residential and commercial establishments using fossil fuels. Globally the natural and man-made emissions are roughly equal. In North America and Europe, however, man-made sources contribute more than 90 per cent of the total. Man-made emissions of sulphur dioxide rose from about 7 million tons per year in 1860 to about 155 million tons per year in 1985, although the emissions during the period 1970–1985 were reduced substantially in several countries as strict pollution standards were imposed.

In industrial economies, generation of electricity in power plants using fossil fuels is the largest single contributor to the emissions of sulphur dioxide (SO_2), and the transportation sector is the largest source of nitrogen oxides. Although emissions of nitrogen oxides were slightly reduced or stabilized during the period 1970–1985 in some of the developed market economies, the total amount of nitrogen released annually is still rising. Motor vehicles are the major source and are more difficult to identify and regulate than the major sources of SO_2 emissions.

Acid deposition far downwind from big pollution sources greatly exceeds emissions from local sources in many regions. In Austria, eastern Canada, the Netherlands, Sweden, and Switzerland more than 60 per cent and in Norway about 75 per cent of the sulphur deposition comes from other areas. Acid rain falling over the Atlantic as far out as Bermuda and the acidity of snow in the Arctic are other examples of long-range transport of acids. Because relatively little of the harm from acid rain is suffered by the communities where it is produced, many countries have been unwilling to bear the costs of preventing it. Nevertheless, the ECE protocol and recent consultations between Canada and the United States indicate significant progress in international co-operation on preventive measures.[22]

A variety of approaches and technologies aimed at the reduction of acid rain are available:

(a) Selection of fuels low in sulphur and nitrogen content;

(b) Combustion modification using limestone injection multi-stage burners, fluidized bed combustion, and post-combustion emission controls using scrubbers, which allow removal of 50 to 90 per cent of the SO_2 in coal-fired electric power plants;

(c) Use of the catalytic converter to reduce emissions of nitrogen oxides in new automobiles that burn unleaded gasoline;

(d) Increased fuel efficiency;

(e) Vehicle sharing and limitation of private automobile use.

C. LAND AND WATER

Rapid growth of population, spread of cash crops, introduction of new technologies developed in other ecological and socio-economic contexts, pressures to earn foreign exchange, and the vicissitudes of the terms of trade for agricultural exports have all disturbed the ecological stability of traditional agriculture in many low-income countries. These disturbances have led to various sequences of deforestation, soil degradation and desertification, and increasing scarcity of water.

1. Deforestation

The world's forests are disappearing at a rate of 15 million hectares each year, with most of the losses occurring in humid parts of Africa, Asia, and Latin America. With the present rate of deforestation, about 40 per cent of the remaining forest cover in the developing countries will be lost by the year 2000.[23] Tropical forests are being cleared both for their lumber and to make way for plantations, pastures, and crops. Migration by landless peasants and other unemployed people into forest areas is encouraged in some countries, but after a few harvests the soil is severely depleted.

The cause of deforestation under these conditions is not simply population pressure but also the desire for foreign exchange. This induces many developing countries to export timber faster than their forests are being regenerated. Overcutting also causes the loss of forest-based livelihoods, increases soil erosion and downstream flooding, and accelerates the decline of rare genetic resources and the loss of endangered species. In South and East Asia and Latin America deforestation in upland watersheds often causes increased downstream flooding in the rainy season. The flooding is followed by abnormally low water flow during the dry season, with severe damage to agricultural productivity in floodplains and valleys. In the Ganges plain alone, flood damage in India and Bangladesh exceeds $1 billion annually.[24] Deforestation also contributes a significant portion of the increasing global emissions of carbon dioxide, as noted earlier.

Increased demand for agricultural land up to the year 2000 in developing countries may be on the order of 80 million hectares. Some of that demand will probably be met out of their present forest land. But many tropical soils are unsuitable for continuous cultivation or intense grazing, and such agricultural expansion may cause ecological damage and loss of productivity. In some developing countries programmes of transmigration and settlement for farming and ranching in tropical forest areas have already caused severe environmental damage, eroding long-term food security.

To alleviate tropical deforestation and to promote sustainable exploitation of the world's forests, nations should assess the value of their forest resources in a comprehensive way and reflect this in their development plans. Once the true costs of deforestation are realized, Governments would be more likely to seek to protect their forest ecosystems. Multipurpose forest management involves production of timber, non-wood forest products, fuelwood, fodder, fibre, and wildlife management; it also contributes to provision of water, shelter and recreation, control of air pollution, and protection of soil, genetic resources, and natural heritage. The following techniques and approaches are essential in a strategy to find this balance:

Agroforestry integrates trees with crop and livestock production systems and is a promising way to link food production, especially in low-potential areas, with improved forest management.

Watershed management is necessary to guarantee food production in high-potential areas. Links need to be maintained between forestry and food production through an integrated approach to watershed management. Incentives must be provided to rehabilitate degraded watersheds.

Monitoring and evaluation systems should include adequate baseline surveys, geographic information systems, and assessment of local environmental impacts and community benefits and involvement.

Protection of genetic resources is fundamental to any forest strategy. The establishment in 1987 of the International Fund on Plant Genetic Resources was an important step toward ensuring that the genetic resources of the tropical forests are conserved and wisely utilized.[25]

The Tropical Forestry Action Plan was initiated in 1985 to coordinate human needs, environmental management, and sustainable forest development. It is slowly gaining recognition by con-

cerned countries. Seeking to find the right balance between development and environmental protection, this plan represents the
first serious international effort to confront the problem of saving
the tropical forest in an integrated way. The International Tropical
Timber Agreement also came into force in 1985. Its main objectives are to improve market intelligence, to assist producing countries to develop better techniques for reforestation and forest management, to encourage increased timber processing in producing
countries, and to support research and development programmes
to achieve these goals.[26] Several developing countries, including
Brazil, Indonesia, and the Philippines, have banned most exports
of logs; more dramatically, Thailand has banned all commercial
logging, even for use by its own wood products industry, and is
removing squatter farmers from forest areas with steep slopes or
shallow soils.[27]

2. Desertification and soil degradation

The world's drylands supported about 850 million people in 1984,
of whom 230 million were on lands affected by severe desertification. Worldwide it is estimated that millions of hectares are
losing their biological diversity each year, as human and animal
pressures have accelerated the removal of vegetation and consequent soil erosion. Two fifths of Africa's non-desert land risks
being turned into desert, as does one-third of Asia's and one-fifth
of Latin America's.[28] Disturbance of the ecological system has
decreased the infiltration of rainwater, increased surface runoff,
lowered ground-water levels, and caused the drying up of surface
water and loss of topsoil and soil nutrients. Under these conditions, drought will more quickly reduce food output and lead to
famine. However, political, economic and social factors are more
important than low rainfall in the process of desertification. Besides rapid growth of human and animal populations and detri-
mental land use practices, the cultivation of cash crops on unsuitable rangelands has forced herders and their cattle onto

marginal lands, thus accelerating soil degradation and outright desertification.

Declines in soil fertility or even total losses of land to agriculture are common in many parts of the world. Soil erosion by wind and water is serious in the arid parts of North Africa and the Middle East, parts of South Asia and South America. The problem is caused in great measure by inappropriate land use and cropping patterns. Substitution of traditional mixed cropping (which includes plants or shrubs along with food crops) by monoculture, and poor management of land and water have caused significant soil erosion and other types of degradation. Salinization affects extensive land areas in many countries in North Africa, the Middle East, and Asia. About half the land under irrigation is affected by secondary salinization and/or alkalinization in varying degrees. Some 40 million hectares of irrigated land are either waterlogged or suffer from excessive salinity or both. Salinization may be removing as much land from production as is added by irrigation. Irrigation has greatly improved farm productivity in areas of uncertain or inadequate rainfall and has been responsible for the adoption of high yielding varieties in many developing countries. Yet inappropriate irrigation has wasted water, polluted groundwater, and damaged the productivity of millions of hectares. Excessive extraction of groundwater for irrigation has depleted aquifers in Asia and Africa. Acidification of peat soils occurs when the groundwater table is lowered. It drastically reduces production of crops and fish (in ponds) as, for example, along extensive coastal areas in southeast Asia.

3. Water resources[29]

Abundance or scarcity of water can mean prosperity or poverty, life or death. It can even be a cause of war. Most countries have deeply worrisome problems concerning the quantity and quality of their fresh water resources, and many countries are suffering from the effects of pollution of their coastal waters. Constraints on the supply of fresh water are increasing, aggravated by droughts, depletion of aquifers, and deforestation, while demand for water is rising rapidly for irrigation, energy generation, industrial production, and urban consumption. (The provision of safe drinking water is discussed in Chapter 12, Health.)

The availability of fresh-water resources per capita varies widely. Many areas of the world are semi-arid, suffering a devastatingly high rainfall variability and recurrent droughts as well. The largest such area, with a rainfall variability of over 40 per cent, consists of North and sub-Saharan Africa, the Arabian peninsula, the southern part of the Islamic Republic of Iran, Pakistan and western India. In the Sahel rainfall is not only unreliable, but is less now than 50 or even 30 years ago. Water supply per capita in Asia is less than half the global average, and the continent's run-off is the least stable of all the major land masses. In Africa two-thirds of the countries have at least one-third less run-off than the global average. But the main problem is under-development of water resources relative to needs and potential, and the uneven distribution of water resources.

In spite of the large increases foreseen in water withdrawals for irrigation, industrial, and domestic uses, total use worldwide by the year 2000 is likely to be less than half the stable renewable supply at the global level. In North Africa and the Middle East, however, meeting the expected demands by the year 2000 could require virtually all of their usable fresh-water supplies. Even under existing patterns of water use, the amount of water needed in Western Asia will probably double between 1980 and 2000. In several countries, including Bahrain, Democratic Yemen, Kuwait, and the Syrian, Arab Republic, total demand for water already equals or exceeds the available supply, or is expected to do so by the year 2000. Use in southern and eastern Europe as well as central and southern Asia also could closely approach the limits of available supplies that can be safely tapped.

At least 19 developing countries in 1975 had total natural water supplies of less than 500 cubic metres per person per year. This translates into some 200 cubic metres or less of actual availability, taking into account losses incurred in the process of tapping and harnessing the natural supplies for particular uses. Ten more countries could be in a similar situation by the year 2000, and another eight by the year 2025. Still others would have less than 1,000 cubic metres per person available per year and could thus be regarded as approaching a situation of severe scarcity.

From 15 to 25 North African and sub-Saharan African countries may face serious problems with water shortages by the year 2025. Most of these countries have agricultural sectors that need higher than average inputs of water and fertilizer for food self-sufficiency. Food self-sufficiency will be an elusive goal as household and industrial demands for water will compete strongly with the agricultural sector for the limited quantities of water available.

Turning to water quality, contamination of water supplies is posing health risks and is drastically increasing the costs of water treatment facilities. Polluted inland water bodies and seas are reducing the productivity of fisheries and increasing the health risks of eating fish caught in those waters. Polluted irrigation water poses health risks, undermines long-term crop productivity, and degrades the recreational use and aesthetic aspects of surface water.

Surface and underground water sources in many areas are contaminated by fertilizers, herbicides and pesticides used in agriculture, and by industrial and residential waste, seepage from waste storage and disposal sites, and acid rain. Toxic chemicals have killed large amounts of aquatic biota and rendered many water sources useless for drinking and even for irrigation.

In the industrial world, where new waste-water treatment facilities have been built in recent years at considerable cost, river water quality has improved in some cases. However, long stretches of numerous rivers still remain heavily polluted. The run-off of pesticides, herbicides, and fertilizers from agricultural lands has become a major problem in such sources of community water supply as artificial lakes and reservoirs, especially in several countries in Latin America.

Most urban centres in the developing countries lack adequate facilities for the collection and disposal of domestic and industrial wastes. This results in urban run-off highly polluted with pathogens and organic materials that may have a serious impact on the quality of nearby surface waters and shallow ground waters. In many cities, open sewers and surface run-off after rain create "rivers of sewage" that contaminate local water supplies.

One of the most acute problems is the increasing flow of nitrates into drinking waters, leading to possibly serious threats to human health. This problem is already widespread in areas of intensive agriculture in Europe and is appearing in the USA and the USSR. The increasing use of fertilizers in the developing countries implies that similar problems can be expected there also. Nitrogen and phosphorus, the two most important causes of excessive plant growth in surface water supplies, are well above natural levels in the water measured by the Global Environmental Monitoring System (GEMS). This project consists of 344 monitoring stations in 59 countries. Many rivers outside Europe contain 2.5 times as much nitrates as the natural average for unpolluted rivers, and levels in European rivers are 45 times higher than natural background levels. Relatively high levels of organochlorine pesticides and the polychlorinated biphenyls (PCBs) were reported by stations in China, Japan, and the United Kingdom. Very high levels were found in Colombia, Indonesia, Malaysia, and the United Republic of Tanzania. OECD time-series data show that biological oxygen demand (the amount of oxygen needed to decompose sewage and other organic wastes) declined in some rivers and increased in others. Nitrates increased in most major rivers and lakes from 1975 to 1985, but phosphate concentrations either remained stable or declined slightly. In most OECD rivers there was a marked drop in concentrations of lead, cadmium, chromium, and copper.[30]

Concern about the protection and rational management of coastal water and marine resources has increased in many countries in the past few years. Shorelands, small islands, coral reefs, estuaries, seagrass beds, and open coastal water foster great varieties of fish and other marine organisms. They also have scientific and educational value and attract tourism. Outbreaks of algal blooms in coastal waters, as well as problems of sewage disposal, have focused the attention of governments on the need for marine environment protection. The incineration of chemical wastes at sea has also triggered considerable concern. In 1987, eight North Sea countries agreed to reduce waste incineration at sea by at least 65 per cent by the end of 1990 and to phase it out altogether by 1994.[31]

In order to ensure that the finite amount of fresh water in the hydrological cycle is adequate to meet the growing demand, new ways must be found to conserve water and to implement existing methods more extensively. New water supplies must also be developed, taking into account likely adverse effects on the environment. Reuse of waste water has been advocated mainly for non-potable purposes, such as agricultural irrigation, cooling, and industrial in-plant recycling. A large proportion of the water used for industrial purposes can be recycled several times, and the efficiency of water use can be increased further by using integrated water recycling systems. Given the typically low price of industrial water supplies relative to prices of other inputs, incentives for using water more efficiently must come from strict water allocations and stringent pollution control requirements, as well as from more rational pricing policies.

The scope for waste water reuse is relatively small so far in developing countries, as many of them do not have sewerage systems that collect it. But there is wide scope for their new industries to have built-in water recycling systems. Developing countries are probably better placed to take advantage of new recycling technologies than the older industrial countries, because building water efficiency and pollution control into new plants is generally much cheaper than retro-fitting old ones. Some of the technologies available are capable of reducing water use and waste water flows by up to 90 per cent. Technology transfer could help to alleviate water supply and pollution problems in the emerging industrial countries.

Raising the efficiency of irrigation is even more important. Irrigation accounts for the bulk of most countries' water use and is generally rather inefficient. Improvements in technical infrastructure and adoption of more efficient management methods, such as lining irrigation canals, can greatly reduce seepage losses. Even more effective would be to educate farmers on optimal use of water, such as avoiding using more water than necessary through assessment of water needs for different crops at various places and times. Co-ordination of the use and management of groundwater and surface water can significantly increase the total efficiency of irrigation. Other options are the use of brackish water and treated waste water for irrigation of salt-tolerant crops and for certain industrial uses.

Although municipal use of water is much less than irrigation and industrial use, the costs of supplying safe drinking water as well as collecting and treating household waste water are large. This is especially so in comparison with per capita incomes in the low-income countries. Conserving water and increasing the efficiency of household and municipal water use would reduce the need for new plants, water mains, and sewer pipes. It would also cut energy and other costs for providing and disposing of municipal water supplies. Efficiency can be increased by reducing losses in the distribution system and using less wasteful designs for new, improved household fixtures and appliances. Domestic waste water could be collected, treated, and used for agricultural purposes.

A region's fresh water also can be conserved by cutting loss through evaporation—by using underground or covered storage instead of storage in open surface reservoirs. The costs, while high, often seem reasonable compared to alternative schemes.

Several technically feasible and economically viable new options are available for increasing fresh water supplies. Of the non-conventional ways, such as seeding clouds to induce precipitation, towing icebergs, desalting sea and brackish water, and transporting water by tankers, the latter two appear to hold the greatest near-term potential. But the available desalination technologies (distillation, electrodialysis, and reverse osmosis) are highly energy-intensive and far too expensive, except for countries having non-marketable supplies of natural gas or for islands that depend on tourism for a large share of their income.

Almost all important stocks of bottom-dwelling fish species are either fully exploited or over-fished; most stocks of the valuable crustacean species, especially shrimp, are also heavily exploited and have generally reached a stage of economic over-fishing, although there is significant potential for aquaculture. There are better prospects for increasing the harvest of small surface-dwelling species; however, the stocks of such species, some used primarily for conversion into fish meal and oil, are subject to considerable long-term fluctuation in abundance. Sustained growth in demand, given these supply constraints, will lead to a continued rise in the real prices of preferred species.[32]

The growing demands on the fisheries sector, particularly for human consumption, could be satisfied by several changes in commercial fishing practices that could significantly increase the supply of fish. These include saving the discards from trawling operations for preferred species, reduction of post-harvest losses through better landing, storage, and marketing facilities, and the wider use of small surface-dwelling species for human food products. Major gains also may be obtained from the culture of additional species through extensive aquaculture systems and fishery enhancement in reservoirs, lakes, and even in the open seas.

Extension of national jurisdiction over fisheries, whilst a precondition for rational management, does not of itself ensure the most efficient conservation and use of fish stocks. It must be reinforced with the legal and operational institutions necessary to design and implement conservation and management schemes. Greater support for fish farming and other types of aquaculture—for example, the award of fishing rights to specific communities—could make a significant nutritional and social impact in rural areas of low-income countries. Such rights often reflect traditional customs that have demonstrated the value of allocating exclusive fishing rights in defined areas to specific groups of fishermen, with the attendant incentive of maintaining sustained production through self-regulation and control.[33]

D. GENETIC RESOURCES

Rapid destruction of the natural environment is quickly reducing both the number of species and the amount of genetic variation within individual species. Perhaps a quarter of the earth's total biological diversity, amounting to about a million species, is in serious risk of extinction during the next 20 to 30 years. This is perhaps 1,000 times faster than the historical rate of extinction. If a forest is reduced to 10 per cent of its original size, the estimated number of species that can continue to exist in it will decline eventually by half. Habitat reduction on this scale has already occurred in many parts of the tropics in recent decades. More than half of the world's species are believed to live in tropical rain forests. They were disappearing at a rate of more than 7 million hectares per year in the early 1980s; this implies a 40 per cent reduction in their total area from the mid-1980s to 2000.[34] Other species-rich habitats in danger include tropical coral reefs, geologically ancient lakes, and coastal wetlands.

Biological diversity must be viewed as a global resource, like the atmosphere or the oceans. New uses for it are being discovered that can relieve both human suffering and environmental destruction. Only a tiny fraction of species with potential economic importance have been utilized; 20 species supply 90 per cent of the world's food, and just three (wheat, maize, and rice) provide more than half. In most parts of the world, these few crops are grown in monocultures that are particularly sensitive to insect attacks and disease. Yet tens of thousands of edible species—many possibly superior to those already in use—remain unexploited. The rapid development of biotechnology will speed up the use of available genetic resources, thereby increasing the value of maintaining the most diverse possible pool of species and genes.

The maintenance of biological diversity is a precondition for sustainable development. Conversely, sustainable development is, in many respects, the key to the maintenance of biological diversity. Hungry people may have no alternative but to convert ecologically unique habitats into arable land. Thus, the effective implementation of conventions to conserve wetlands, for example, is dependent on helping people to raise the productivity of existing arable land, thereby taking the pressure off these unique habitats.

A strategy in this area could be built around two primary objectives:

(a) Conserving sufficient inter- and intra-specific diversity to ensure that mankind has the genetic resources to respond to new pests and diseases and to potential problems such as deterioration in growing conditions as a result of climate and other environmental changes;

(b) Promoting the utilization of appropriate genetic resources and biodiversity, and raising the economic and social importance of natural resources in specific ecosystems for agro-forestry, livestock, fish, and game cropping in natural savannah areas.[35]

Compared with the magnitude of the problem, the action being taken so far by Governments and the international community to promote conservation and sustainable use of biological diversity is inadequate in the extreme. There is a pressing need for a comprehensive biodiversity strategy. Crucial issues include the provision of adequate compensation for the conservation of genetic resources, use of part of the compensation for more active conservation, and wider access to these and other genetic resources in the field and in gene banks, including those produced through biotechnology. The World Conservation Strategy, the Environmental Perspective to the Year 2000 and Beyond,[36] and the Report of the World Commission on Environment and Development[37] propose three main objectives for all conservation policies and practices: to ensure the sustainable utilization of species and ecosystems; to maintain essential ecological processes and life-support systems; and to conserve genetic diversity. The World Conservation Strategy emphasizes the formulation of national conservation strategies as a priority for national action. So far only about 35 countries have started to do so, but a global network of gene banks has been established to house the World Base Collection of crop germplasm, and more than 100 countries are collaborating in it.[38]

E. HAZARDOUS WASTES*

The present methods of storage and disposal of many chemical wastes and other toxic substances pose severe risks to human health and to the viability of other species and ecological processes. All countries produce and dispose of hazardous substances on an increasing scale, but many of them, especially developing countries, lack awareness of the hazards. They also lack the data and analytical capacity needed for the safe management of hazardous wastes. After decades of uncontrolled dumping, industrialized countries and an increasing number of developing countries have discovered that the cost of ignorance and neglect is extremely high in terms of air, water, and land pollution and consequent harm to health and productivity.

The traditional low cost methods of hazardous waste disposal are landfill, storage in surface impoundments, and deep-well injection. Recently, thousands of landfill sites and surface impoundments used for dumping hazardous wastes have been found to be entirely unsatisfactory; corrosive acids, persistent organics, and toxic metals have accumulated in them for decades. Estimates of the costs of cleaning up existing dangerous sites range from $1 billion in Denmark to $10 billion in the Federal Republic of Germany and $23 to 100 billion in the United States. Some of the unsatisfactory dumping has exposed people directly to hazardous chemicals. In two major cases in the Netherlands and the United States, homes were built on reclaimed land containing paint solvents, pesticides, chemicals used in making plastics, and the sludge from the bottom of stills. Hundreds of families had to be evacuated from the sites in both cases. For the U.S. site, the cleanup costs reached tens of millions of dollars and there were many serious health problems in children living on and near the site. In Japan in the 1950s and 1960s, mercury discharged from a chemical factory into the sea contaminated fish eaten by local people; nearly

---

* This section is based mainly on UNEP, *The State of the World Environment 1989, op. cit.*, Chapter 4.

two thousand people suffered neurological disorders and about four hundred died. Although dumping of waste at sea is now controlled under international and regional contentions, several countries are still using this method for the disposal of hazardous waste, and underground storage of hazardous waste is practised on a limited scale in a few developed countries.

Several physical, chemical, and biological methods can be used to reduce the bulk or toxicity of the waste. Of all the treatment technologies available, properly designed incineration systems can provide the highest overall degree of destruction and control for the broadest range of hazardous waste streams. Ideally, incineration should produce carbon dioxide, water vapour, and inert ash. But small quantities of a multitude of other more dangerous emissions may be formed. Such emissions appear to pose little increased risk to human health, but more detailed studies are needed. Rising costs, scarce treatment capacity, and public opposition to new treatment and disposal facilities plague hazardous waste disposal programmes virtually everywhere. Incineration at sea in specially designed ships costs much less than land–based incineration, since emissions are not as tightly controlled. However, there is now a trend to limit marine incineration or ban it altogether.

As controls on hazardous waste disposal have been tightened in some countries, industries have increasingly resorted to exporting their waste to foreign countries. Recent publicity about the dumping of hazardous wastes in some African countries has triggered widespread concern. The shipment of hazardous wastes from the North to the South is likely to grow even if illegal dumping is prevented. Developing countries may accept hazardous wastes in return for hard currency or needed industrial goods, even though it is extremely difficult for them to ensure that the wastes are properly handled and disposed of. Export of hazardous wastes transfers the risks involved to the importing countries, without necessarily transferring the knowledge or managerial capability to deal with them. Transboundary transfer of hazardous wastes may magnify such risks, therefore, and it weakens incentives for reduction of waste generation at the source. Reduction at the source appears to be the most reliable way to reduce the impact of hazardous waste, and is probably the cheapest in the long run.

Despite some encouraging examples of new low-waste technologies, recycling, and other innovative measures, few of the potential gains have so far been achieved. About 4 to 5 per cent of hazardous wastes are being recycled in some OECD countries, but using existing technologies there is a great potential for recovering up to 80 per cent of waste solvents and 50 per cent of the metals in liquid waste streams in the United States. Japan seems to have advanced the furthest of any major industrial country toward recycling and reusing its industrial waste, largely thanks to a cooperative relationship between industry and government. In Japan, the United States, and Western Europe, there are waste exchanges operating on the simple premise that one industry's waste can be another's raw material. They have succeeded to varying degrees in promoting the recycling and reuse of industrial waste. The United States Environmental Protection Agency has estimated that existing technologies could reduce the total amount of hazardous wastes generated in the United States by 15 to 30 per cent by the year 2000. More vigorous research and development in recycling and waste minimization technologies, together with technical and financial support to encourage investments in them and, in some cases, taxes on waste generated, could probably cut the production of hazardous wastes by one third in many industrialized countries by the year 2000.

Until more production processes that produce far less hazardous waste can be devised and implemented, technical and regulatory measures will be necessary. They will be needed to ensure safe handling and disposal of the existing output of waste, especially in the developing countries. These measures should include methods to evaluate alternative means and sites of waste disposal and to assess the implications of importing such wastes. But few developing countries have established the basic foundation of a hazardous waste management system. Most have no regulation, no trained manpower, and no facilities capable of adequately treating and disposing of hazardous wastes. An active exchange of information and experience between developed and developing countries could do much to advance the latter's capabilities to deal with such wastes. Special emphasis should be put on strategies of waste minimization, recycling, and reuse that could yield large economic and environmental gains.

More than 100 countries signed the Final Act of the Basel Convention on the Control of Transboundary Movements of Hazardous Wastes and Their Disposal in March 1989.[39] This Act deals with exchange of information, technical assistance, and control measures. Under the terms of the Convention, the signatories cannot send hazardous waste to another signatury that bans imports of it, or to one that does not have the facilities to dispose of the waste in an environmentally sound manner, or to any country that has not signed the Treaty. An exporting country must have the importing country's consent, and must first provide detailed information to the importing country to allow it to assess the risks. When an importing country proves unable to dispose of legally imported waste in an environmentally acceptable way, then the exporting State has a duty either to take it back or to find some other way of disposing of it in an environmentally sound manner. Shipments of hazardous waste must be packaged, labelled, and transported in conformity with generally accepted and recognized international rules and standards. The Treaty calls for international co-operation involving the training of technicians, the exchange of information, and the transfer of technology. It also asks that less hazardous waste be generated and that such waste be disposed of as close to its source as possible.

The ultimate goal of the Convention was to make the movement of hazardous waste so costly and difficult that industry will find it more profitable to cut down on waste production and recycle what waste they produce. But a total ban on the movement of hazardous waste is neither practical nor desirable. The Executive Director of UNEP has noted that only about 20 per cent of the hazardous waste generated in and exported from industrialized States is shipped to developing countries. In the near future, developing countries will be exporting hazardous waste to developed countries. Nigeria is already shipping hazardous waste to the U.K. This Convention can give great impetus to minimizing the production of hazardous wastes and the risks of dealing with them, once the necessary 20 countries have deposited their instrument of ratification with the Secretary-General. As of 12 December 1989, more than 40 countries had signed the Treaty itself, but only Jordan had deposited its instrument of ratification.

F. ENVIRONMENTAL IMPACTS OF NEW TECHNOLOGIES AND MATERIALS*

Since the late 1970s the world has experienced a technological revolution propelled by extraordinary scientific progress and rapidly advancing technology. Computers, telecommunications, robotics, biotechnology, lasers, and new materials have brought the global economy to the threshold of a new industrial age. These technological advances are generating profound economic and social changes in many countries, but there is little information on their risks to mankind and the environment. The characteristics of a technology that make it beneficial to one group of people may make it harmful to another and/or to the environment. Advanced technologies frequently use potentially hazardous materials or processes. And in spite of the many precautions and back-up systems used to avoid accidents, some catastrophes have recently occurred. Proponents of advanced technologies point out that they are often safer than some technologies already in use, but no technology is without risk.

Biotechnology, with its advanced techniques of genetic engineering, will have both beneficial and deleterious environmental effects, but the knowledge of those effects is still in its infancy. Industrial applications of genetic engineering probably will be introduced subject to strict safety measures to ensure that genetically engineered organisms are contained. The possibility of accidental release of such organisms, however, cannot be ruled out.

---

* This section is based largely on UNEP/GC.15/7/Add.3, paras. 22–28.

Likewise, the deliberate release into the environment of such organisms for agricultural or environmental purposes may cause health hazards and/or damage to particular ecosystems.[40]

The semiconductor industry uses large quantities of toxic metals, chemicals, and gases. It may be creating great health and safety problems for its workers, the public generally, and the environment. More or less similar problems may be encountered in manufacturing new types of optical fibres, ceramics, composites, and other new materials. An important issue is that most such new materials cannot be easily decomposed; their disposal will create problems never previously encountered. Video display terminals have come into general use in most countries with the increasing use of computers. The manufacture of such terminals creates environmental problems similar to those experienced in the semiconductor industry.

Prevention generally is better than cure. Information on new technologies should be disseminated, therefore, as soon as it is available to allow an assessment of the various risks to society and the environment, and to identify the gaps in knowledge calling for further research by the scientific community. Once the risks have been assessed, measures should be taken to prevent or minimize possible hazards.

4. The Environmental Perspective to the Year 2000 and Beyond

In its resolution 42/186, the General Assembly of the United Nations adopted the Environmental Perspective to the Year 2000 and Beyond:

> "as a broad framework to guide national action and international co-operation on policies and programmes aimed at achieving environmentally sound development. . . ."

The resolution noted the

". . . perceptions generally shared by Governments of the nature of environmental problems, and their interrelations with other international problems, and of the efforts to deal with them . . .,"

as presented in the Introduction to the Environmental Perspective (para. 3). It welcomed

"as the overall aspirational goal for the world community the achievement of sustainable development on the basis of prudent management of available global resources and environmental capacities and the rehabilitation of the environment previously subjected to degradation and misuse, and the aspirational goals to the year 2000 and beyond as set out in the Environmental Perspective, namely:

"(a)   The achievement over time of such a balance between population and environmental capacities as would make possible sustainable development, keeping in view the links between population levels, consumption patterns, poverty, and the natural resource base;

"(b)   The achievement of food security without resource depletion or environmental degradation and restoration of the resource base where environmental damage has been occurring;

"(c)   The provision of sufficient energy at reasonable cost, notably by increasing access to energy substantially in the developing countries, to meet current and expanding needs in ways which minimize environmental degradation and risks, conserve non-renewable sources of energy, and realize the full potential of renewable sources of energy;

"(d)   The sustained improvements in levels of living in all countries, especially the developing countries, through industrial development that prevents or minimizes environmental damage and risks;

"(e) The provision of improved shelter with access to essential amenities in a clean and secure setting conducive to health and to the prevention of environment-related diseases which would, at the same time, alleviate serious environmental degradation;

"(f) The establishment of an equitable system of international economic relations aimed at achieving continuing economic advancement for all States based on principles recognized by the international community, in order to stimulate and sustain environmentally sound development, especially in developing countries" (para. 4).

The General Assembly also agreed "that the recommendations for action contained in the Environmental Perspective should be implemented, as appropriate, through national and international action by Governments, intergovernmental and non-governmental organizations and scientific bodies" (para. 5).

In addition to the recommendations for action set forth in the Environmental Perspective to the Year 2000 and Beyond, the following principles are relevant to many environmental issues. Each Government should be responsible for educating its own citizens regarding their effect on the environment, as both producers and consumers, and for otherwise motivating them to adopt less harmful practices. The developed countries have most of the available pool of technical skills, and therefore most of the responsibility, for devising less harmful techniques of production in all fields, and for assisting the developing countries to acquire and use them. Also, as their standards of consumption tend to be advertised in and therefore copied by the citizens of developing countries, they have the greater responsibility for promoting less harmful patterns of consumption. The developing countries have the primary responsibility, however, for evaluating and modifying foreign consumption patterns so as to harmonize them with their local climate, resources, and culture in order to maintain the productivity of their resource base and the healthfulness of their environment.

NOTES

1. The Governing Council of UNEP, the UN Environment Programme, in its decision 15/2 of 1989, "invites the attention of the General Assembly to the understanding of the Governing Council with regard to the concept of "sustainable development", as follows: "Statement by the Governing Council on Sustainable Development"

"Sustainable development is development that meets the needs of the present without compromising the ability of future generations to meet their own needs and does not imply in any way encroachment upon national sovereignty. The Governing Council considers that the achievement of sustainable development involves co-operation within and across national boundaries. It implies progress toward national and international equity, including assistance to developing countries in accordance with their national development plans, priorities and objectives. It implies, further, the existence of a supportive international economic environment that would result in sustained economic growth and development in all countries, particularly in developing countries, which is of major importance for sound management of the environment. It also implies the maintenance, rational use and enhancement of the natural resource base that underpins ecological resilience and economic growth. Sustainable development further implies incorporation of environmental concern and considerations in development planning and policies, and does not represent a new form of conditionality in aid or development financing.' "—*Official Records of the General Assembly, Forty-first Session, Supplement No. 25* (A/4425), UNEP/GC, 15/12 decision 15/2, Annex II.

2. If developing countries had been required to meet the environmental standards that prevailed in the United States, they would have incurred direct pollution control costs of $5.5 billion in 1980 with respect to their exports of manufactures to OECD countries, which amounted to $48 billion. In addition, it has been estimated that, if the pollution control expenditures associated with the materials that went into the final product were also counted, the costs would have risen to $14.2 billion. This is probably an underestimate, as it relates only to the impact of environmental pollution and does not allow for the costs of soil degradation, deforestation, desertification and other deterioration of resources. Source: A/42/427, Annex.

3. FAO, "Long-term Strategy for the Food and Agricultural Sector" (C 89/19, August, 1989, para. 95).

4. "There is general agreement that if present emissions trends continue, a rise of global mean temperature could occur in the first half of the next century that would be greater than any in the history of civilization." "The Full Range of Responses to Anticipated Climatic Change", UNEP and the Beijer Institute, April 1989, p. xi.

5. *Ibid.*, pp. v–vi.

6. UNEP, *The State of World Environment 1989* (UNEP/GC.15/7/Add.2), paras.

60 and 61. The lower projected increase assumes that "primary energy use will continue at the present rate and reach 720 Exajoules/year in 2050". The higher projection is based on a scenario of accelerated energy use, to reach 1,150 Exajoules/ year in 2050. Many climate-change models have assumed high fossil fuel consumption growth rates of about 4 per cent and concluded that the doubling date of CO_2 concentration would occur around the year 2030. However, assuming annual growth rates of 2 to 3 per cent would extend the period to around the year 2060, while rates of 1 to 2 per cent would delay it far beyond the middle of the next century. (*World Economic Survey 1989*, United Nations publication, Sales No. E.89.II.C.1, p. 108.)

7.   FAO, C 89/19, *op. cit.*, para. 121.

8.   See UNEP/02L. Pro.1/5, Appendix I.

9.   *World Economic Survey 1989*, United Nations publication, Sales No. E.89.II.C.1, p. 108.

10.   UNEP, *Environmental Data Report,* Basil Blackwell, 1987, p. 4.

11.   UNEP, *The State of the World Environment 1987* (UNEP/GC. 14/6), Nairobi, Kenya, April 1987, p. 10.

12.   *World Economic Survey 1989, op. cit.*, p. 108, and Fig. V.3, p. 109.

13.   Stewart Boyle, "Global warming—a paradigm for energy policy?", *Energy Policy,* Feb. 1989.

14.   UNEP, *Environmental Data Report,* Basil Blackwell, 1987, p. 6.

15.   *World Economic Survey 1989, op. cit.*, p. 106.

16.   Ibid.

17.   UNEP, *The State of the World Environment 1989*, para. 82.

18.   *Ibid.*, para. 11.

19.   A decline of 1 per cent in total ozone concentration would increase the intensity of UV-B on the earth's surface by about two per cent, and would increase the incidence of skin cancer by about two per cent. See UNEP, *The State of the World Environment 1987, op. cit.*, p. 14, and United States National Academy of Science estimates, as reported in *Time* magazine, "The Heat Is On, 19 October 1987, p. 60.

20.   UNEP, *loc. cit.*, para. 14.

21.   *The New York Times*, 11 October 1989, p. A 27.

22.   Several international organizations, such as ECE, EEC and OECD have in the past few years adopted strategies to mitigate acid rain. The ECE sulphur-reduction protocol, agreed to at Helsinki in July 1985, entered into force in September 1987; it is the first international treaty specifying measurable reductions of air pollution. The protocol binds the concerned countries to reduce their sulphur emissions by at least 30 per cent from 1980 levels as soon as possible, and by 1993 at the latest. However, some of the largest sulphur emitters had not yet joined in 1989, including Poland, the United Kingdom, and the United States. A similar protocol to limit nitrogen oxide emissions is being negotiated. The draft protocol calls for a freeze in nitrous oxide emissions at 1987 levels by 1994.

23.   UNEP, *The State of the World Environment 1987, op. cit.*, April 1987, p. 30.

24.   World Bank, "Environment, Growth and Development", Washington, D.C., 16 March 1987 (mimeograph), p. 3.

25.   FAO C, 89/19, *op. cit.*, para. 112.

26.   UNEP, *The State of the World Environment 1989, op. cit.*, para. 27.

27.   World Watch, Vol. 2, No. 5, Sept.–Oct. 1989, p. 8.

28.   World Bank, "Report: 'Sound Environmental Management Should Be Integral Part of Economic Policy-Making' ", *World Bank News VI* (15), April 16, 1987, p. 12.

29.   Except as otherwise noted, this section is based primarily on the Report of the Committee for Development Planning on its twenty-fifth session, 9–12 May 1989, *Official Records of the Economic and Social Council, 1989 Supplement No. 11* (E/1989/29), sections IV A and B.

30.   *The State of the World Environment 1989, op. cit.*, paras. 16–19.

31.   *Ibid.*, paras. 22–23.

32.   FAO, *op. cit.*, para. 23.

33.   *Ibid.*, paras. 100, 115–118. The 1984 FAO World Conference on Fisheries Management and Development endorsed a strategy for fisheries management and development. Two of its elements are particularly relevant to the issues of sustainable development: (a) principles and practices for the rational management and optimum use of fish resources; and (b) the special role and needs of small-scale fisheries and rural fishing and fish farming communities. The strategy also underlines the importance of further efforts to develop aquaculture and calls for increased emphasis upon environmental considerations. (*Ibid.*, para. 119.)

34. UNEP, *The State of the World Environment 1987, op. cit.*, para. 85.

35. FAO, *op. cit.*, para. 120.

36. General Assembly resolution 42/186, annex.

37. A/42/427, annex.

38. Pilot data banks and conservation schemes have been developed to offer access to information on animal genetic resources and analysis of it. A global network of Microbiological Resources Centres (MIRCENs) now exercises regional responsibility for the collection, maintenance, and application of microbial genetic resources. The first national parks were established more than a century ago, and many other types of protected areas have evolved in recent years. These range from scientific reserves to multiple-use areas such as biosphere reserves where some sustained utilization of natural resources is permitted. As of 1985, there were over 3,500 protected areas covering about four million square kilometres, or about 3 per cent of the global land area.

39. See UNEP/IG.80/3.

40. A Working Group on Biotechnology Safety was established in 1985 jointly by UNEP and the World Health Organization (WHO). The Group has been reviewing the different aspects of bio-safety and has emphasized the need for a set of guidelines, training programmes, the exchange of information, and notification schemes in regard to field testing and the use of genetically modified and novel organisms.

5.
Energy

THE ENERGY SECTOR has passed through three distinct periods during the past forty years. After World War II and up to 1973, the energy market was characterized by a rapid growth in energy consumption fueled by cheap and plentiful supplies of energy, especially oil. In the 1970s, the energy market changed decisively when large oil price increases in 1973–1974 and again in 1979–1980 were accompanied by apprehensions about the security of supplies. Higher energy prices resulted in sluggish demand during the first half of the 1980s. This slow demand reflected energy conservation and improved efficiency in energy use as well as low economic growth rates in developed countries and even negative growth in many developing countries. In the end energy prices were sharply reduced.

Oil prices collapsed in 1986. Their subsequent stabilization as well as the resumption of higher growth rates in the economies of the developed market economies and several developing countries in Asia have once again brought about higher than expected increases in energy demand, including oil. Perceptions of energy scarcities have been replaced by widespread expectations of surplus capacities. This is true despite several indications that the world energy situation may be on the threshold of new problems of increasing supply concentration in the medium term, as well as of environmental problems that were hardly even imagined a few years ago.

Because of the long lead times required for energy projects, the structure of the world energy market cannot be expected to change drastically in the next ten years. Policy decisions during the 1990s, however, particularly those arising from environmental considerations, may set the stage for fundamental changes in the world energy picture at the beginning of the next century.

A. HISTORICAL TRENDS AND THE CHANGING ENERGY MARKET

Between 1960 and 1973 world consumption of commercial energy and world GDP grew at average annual rates of 5.1 and 5.8 per cent respectively. Between 1973 and 1987 these rates were only 1.9 and 2.6 per cent respectively. The large increases in oil prices in 1973–1974 and 1979–1980 and the slowdown in world GDP that led to a reduction of world energy consumption served to confirm that prices and GDP are major determinants of energy demand.

The relationship between energy demand and economic growth can be measured by the energy intensity, defined as the amount of energy required to produce a given unit of economic output (i.e., energy consumption divided by GDP). Energy intensities for the developed market economies, the economies of Eastern Europe and the USSR, the developing countries and the world as a whole are displayed in table 5.1 for the period 1970 to 1986. Figure 5.1 shows the evolution of these intensities and suggests that energy intensity trends largely reflect the level of economic development and the structure of the economy.

Market responses to changes in relative prices and to measures undertaken by governments have led to structural changes in the demand for energy and the composition of supply. In developed

ENERGY INTENSITIES
(1977=100)

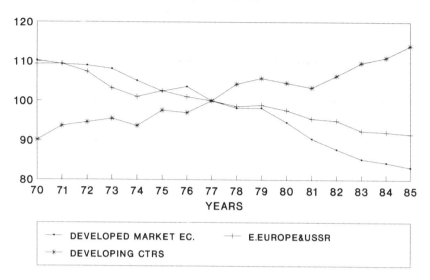

Figure 5.1
Source:Diesa/UN Secretariat,Energy Stat.
Yearbook,Nat.Acc.Database UN Stat.Office

market economies, conservation and greater energy efficiency have resulted from the switch to less energy-intensive capital goods and consumer durables, and from the application of energy-efficient electrical machinery in industry, heating, and air conditioning. Increased efficiency in the transport sector has contributed to overall improvement in energy use. For example, in the early 1970s automobiles in North America were much less fuel-efficient than their European and Japanese counterparts, but this has changed significantly.

As a result, energy intensity in the developed market economies declined by 27 per cent, from 3.60 barrels of oil equivalent per $1000 of real GDP (boe/$1,000) in 1973 to 2.67 in 1986. It declined slowly but steadily until 1979. Following the 1979–1980 increase in energy prices, it fell more rapidly until 1986. Although the rate of growth of real GDP averaged 2.4 per cent annually during that period, primary energy consumption remained almost stagnant.

For the period 1970 to 1986 in Eastern Europe and the USSR, energy intensity fell by 17 per cent, from 10.02 boe/$1,000 to 8.32 boe/$1,000. Much of the decline occurred in the 1971–1974 planning period. Little change took place between 1975 and 1979, but further reductions were recorded in the period from 1980 to 1986. Despite this decline, energy intensity in these economies is still much higher than in other developed economies.

Energy intensity reflects different characteristics of the development process. Thus, the high energy intensity in Eastern Europe and the USSR may be attributed in part to the energy-intensive heavy industries that grew rapidly in the 1960s until energy intensity peaked. But it may also be attributed to the low efficiency of dominant technologies and types of fuels used, particularly in the industrial sector.

In Eastern Europe and the USSR, as elsewhere, the relative decline in overall energy intensity has been accompanied by progress in inter-fuel substitution, particularly in the industrial sector. The share of coal in total energy use fell from 47.8 per cent in 1973 to 35.7 per cent in 1987, and the share of natural gas increased from 21.4 per cent to 35.6 per cent during the same period. The share of oil in total energy consumption rose slightly from 29.6 per cent in 1973 to 31.8 per cent in 1980, then it declined to 26.3 per cent in 1987. Since 1981 the share of oil in secondary electricity generation, in industrial activities, and in residential- commercial-agricultural use declined as large supplies of natural gas from the Soviet Union became available.

Measures to encourage energy conservation, improvement in energy efficiency, and inter-fuel substitutes have been rather limited in developing countries. The amount of energy consumed per unit of output is still rising. It should eventually reach a plateau, then it may decline. The replacement of non-commercial energy (i.e., wood and farm waste) by commercial energy such as fossil fuels and electricity during the transition from a rural less developed society to an urban industrial society is a common feature of the development process. It leads to a rapid growth in energy intensity, accentuated by the growth in energy-intensive industry in the early phase of industrialization.

Energy intensity in developing countries, therefore, has been rising since 1970. From 1970 to 1986 it increased by 29 per cent, from about 3.02boe/$1,000 to about 3.89 boe/$1,000. During the period 1971 to 1974, the intensity of oil consumption increased but coal intensity decreased. There was little change between 1974 and 1980, but since 1980 oil intensity seems to be declining whereas coal intensity is rising again. Energy intensity in the members of OPEC has been rising rapidly since 1977, but it has declined in other oil-exporting countries, particularly China. In the oil-importing developing countries, energy intensity increased rapidly between 1970 and 1973, but since 1973 it has increased only moderately.

The shares of world commercial energy consumption and GDP by socio-economic groups of countries are shown in figure 5.2. Between 1970 and 1986, the shares of world energy consumption and GDP of the developed market economies decreased, while those of the developing countries and Eastern Europe and the USSR increased.

Fuelwood is the main source of energy for many developing countries, but because it is mostly collected on a noncommercial basis for use in home heating and cooking, it is not usually included in official energy statistics. Among the developing countries, the largest fuelwood producers and consumers are India, Brazil, China, Indonesia, and Nigeria. Fuelwood accounts for about 80 per cent of the total energy consumption in some countries in sub-Saharan Africa.[1]

Table 5.2 shows that during the period 1970 to 1986, the growth of energy consumption was slower than the growth of GDP for the industrialized economies. In the developed market economies the average GDP growth rate was 2.9 per cent, while the average growth rate in energy consumption was 0.9 per cent; the GDP elasticity of demand for energy (energy growth rate divided by GDP growth rate) was 0.3. In Eastern Europe and the USSR, GDP grew at an average annual rate of 4.5 per cent, although energy consumption grew faster than GDP in this region

STRUCTURE OF THE COMMERCIAL ENERGY CONSUMPTION

ENERGY 1970

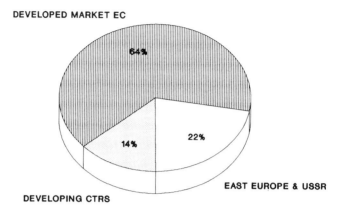

ENERGY 1986

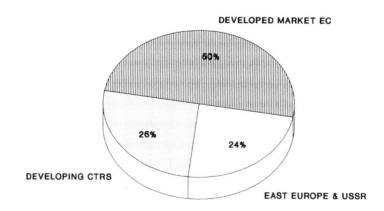

Figure 5.2

in most of the 1970s, but during the period 1970 to 1986 it grew only an average of 3.3 per cent. In developing countries, however, energy consumption grew faster than GDP; the difference was especially large in OPEC.

B. FUTURE TRENDS IN ENERGY CONSUMPTION AND PRODUCTION

Energy consumption is expected to grow worldwide with continuing demographic and economic growth, but considerable uncertainty prevails with regard to future improvement in energy efficiency and conservation. In the baseline scenario, energy consumption worldwide is expected to grow from 1987 to the year 2000 at about 2.8 per cent per year (see figure 5.3). This rate is higher than those projected in studies of energy demand and supply made by the Commission of the European Communities (about 2 per cent), the International Institute for Applied System Analysis (2.15 per cent), and the 1986 World Energy Conference (1.7 per cent) (see table 5.3).[2] It should be noted that these scenarios reflect what the organizations considered as low energy paths a couple of years ago.

Energy consumption in the developed market economies is expected to rise at an average annual rate of about 1.6 per cent from 1987 to the year 2000. This is consistent with a rate of growth of GDP of about 3.1 per cent per year and further reduction in the GDP elasticity of demand for energy, from a current level of about 0.6 to an average of 0.52 over the remainder of the century.

Demand for electricity is expected to grow faster than total primary energy demand and at about the same rate as GDP. Although the outlook for nuclear power in the developed market economies is uncertain, it is expected to represent about 15 per cent of total electricity production by the year 2000.

Energy production in the developed market economies is projected to increase from 57 million barrels per day of oil equivalent

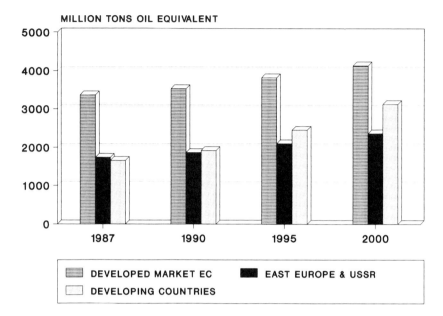

COMMERCIAL ENERGY CONSUMPTION

MILLION TONS OIL EQUIVALENT

Legend:
- DEVELOPED MARKET EC
- EAST EUROPE & USSR
- DEVELOPING COUNTRIES

Figure 5.3

(mbdoe) in 1986 to 67 mbdoe in the year 2000. The share of conventional oil and natural gas liquids in total primary energy production is expected to decline from 25 per cent to about 18 per cent during the same period, mainly owing to the rapid decline in United States oil production. Efforts to raise reserves through extensions of known fields or implementation of large enhanced oil recovery projects may, if reasonably successful, limit the rate of this decline. Nevertheless, the developed market economies will have to rely on more imports of oil, particularly from OPEC.

Natural gas production, currently at about 12 mbdoe and apparently offering good geological prospects, is not expected to decline. A gradual rise in coal and lignite production is expected to the year 2000, from 20 mbdoe in 1986 to 21 to 24 mbdoe. Recently it was estimated that coal reserves in the developed market economies represent over 200 years of coal consumption at the prevailing rate.[3]

A one per cent rise in GDP in Eastern Europe and the USSR currently requires a rise in energy input of about 0.77 per cent. With the efficiency improvement indicated by recent trends, one might expect the energy coefficient to decline to an average of 0.7 per cent for the period 1987 to 2000. Given an expected rate of growth of GDP of about 3.6 per cent per year, this would imply a rise in energy consumption of about 2.4 per cent annually. The industrial sector accounted for over one half of final energy use in 1987; its share is expected to fall marginally, and that of the transportation sector to increase gradually.

Although the heavily oil-dependent transportation sector would rise relative to less oil-dependent sectors, inter-fuel substitution and better efficiency would reduce slightly the relative role of liquid hydrocarbon by the end of the century. The large natural gas reserves in the USSR will ease the changeover from oil to coal. The consumption of electricity is expected to increase faster than that of other forms of energy. Increasing dependence on nuclear energy for their electricity supplies is expected in Eastern Europe and the USSR. Nuclear power is projected to account for some 12 per cent of their energy use by the year 2000.

In the developing countries, including China, the next decade will witness continuing replacement of non-commercial energy by fossil fuels. The GDP elasticity of demand for energy is expected to average about 1.0. Energy consumption would thus increase at the expected GDP average growth rate of about 5 per cent annually during the period 1987 to 2000. The rapid growth of energy consumption in developing countries is due to high population growth and large unsatisfied energy needs. The share of final consumption represented by the residential-commercial-agricultural sectors would decline in favour of industry and transportation.

Achieving an improved balance among commercial energy sources is more difficult in developing countries than in industrialized economies. Developing countries will still be heavily dependent on liquid hydrocarbons at the end of the century. Production of crude oil and natural gas liquids will rise from approximately 30 mbdoe in 1987 to 46 to 50 mbdoe by 2000. Some 30 to 34 mbdoe will be produced by OPEC. Currently OPEC member countries hold about 77 per cent of total world proven oil reserves of approximately 990 billion barrels, and they are capable of raising output capacity to meet the growing oil demand. Natural gas production in the developing countries is expected to more than double the current level of about 4 mbdoe.

Many developing countries have large unexploited hydro-power sites. They can be used to increase domestic energy production to meet their growing electricity demands, provided that the sizeable investment required can be financed. The electricity supplied by nuclear energy in a few large developing countries so far constitutes less than 1.0 per cent of the total energy produced in developing countries. This level is expected to reach 2 per cent by the end of the century.

The pattern of world energy trade is expected to change significantly. Between 1975 and 1985 the share of OPEC in world exports of crude oil dropped from 61 to 40 per cent. Since 1986, their share has been increasing again. Because lower oil prices have led to significant declines in exploration and related investments, this trend is expected to become more pronounced during the 1990s.

Net imports of liquid hydrocarbons by the developed market economies from the developing countries are expected to rise from 13 mbdoe in 1987 to 20 mbdoe by 2000. Nearly half of this would flow to the United States, where current oil imports account for nearly one half of consumption and are expected to continue increasing. The Council for Mutual Economic Assistance (CMEA) group is projected to swing from net exports of 1.6 mbdoe in 1987 to net imports of 2 mbdoe in the year 2000. These net oil imports would be largely offset by exports of natural gas to Western Europe. Imports of sea-born liquified natural gas by Japan and the United States will also be significant. The current balance of international trade in coal between developed and developing countries is expected to be reversed. The developing countries as a group had net imports of about 0.3 mbdoe in 1986 but would have net exports of about 1.0 mbdoe in the year 2000. These exports would come mostly from China.

Oil will remain the most widely traded energy source. Its share in world energy demand is expected to increase through the year 2000. As the demand for OPEC oil has been rising steadily and excess production capacity has been shrinking since 1986, the downward pressure on the price of oil has eased. In the past three years, the demand for OPEC crude oil has increased substantially from about 15 million barrels a day in early 1986 to more than 20 million barrels a day in early 1989. The nearly 12 to 14 million barrels per day of OPEC excess capacity that has been displaced from the market by 1985 has been reduced to about 6 million barrels a day. The current sustainable OPEC crude oil production capacity is about 26 million barrels per day.[4]

It is widely believed that non-OPEC production has already peaked and is currently declining, and that growing oil demand will be met in the future by expansion of OPEC output. It appears that the time needed for demand to adjust to the 1986 decline in oil prices has passed as demand for oil has been more responsive to price than had been anticipated. In the past two years oil demand increased at an average rate of about 2.75 per cent per year in the market economies. This trend may continue for the next few years. The increasing demand for oil is related to the effect of lower oil prices as well as to the sustained growth in the developed market economies and in the newly industrializing developing countries.

Given the current circumstances, it is not likely that normal growth in demand will by itself lead to sharp and persistent oil price increases in the next few years. Short-term supply disruptions or sudden increases in oil demand due to seasonal climate conditions may cause only temporary volatility in oil prices. Sometime around the mid–1990s, however, as the equilibrium between supply and demand begins to be restored and the market tightens, prices may be expected to move up more rapidly.

Many small high-cost fields in non-OPEC countries will be exhausted later in the decade, and oil production capacity will become more concentrated. Large low-cost fields, located mainly in the Middle-East, will increase their share in rising world oil demand. The maintenance of discipline among producers will become easier, and the possibilities for co-operative action will be enhanced. Nonetheless, given past experiences, it seems unlikely that the price of oil will be sustained for any appreciable period above $25 per barrel (in 1987 dollars) during the rest of the century.

The maintenance of oil prices below $15 per barrel (in 1987 dollars) for extended periods is also unlikely, since this would stimulate further expansion of oil consumption and result in "shutting in" production in high cost regions. In addition, given the heavy dependence of OPEC member countries on revenues generated by the sale of their oil, it is unlikely that they will jeopardize the development of their economies by letting the price fall below $15 per barrel.

During the second half of the 1980s, lower oil prices appear to have created a new climate for energy policies. Growing environmental concerns have contributed to new uncertainties, however, about the future development of the world energy market. The evidence, discussed elsewhere in this report, that fossil fuels are major contributors to the greenhouse effect as well as to acid rain, together with the widespread public resistance to nuclear energy, is influencing energy investments and development strategies in a number of countries. Increased use of natural gas and continued research and development programmes aiming at cleaner and more efficient coal burning methods could contribute to easing the problem of global warming. Because humanity needs energy and a clean environment for its development and survival, co-operation and understanding between all major parties is necessary.

NOTES

1. *World Resources* 1988–1989, report by the World Resources Institute and the International Institute for Environment and Development, in collaboration with the United Nations Environment Programme (New York Basic Books, Inc., 1988).

2. Report submitted by the International Atomic Energy Agency, addendum, (A/44/339/No. 11), p. 7.

3. (E/C.7/1985/4), p. 12.

4. Subroto, Secretary-General, OPEC, *Long-term prospects for oil market stability*, Energy Policy, October 1989, p. 449.

TABLE 5.1 *Energy intensities*
(boe/$1,000 GDP)

Region	1970	1975	1980	1985	1986
Developed market economies	3.66	3.40	3.14	2.76	2.67
Eastern Europe & the USSR	10.02	9.40	8.95	8.40	8.32
Developing countries	3.02	3.27	3.50	3.82	3.89
OPEC	1.31	1.45	1.95	2.80	3.09
Oil-exporting	5.14	5.92	6.02	5.78	5.78
Oil-importing	2.73	2.90	2.97	3.01	3.02
World	4.12	3.98	3.82	3.60	3.56

Source: United Nations Secretariat, Department of International Economic and Social Affairs, based on Energy Statistics Yearbook, *United Nations publication, various issues; and the national accounts data base of the United Nations Statistics Office.*

TABLE 5.2 *Economic growth and commercial energy consumption,*
1970–1986

Region	Average growth rates in percentage		Elasticity of demand for energy[a]
	GDP	Energy con-sumption	
Developed market economies	2.9	0.9	0.31
Eastern Europe & the USSR	4.5	3.3	0.73
Developing countries	4.5	6.2	1.38
OPEC	3.4	9.1	2.68
Oil-exporting	5.6	6.4	1.14
Oil-importing	4.4	5.1	1.16
World	3.4	2.4	0.71

Source: Ibid.

[a] *GDP elasticity of demand for energy equals energy growth rate divided by GDP growth rate.*

TABLE 5.3 *World total primary energy demand*
(In million tons of oil equivalent)[a]

Source of forecast	1980	1990	2000	2010
Commission of the European Communities (1986)	7,270		10,800	
International Institute for Applied Systems Analysis (1985)	6,800	8,000	9,900	11,300
World Energy Conference (1986)	7,700	9,400	11,100	13,300

Source: See footnote 4.

[a] *There are differences in the data for 1980 depending on whether so-called non-commercial energy sources in developing countries, mainly fuelwood and animal dung, have been included. Also the use of different conversion factors to convert hydro-, wind-, and solar-produced electric energy to primary energy results in different data.*

6.
Agriculture

A. 1960 TO THE PRESENT

SINCE THE EARLY 1960s the outstanding development in world agriculture has been the significant improvement in the levels and quality of food consumption. The challenge of feeding some 1,800 million people more than in the early 1960s has been met. Earlier fears of chronic food shortages over much of the world have proved to be unfounded. In many areas and for many groups of people, however, hunger and malnutrition are rife. According to the Fifth World Food Survey made by the Food and Agriculture Organization of the United Nations (FAO), between 350 and 510 million people are still seriously undernourished in the developing countries (excluding China), with more than half of them living in Asia.[1]

The key factor that enabled the world's expanding population to be better fed was the transformation of agriculture, first in the developed market economies but increasingly in the developing countries, particularly following the Green Revolution. Rice yields rose by 42 per cent in developing countries between 1969–1971 and the mid 1980s, wheat yields by 84 per cent. Production growth in the developing countries averaged 3.2 per cent a year

PER CAPITA OUTPUT OF STAPLE FOOD CROPS
(CEREALS,PULSES,ROOTS AND TUBERS)

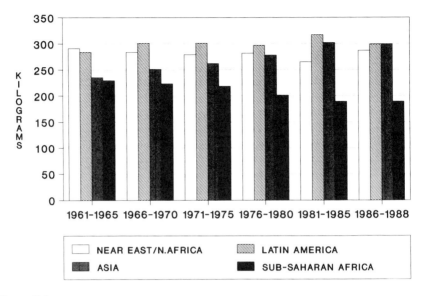

Figure 6.1

in 1961–1988. In sub-Saharan Africa, however, sluggish growth during the 1960s worsened in the 1970s and, aggravated by droughts, became a full-scale crisis in the early 1980s (table 6.1 and figure 6.1).

The developed countries account for about half of world agricultural production, and they experienced a marked slow-down in production growth (see table 6.2 and figure 6.2). This reflected a slow-down in the demand for agricultural products in these countries due to a decline in their population growth rates and the already prevailing high levels of per capita consumption. Slower growth of demand in domestic markets was compounded by a slow-down in the growth of their export markets. The slow-down in production in the developed market economies from 2 per cent in the 1960s and 1970s to less than 1 per cent in the 1980s was in many cases brought about by supply control measures that

GROWTH RATES OF AGRICULTURAL PER CAPITA
PRODUCTION, 1960-1988

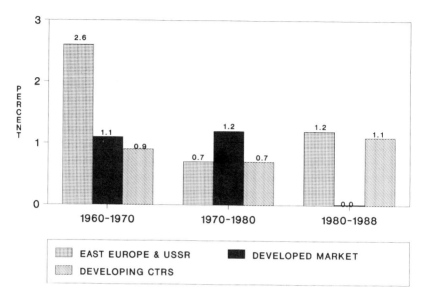

Figure 6.2

became necessary to counteract support policies that tended to increase production in excess of demand.

At the same time the world food system came to rely increasingly on trade. In the early 1960s, 8 per cent of world agricultural production entered international trade, but by the mid–1980s this share had grown to 12 per cent. For cereals the picture is more complex. During the 1960s trade in cereals expanded steadily from 87 million tons to 111 million tons. But during the 1970s cereal trade boomed, reaching 214 million tons by 1981–1982. Since then it has stagnated and even declined. Net cereal imports by the developing countries remained more or less constant, however, at about 20 million tons in the 1960s. Then it more than tripled during the 1970s and reached almost 70 million tons by the end of the decade, increasing to 86 million tons in 1988. By contrast, net cereal imports in sub-Saharan Africa remained stationary in the 1980s at a level of about 8 million tons (table 6.3). Combined with an annual fall of 1 per cent in per capita production for the same period, this led to a serious decline in the region's food availability.

Another important development was the greater integration of agriculture with the world economy. A rising share of output was marketed, more off-farm inputs were purchased, institutional credit was expanded, and more off-farm income was earned by agricultural households. These increased links with the monetary economy and the rising share of output traded internationally made the agricultural sector more open to external economic developments. As a consequence, international economic conditions have come to play an increasingly important role in agriculture. Fluctuating exchange rates, commodity price instability, soaring external debt, and rising real rates of interest have affected food supplies and agricultural development.

Food security became a leading issue in the wake of the world food crisis in the early 1970s. The World Food Conference held in Rome from November 5 to 16, 1974 sought to eradicate hunger and malnutrition by both national and international measures.[2] The need to increase food production in the developing countries was stressed. Greater external assistance was to be mobilized, and a minimum 10 million tons annual food aid target was set. Internationally coordinated stock policies were recommended, but in practice attempts to negotiate an International Grains Agreement with Economic provisions (on stocks and/or prices) failed.

The moderately good record of the developing countries in terms of production and improvement in food consumption levels is more mixed when examined at the level of regions or individual countries. For some countries (e.g., major Asian countries), new food supplies came predominantly from growth in domestic production; in others food imports played an important role (e.g., many countries in the Near East/North African region). Other countries failed to benefit from either of the sources, and some of them suffered absolute declines in per capita food supplies. There was devastating drought in the African region and overall economic stagnation that led to poor agricultural performance both in Latin America and sub-Saharan Africa.

Production growth generally resulted more from higher yields than from expansion of area under cultivation. Countries that followed policies encouraging, or at least not discouraging, farmers to use yield raising technologies (improved seed varieties and the associated off-farm inputs, irrigation and better management) generally scored best in production growth. These policies cover a wide variety of interventions, some agriculture specific, others less so. More profitable production was achieved by, for example, public investment in irrigation or other infrastructure, removal of institutional constraints, or more remunerative prices. But more commonly it was achieved by varying mixes of these and other policies. Some countries achieved agricultural progress by putting emphasis on alternative policy mixes: China's experience in the late 1970s to the mid–1980s is an example of policy reform relaxing institutional constraints and allowing more scope for economic incentives to work. Saudi Arabia is an example of heavy public investment and subsidization of inputs and producer prices. India has emphasized irrigation technology diffusion and spread of high yielding varieties. Malaysia is an example of successful long-term development of export crops emphasizing research and development and with a keen eye on export markets. There are also a number of African countries whose policies proved the validity of giving priority to agriculture in their national development strategies.

The choice and effectiveness of the mix of policies has depended on initial conditions and on the ability of Governments to implement them in the appropriate sequence. Price policies proved an effective means of encouraging production in countries where the physical and institutional infrastructure was already in place. Non-price policies (promotion of infrastructure, research, marketing, credit) were instrumental in countries lacking these initial conditions. Valuable policy lessons can be learnt equally from countries that implicitly or explicitly failed to improve the policy environment of agriculture, e.g., by maintaining overvalued exchange rates and keeping domestic terms of trade unfavourable for agriculture.

It must also be recognized that differences in natural resource endowments have made it more difficult for some countries, e.g., semi-arid ones, to encourage agricultural growth by means of yield-raising modern varieties. In such cases, significant gains in production and productivity were difficult to achieve, even when inappropriate policies did not stand in the way of exploiting existing technological potential for these areas. The growth of domestic food production in many low-income, food-deficit countries, especially in Africa, may cause environmental damage as the pressure of rising demand on scarce natural resources increases.

Other constraints to agricultural growth in the developing countries that could have been relaxed by policy interventions, and indeed have been in a number of cases, must be emphasized. In particular the access by smaller farmers and the landless to productive assets, technology, credit, and services. This is true especially in those countries where agricultural production growth is constrained by inadequate demand. In such cases, policies that increased income earning opportunities of the poor, including promotion of equitable agriculture and rural development, have provided a stimulus to agricultural growth. The overall economic crisis and its adverse effects on the incomes of the poor in Latin America contributed to the decline in the region's agricultural growth in the 1980s. For these countries reduced exports to the developed countries combined with the debt burden, depressed employment, and economic activity resulted in a slow-down in domestic demand for agricultural output.

Finally, the disarray in international agricultural trade conditions has affected agricultural growth in most developing countries. Protectionism in the main industrial countries has restrained exports of traditional products of the developing countries such as sugar, meat, and tropical products. Exports of agricultural products in countries with overvalued exchange rates and inefficient parastatals have declined while other countries with better policies have made inroads into the foreign markets. The heavy subsidization of industrial country exports of temperate zone foodstuffs (cereals, livestock) created difficult conditions for the developing countries exporting these products. By keeping world prices low, it provided a disincentive to production and to required policy reforms of importing countries, although they benefited from lower import prices in terms of foreign exchange outlays.

B. PROSPECTS TO THE YEAR 2000 AND POLICY ISSUES[3]

The projections presented here come mainly from the FAO study "Agriculture: Toward 2000", completed in 1987. They are not mere extrapolations of trends. Rather, they reflect a broadly optimistic view of the prospects of developing countries when a "composite" scenario is built on the basis of alternative scenarios presented in Chapter 3. The population projections are those of the UN medium population growth variant as assessed in 1984.

Projections of domestic final demand are made by country and commodity on the basis of GDP and population growth projections. Intermediate demand is derived in conjunction with the production projections as a function of livestock production (feed) and of harvested area (seed). The production projections are made on the assumption that the developing countries will continue to give priority to domestic production over imports of deficit food products and adopt appropriate policies to raise self-sufficiency if this can be achieved economically. Much of the production analysis rests on the proposition that when self- sufficiency in the year 2000 seems unfeasible, the targets are revised downwards. The evaluation of technical and economic feasibility of production increases takes into account agricultural resources, technology, productivity trends, and the costs involved.

The demand projections of the developed countries are confronted with their production trends to define possible net trade positions. Implied import requirements and export availabilities of all countries are aggregated to form an initial estimate of world balances. Further iterations ensure that adjusted exports and imports of each commodity are brought into balance at the world level, and that related production levels are consistent with explicit technological and resource constraints in developing countries. An assumption is that the developed market economies as a group will moderate their import substitution policies. Thus they will avoid further declines of their net imports of competing commodities such as sugar and vegetable oils from the developing countries. More generally, efforts to contain protection and move towards a more market-oriented world agricultural trading system are assumed to lead to a gradual process of attenuation rather than a radical reversal of the unfavourable trends for the developing countries' agricultural exports.

Tables 6.4 and figure 6.3 summarize the projections for the developing countries. On the aggregate, the production growth rate of agriculture at 3.1 per cent is equal to that of past trends but with significant regional differences. The prospects for an upturning African agriculture are far from clear, but in these projections assume that it will return to a growth rate of 3.5 per cent, matching that of the population. The 3.1 per cent growth rate of agriculture in Asia will be lower than in the 1980s because of increasingly binding resource and technology constraints, and because of the expected slow-down in population growth to 1.65 per cent per annum.

This assessment suggests that the developing countries will continue to be large and increasing net importers of cereals. The net imports could increase at a much slower ratio than in the past, however, if appropriate policies for agricultural development are adopted. Self-sufficiency may not improve significantly—in fact it will decline in Africa—but its rapid erosion will be checked.

The overall economic prospects for developing countries in Africa and Latin America are unfavourable. Incomes are likely to grow very slowly, if at all, in those countries. Under these conditions, the incomes of the poor will not rise enough to eliminate poverty and undernutrition. FAO projects the persistence of undernutrition around the estimated present level of some 500 mil-

PROJECTION OF NET CEREAL IMPORT
REQUIREMENTS OF DEVELOPING COUNTRIES

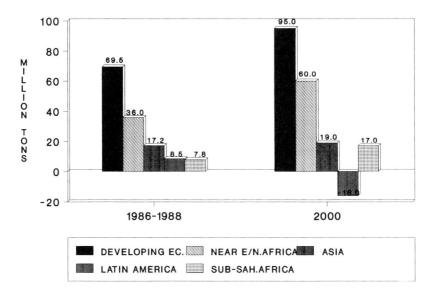

Figure 6.3

lion people, with the number of undernourished persons growing rapidly in sub-Saharan Africa, although the majority of under-nourished persons would still be in Asia.[4]

The assumption of slow progress towards improved access to the main markets for tropical agricultural products and nearly saturated consumption levels for these products implies that agricultural exports from the developing countries will also continue to grow very slowly.

In the developed market economies, the agricultural growth rate will slow down to just under 1 per cent per annum in line with the slow growth of domestic and foreign demand. Current policy reforms in Eastern Europe and the USSR introduce a high degree of uncertainty, but the present assessment is that moderate success in such policy reform would suffice to check the rapid growth of net food imports and to reduce them significantly by the year 2000.

Policies to promote agricultural development must be seen in the wider context of present macroeconomic policy reform efforts. If these are successful, they will also benefit agriculture. Current efforts to reduce agricultural trade distortions should help developing countries that have low costs of agricultural production, though low-income food deficit countries may suffer if trade liberalization raises some food prices. For tropical products, including semi-processed and processed products, trade should be liberalized to the fullest extent possible. Complementary programmes should be implemented to enhance the developing countries' opportunities to diversity their agricultural trade.

In the debate on world food security, issues of inadequate access to food of the poor and endemic undernutrition at the local level in many countries are likely to overshadow the issues of adequacy and stability of global supplies. Undernutrition and food security are intimately linked with issues of poverty alleviation and human resources development. The overall economic crisis and policies for structural adjustment have created an unfavourable environment. The unfavourable income growth prospects for many developing countries will mean the continuation of poverty and undernutrition in the foreseeable future. The need for national and internationally supported direct interventions will remain acute and be a subject in the policy debate over the next decade. The future prospects will depend greatly on the formulation and implementation of more effective policy measures to deal with the issues reviewed earlier (in section 1 of this chapter). Food aid can play a role in these efforts provided it is made available and used in such a way that possible adverse effects, such as disincentives to local food production, are avoided.

Improved technology has underpinned much of the agricultural growth in both the developed and the developing countries. Some countries have been at a disadvantage because the available technology was less suitable for their ecologies and farming systems. R&D for agriculture will be essential for agricultural development in the 1990s, but more emphasis should be put on identifying and promoting more efficient ecologies and farming systems. They offer high pay-offs not only in terms of potential increases in global production, but also in terms of rural income generation, poverty alleviation, and improved nutrition.

NOTES

1.   Undernourished: persons with estimated calorie intakes below 1.2 and 1.4 times (alternative assumptions as to thresholds) the basal metabolic rate (energy requirements in a state of fasting at complete rest in a warm environment). These levels are approximately equivalent, for example, to between 1,450 and 1,610 calories in India or 1,550 and 1,720 calories in Egypt. For methods of estimation and other details see FAO, *The Fifth World Food Survey*, Rome, 1985.

2.   E/CONF. 65/20 (United Nations publication, Sales No. E.75.ll.A.3). For the report of the conference, see *Report of the World Conference on Agrarian Reform and Rural Development*, Rome, 12–20 July 1979 (WCARRD/REP).

3.   Issues of natural resources, environment and sustainability in relation to agriculture are discussed in chapter 7, below.

4.   The prospects for undernutrition are discussed in more detail in Chapters 3 and 12.

TABLE 6.1. *Per capita output of staple food crops (cereals, pulses, roots and tubers in grain equivalent)[a] in kilograms[b]*

	1961–1965	1966–1970	1971–1975	1976–1980	1981–1985	1986–1988
World	348	373	384	398	408	397
Developed market economies	590	674	738	813	895	825
Eastern Europe & the USSR	647	761	805	846	769	845
Developing countries	243	255	262	271	286	284
Excluding China	243	244	245	248	255	251
Africa (sub-Saharan)	229	223	218	201	189	189
Near East/North Africa	291	284	279	282	265	287
Asia	235	251	262	278	302	299
Asia excluding China	229	230	233	244	259	252
Latin America	284	301	301	297	317	299

Source: FAO, Agriculture: Toward 2000 (C 87/27) for 1961–1985 and FAO Secretariat estimates for 1986–1988.

[a] *Aggregated on the basis of calorie content weights.*

[b] *One kilogram equals approximately 2.2 pounds.*

TABLE 6.2. *Growth rates of agricultural production in 1961–1988 (In percentage per annum)*

	1960–1970	1970–1980	1980–1988	1980–1985	1986	1987	1988
	Total production						
World	3.0	2.4	2.1	2.7	0.9	0.9	0.5
Developed market economies	2.2	2.0	0.6	1.3	−1.3	−0.1	−3.8
Eastern Europe & the USSR	3.7	1.5	2.0	2.0	6.3	−0.6	−1.0
Developing countries	3.5	3.0	3.2	4.0	0.8	2.0	3.9
Excluding China	(2.7)	(2.9)	(2.7)	(3.1)	(0.3)	(0.6)	(5.3)
Sub-Saharan Africa	2.8	1.3	2.1	1.8	3.5	−3.4	5.7
Near East/North Africa	2.9	3.0	3.1	2.9	4.4	−0.6	5.0
Asia	3.9	3.2	3.9	5.1	1.1	2.5	4.1
Asia, excluding China	(2.4)	(3.1)	(3.2)	(4.2)	(0.2)	(−0.4)	(7.3)
Latin America	3.0	3.2	2.0	2.2	−2.6	4.4	2.2
	Per capita production						
World	0.9	0.5	0.4	0.9	−0.8	−0.9	−1.3
Developed market economies	1.1	1.2	0.0	0.7	−1.9	−0.8	−4.5
Eastern Europe & the USSR	2.6	0.7	1.2	1.3	5.5	−1.4	−1.8
Developing countries	0.9	0.7	1.1	1.8	−1.3	−0.1	1.8
Excluding China	(0.2)	(0.4)	(0.2)	(0.6)	(−2.1)	(−1.8)	(−2.8)
Sub-Saharan Africa	0.2	−1.7	−1.0	−1.2	0.3	−6.4	2.4
Near East/North Africa	0.1	0.3	0.2	0.1	1.4	−3.4	2.1
Asia	1.4	1.1	2.0	3.2	−0.8	0.6	2.2
Asia, excluding China	(0.0)	(0.8)	(0.9)	(1.8)	(−2.0)	(−2.6)	(5.1)
Latin America	0.2	0.8	−0.2	0.0	−4.7	2.2	0.1

Source: Ibid.

TABLE 6.3. *Import dependency of developing countries*

	Net exports or imports ($-$) of cereals by region, including rice in milled form Annual averages (millions of tons)			
	1961–1963	1969–1971	1979–1981	1986–1988
Developed market economies	20.2	22.6	113.0	116.6
Eastern Europe & the USSR	0.3	-0.1	-43.1	-33.1
Developing countries	-18.1	-20.4	-67.1	-78.6
Excluding China	-13.1	-18.0	-55.2	-71.5
Africa (sub-Saharan)	-1.1	-2.5	-7.7	-7.8
Near East/North Africa	-4.2	-6.5	-23.2	-36.0
Asia	-10.8	-11.4	-20.6	-17.2
Asia, excluding China	-5.8	-9.0	-8.7	-10.1
Latin America	-0.1	3.5	-8.1	-8.5

	Shares of net imports in apparent consumption (percentage)			
	1961–1963	1969–1971	1979–1981	1986–1988
Developing countries	4.9	4.1	9.3	9.0
Excluding China	4.9	5.2	11.7	12.4
Africa (sub-Saharan)	3.3	6.2	16.0	13.4
Near East/North Africa	9.8	12.3	28.4	32.9
Asia	4.4	3.3	4.3	2.9
Asia, excluding China	4.1	4.9	3.7	3.5
Latin America	0.1	—	8.5	7.7

Source: Ibid.

TABLE 6.4. *Growth of population, GDP, total agricultural demand and gross agriculture production in developing countries to the year 2000[a]*
(In percentage per annum)

	1985–2000		1983/85–2000[b]		1986/88–2000[b]	
	Popula-tion[a]	GDP	De-mand	Pro-duction	De-mand	Pro-duction
Developing countries	1.9 (2.0)	4.9	3.1	3.0	3.2	3.1
Excluding China	2.2 (2.3)	4.4	3.0	2.8	3.0	2.9
Sub-Saharan Africa	3.3 (3.2)	3.5	3.5	3.4	3.9	3.5
Near East/North Africa	2.5 (2.8)	4.0	3.1	3.0	3.1	2.9
Asia	1.5 (1.8)	5.7	3.1	3.0	3.1	3.1
Asia, excluding China	1.8 (2.1)	4.8	2.8	2.6	2.8	2.7
Latin America	2.0 (3.0)	4.5	2.8	2.7	2.9	2.8

Source: Ibid., and FAO Secretariat projections.

[a] *The population growth rates in parentheses are those of the latest (1988) United Nations assessment.*

[b] *Projections of demand and production are shown on two alternative base years (three-year averages); the original one of the study 1983–1985 and the latest available three-year average 1986–1988.*

7.
New Technologies

THE DEVELOPMENT of new technologies and their rate of diffusion among industries and countries are the principal forces behind structural change. By a process of innovation, new technologies create new products or production processes and change organizational structures. This process of innovation is largely a function of economic variables such as changing patterns of final demand and relative prices of different productive inputs. Examples of productive input are different types of machinery, raw and intermediate materials, and labour skills.

The developed and developing countries are on different levels of scientific and technological development. The serious concern is that the widening technology gap between countries might threaten the future North-South trade much more than the disparities in income levels. One indicator of technological development, the number of scientists and engineers in developing countries, is about one-tenth of that of developed countries. This gap has been increasing. Another indicator is research and development (R&D) expenditures. They have tripled in developed countries in the decade of 1970–1980, from $60 billion to $195 billion; in developing countries they are slightly above $10 billion, and the gap between the developed and developing countries widened about 3 times during the years 1970–1980.[1]

Africa had only 0.4 per cent of the world's total number of scientists and engineers in 1980, the Arab States 0.9 per cent, and Latin America 1.8 per cent. The distribution of R&D expenditures was similar. In 1980 Africa, Arab States, and Latin America spent 0.3, 0.5, and 1.4 per cent respectively of world R&D expenditures.

Technological underdevelopment can be described as weak capacity to support four major elements of development: (a) modern production facilities; (b) useful and available knowledge; (c) effective organization and management; and (d) technical abilities and skills. These weaknesses give rise to four different vicious circles resulting in an overall vicious circle of technological underdevelopment. In order to break the circle of technological underdevelopment and poverty, Governments must intervene in areas where they can reverse the negative trends. For example, the number of scientists and engineers on a per capita basis in the Republic of Korea has now reached half that in the Federal Republic of Germany. Moreover, political will, education, access to information, and risk-taking leap-frogging are needed as developing countries choose and engage in appropriate aspects of the technological development and promote and encourage innovation.

The level of technological development is increasingly seen as the dominant factor in determining a country's capacity to compete in the world market. It is evident that technological change moulds the patterns of international trade (as revealed in figure 7.1 and table 7.1). The developed market economies imported high R&D intensity products valued at $256.6 billion in 1987; they are growing at 15 per cent and faster than other imports. Imports of medium R&D intensity products were $630.3 billion in 1987; they grew at almost 20 per cent in the 1970s and at about 9 per cent during the 1980s. Imports of low R&D intensity products were $552.9 billion in 1987, and the rate of growth in 1980–1987 was less than 5 per cent.

During the last two decades many Asian developing countries have been catching up fast. They expanded their market shares of both high and low R&D intensity products. Other developing

DEVELOPING COUNTRIES' SHARES OF DEVELOPED MARKET ECONOMIES' IMPORTS OF MANUFACTURES BY R&D INTENSITY

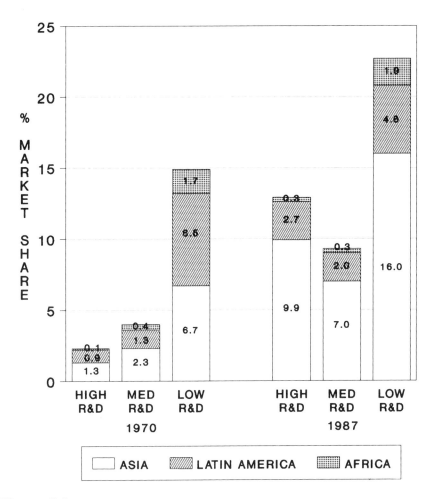

Figure 7.1

countries performed rather poorly, except some Latin American countries that competed relatively well in high R&D intensity products.

The analysis of the developing countries' exports of manufactures by disaggregated R&D categories reveals the competitiveness of their industries in the international market. During the period 1970–1987, they increased their shares in all the high R&D intensity categories of their exports to developed market economies except for drugs and medicines. Table 7.2 shows that some developing countries achieved a competitive edge in the high R&D intensity area of microelectronics and information technology during the years 1970–1987. Their exports of high R&D intensity products were valued at only $33.6 billion in 1987, but they were still growing at more than 15 per cent. Exports of medium R&D intensity products were $60.3 billion in 1987, and they were growing at around 15 per cent per annum. Exports of low R&D intensity products were $130.4 billion in 1987, but in the last few years their growth rate declined to only 6 per cent.

Information technology, new materials technology, biotechnology, space, and nuclear technology are widely recognized to be the five most important new technologies. OECD has identified five characteristics that determine the economic impact of a technology: (a) generating a broad range of new products and services; (b) reducing costs and/or improving performance of existing processes, services, and products; (c) winning social acceptance; (d) stimulating private industrial interest; and (e) yielding applications in various sectors of the economy.[2] Rated according to those characteristics, the five technologies were ranked to indicate their relative economic significance as well as their probable employment impact in the 1990s. These rankings suggest that information technology is perceived to generate the greatest economic and employment impact, followed by materials technology, biotechnology, space technology, and nuclear technology. In another assessment, by the U.S. Department of Commerce, selected advanced materials, biotechnology, micro-electronics, and information technology were ranked as the ones with the greatest expected economic impact in the year 2000.[3] Fast adoption of these technologies may widen the gap between developed and developing countries in terms of economics and know-how.

Technological development changes the composition of output and trade by increasing productivity, and thus the employment structure. Already 15 per cent of the labour force in the United States is employed in "high-tech" industries and information processing activities. But less than one-quarter of those so employed are in specialized occupations such as computer specialists and engineers. Three quarters are in production, distribution, and other service occupations. Therefore, the implications of technological development for the occupational structure of employment are subject to a high degree of uncertainty. In the United States, for example, clerical, professional, and technical workers increased their share of occupational categories by more than one third between 1960 and 1980 (table 7.2). There will be little change in the 1990s in the share of those two groups of occupations in total employment, but the share of professional and technical workers will increase and that of clerical workers will fall. By the year 2000, 20 per cent of the U.S. labour force is expected to be in the category of professional and technical workers, as against 11 percent in 1960.

A. MICRO-ELECTRONICS AND INFORMATION

There are large gaps in the world in the access to information. For instance, in 1986 the developed countries had about 1,000 radio receivers per 1,000 inhabitants, followed by Latin America and the Caribbean with 327, the Arab States with 247, Asia with 162, and Africa with 142. The distribution of the number of telephone main lines in service is even more uneven. Europe had 154.4 million main lines in service in 1987, followed by North America with 136.8 million, Asia with 126.2 million, Latin America with 21.7 million, Australia with 8.4 million, and Africa with

6.5 million. On a per 1,000 inhabitants basis, the U.S. has 10 times more telephone lines than Latin America, 12 times more than Asia, and 48 times more than Africa. In 1990 the U.S. market for the transmission of telegraphic and telex messages and data was estimated to be 60 times larger than the African market and 30 times larger than the Latin American market.

The evolution of information technologies has shown an explosive improvement in their cost/performance ratio. This has induced further expansion of the microelectronics and informatics industry. In OECD countries, only an estimated 10 to 20 per cent of the benefits derived from information-technology-based innovation has so far been reaped; the rest will be acquired in the next 10 years. Similar trends are observed in applications of information technologies, such as the automation of telecommunications and the linkage of computers by data transmission. These applications, together with word processing and computerization of management systems, have transformed finance, banking, business management, and public administration. Information systems developments are continually being applied by private and public sectors to increase the productivity, quality, and efficiency. Recently large companies have begun to use information systems to transmit technical and economic information among numerous computer systems at different geographical locations. In manufacturing and to some extent in agriculture, many processes have been automated, some requiring highly flexible, self-regulating machines, or robots. The engineering industry has been transformed by computer-assisted design (CAD) and three-dimensional computerized screen displays.

More technical advances are expected in automation in the 1990s. Examples are programmable automation, or computer-integrated manufacturing that has the capability of integrating information processing with physical tasks performed by programmable robots (see table 7.3).

The growth of the computer and telecommunication industries is still rapid and pervasive. As proxied by selected industrial categories, the world demand for telecommunication equipment has been growing at an annual rate of 8 per cent during the 1980s.

World demand for computer equipment and services is estimated to grow more rapidly than telecommunication equipment and services for the period 1985–1990, with the U.S. share standing at about 45 per cent (figure 7.2). Even faster growth has been recorded for the semiconductor industry, which produces the key components used in all computerized applications. This sector may account for 4 per cent of total world manufacturing output by the year 2000 (equivalent to $200 billion in 1980 prices).

The world production of information technology systems is estimated to grow from $390 billion in 1986 to $1200 billion in 1995, with software achieving the highest annual growth rate of 20 per cent during 1986–1995. Production of hardware in 1995 will account for 52 per cent, software 36 per cent, and telecommunications and computing services 12 per cent (figure 7.3). In the U.S. alone, expenditure on computers, data processing equipment, and telephone and telegraph systems is projected to grow at an average rate of 20 per cent until 1995. The world market for telecommunications and broadcasting satellites in the 1990s will be dominated by developed countries; Latin America, for example, will account for only 2 per cent. The world market will be about 7 billion in 1986 U.S. dollars in the late 1990s, but it will grow less rapidly in the late 1990s than in the 1980s and early 1990s (figure 7.4).

The diffusion of informatics in developing countries is still in an embryonic stage. They accounted for only 5.7 per cent of the total number of computers in the world in 1985. The developing countries have so far used the computers mainly for standard functions of inventory control, accounting, and payroll. Recently, however, some activities in microelectronics such as assembly of mature components and final testing have relocated from Hong Kong, Singapore, and Taiwan province of China to new locations in the Caribbean, China, Indonesia, the Philippines, Sri Lanka, and Thailand. The semiconductor market in South and East Asia has expanded rapidly; the Republic of Korea, Hong Kong, and Singapore are projected to raise their semiconductor sales from $2 billion in 1986 to $5.4 billion in 1990. During 1981–1986, the Brazilian electronics market grew to about $8 billion, thus be-

WORLD MARKET FOR TELECOMMUNICATION AND COMPUTER GOODS AND SERVICES

1985
(Total value: $ 498 billions)

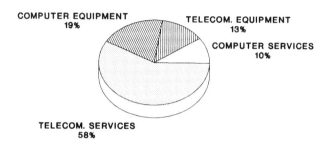

COMPUTER EQUIPMENT
19%

TELECOM. EQUIPMENT
13%

COMPUTER SERVICES
10%

TELECOM. SERVICES
58%

1990
(Total value: $ 884 billions)

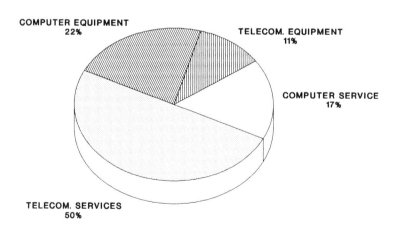

COMPUTER EQUIPMENT
22%

TELECOM. EQUIPMENT
11%

COMPUTER SERVICE
17%

TELECOM. SERVICES
50%

Figure 7.2

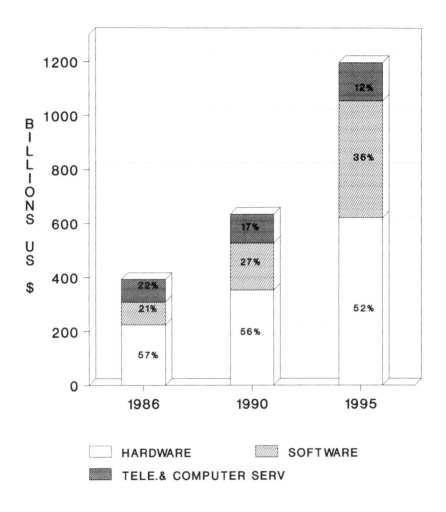

Figure 7.3

MARKET FOR TELECOMMUNICATIONS & BROADCASTING SATELLITES

1986-1990
(Total value: $ 4.1 billions, annual average)

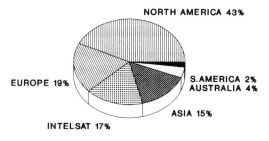

1996-2000
(Total value: $ 6.1 billions, annual average)

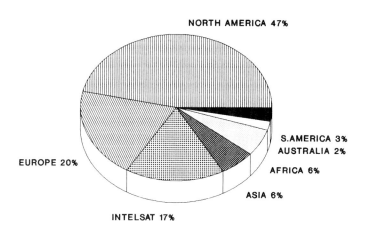

Figure 7.4

coming the tenth largest in the world and slightly larger than that of the Republic of Korea; Brazilian-controlled firms have rapidly expanded their production of computers. India has been particularly successful in software. It has achieved a niche in the international software market through its government policies of tax breaks and liberal foreign exchange regulations for this sector. India increases its software exports each year by about 40 per cent and plans to produce $100 million worth of software annually by the early 1990s.

Telecommunications technologies and micro-computers offer potential opportunities of fulfilling the developing countries' needs, including above all access to information and telephone services. Also, telecommunications technologies may be instrumental in improving the market mechanisms for small businesses and developing the rural areas and underdeveloped regions in developing countries. Micro-computers have found many applications in small and medium-scale enterprises and in education in developing countries due to their speedy improvement in cost/performance ratio and the widespread availability of inexpensive software.

Several surveys conducted in China during 1981 and 1986 indicated that its growing small and medium enterprises primarily needed market, industry, product, resources, and scientific information.[4] This implies that China and other developing countries need to apply modern computer workstations, personal computers, and other appropriate technologies for the construction and utilization of distributed systems of data-bases where information can be stored and accessed by a cluster of small and medium enterprises. In 1983–1986 alone, China increased its computer imports from $70.8 million to $300.4 million.

Information technologies are essential for monitoring and reducing pollution. Microelectronic devices have lowered energy consumption and harmful emissions, particularly in the transportation sector. However, the fast growth of hardware production has created new environmental problems and serious health risks. The semi-conductor industry dumps 65,000 tons annually of potentially toxic materials and releases toxic gases such as artine, phosphine, and diforane.[5]

B. NEW MATERIALS*

Many new materials have been developed during the past three decades as research has been directed toward more consistent quality and reliability, improved durability, and ease of processing. These materials include new metal alloys, plastic-coated metals, elasto-thermo plastics, laminated glass, and fibre-reinforced ceramics. Such new materials (or multimaterials) are developed by the combination of two or more basic categories of traditional materials. The uses of these new materials are becoming widespread in almost every industrial sector (figure 7.5).

The declining trend is accelerating in the amount of raw materials required to produce one unit of industrial production. For instance, during 1973–1985, the per unit consumption of raw materials in Western industrialized countries decreased by 42 per cent in the consumption of tin, 37 per cent in steel, and 32 per cent in zinc. The two types of technological innovations—substitution of one material by another, and materials saving—that occurred in the 1970s have resulted in significant reduction of traditional raw materials consumed in the manufacture of inter-

---

* "New materials" or "advanced materials" refer to substances possessing new compositions or microstructures, advanced properties or performance, and unusual application potentials.

"New materials" can be defined as: (1) specialty polymer materials (characterized by their super-function polymer membranes performing a function unavailable in the conventional polymer materials; (2) fine ceramics (characterized by their production with great precision from synthetic fine powder to render advanced functions); (3) new metal materials (characterized by their functions, which are different from conventional metals, such as expansion and contraction like rubber, and change in shape corresponding to temperature variation); and (4) composite materials (characterized by their functions improved by combining two or more materials).

FIGURE 7.5 *The linkages between basic materials, multimaterials and industrial sectors*

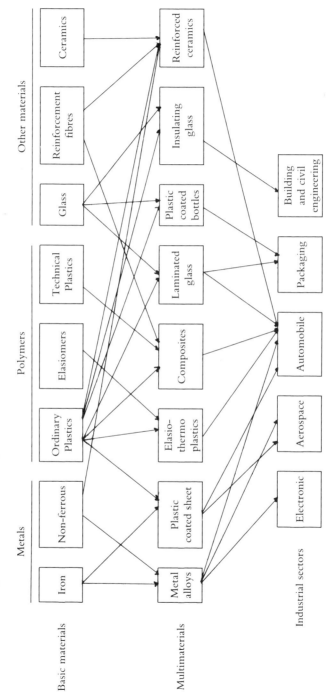

Source: J.M. Poutrel, "Advances in material technologies and their economic impact," Bureau d'information et de prévisions economiques (BIPE), paper presented to the United Nations Centre for Science and Technology for Development, 1986.

mediate and final products. Also, improved properties and efficiency due to new processing methods have led to "dematerialization," that is, the use of less raw material relative to the weight and value of the final product. Intangible investments in software, marketing and R&D will in the future constitute a larger share of the production cost while that of raw materials and energy expenditures will decline.

The long-term trend of substitution of new materials for old is expected to accelerate as a consequence of the demand for enhanced performance in such industries as electronics, communications, information and data processing, transportation, energy, machine-building, manufacturing, and chemicals. The largest changes are expected in the substitution of ceramics, polymers, and composites for metals. Advanced-materials technologies are expected to revolutionize the automobile and aircraft industries in the next decade and beyond. High-performance plastics and ceramics will be increasingly utilized to enhance fuel efficiency by using ceramic engines and to reduce the weight of car bodies by using plastics and resin-based composites. In 1985 high-quality plastics and composites replaced an estimated 9 per cent of the steel formerly used in U.S. motor vehicles. They will replace more than 19 per cent in the year 2000. High-performance composites may substitute 40 per cent of aluminium in commercial aircraft by 1995, and 5 per cent of the metal currently used in construction and heavy equipment.

Estimates of growth in world demand for the period 1985–1990 suggest that the fastest growth is likely to be in ceramics and materials for electronics with annual growth rates of 16 per cent and 12 per cent respectively. In the U.S. polymers and inorganic materials (ceramic glass) are expected to grow faster than metals and other materials during the years 1990–2000 (table 7.3). The moderate growth rates of aggregated categories are averages of high growth rates of new materials and slow or even a negative growth for traditional materials. For instance, structural ceramics are expected to grow by 15 to 30 per cent during the period 1987–2000, and superconductive materials by 32 per cent from 1986–2000; during the period 1983–2000, gallium is estimated to grow by 10.1 per cent and vanadium by 8.9 per cent, as contrasted to 0.8 per cent for silver and 1.2 per cent for tin. The U.S. demand for these materials may rise from $243 billion in 1970 to $370 billion in the year 2000; the percentage share of polymers is estimated to increase from 14 per cent in 1970 to 26 per cent in the year 2000. This is in contrast to metals that will decrease from 49 per cent in 1970 to 38 per cent in 2000, and other materials (including wood) from 29 per cent in 1970 to 19 per cent in the year 2000. The Japanese market for new materials is projected to increase from $2.2 billion in 1981 to $24 billion in the year 2000.

The most recent development of advanced high-temperature superconductive materials, which are metal oxides, is expected to find many commercial applications. The world market for these materials may increase from $400 million in 1986–1987 to $20 to $34 billion in 2000.

The impact of new materials on the world economy is of great concern to the countries that will be seriously affected. An assessment of the impacts of new materials on Japan, which is heavily dependent on raw materials, suggests that it will benefit greatly. For instance, Japan may reduce its fuel consumption by 15 per cent and its total oil fuel consumption by 3 per cent by using ceramics for producing major parts of engines. It may also substitute ceramics for expensive rare metals as heat resistant materials. By developing hydrogen storage alloys, Japan may utilize hydrogen as an energy source in addition to electricity and gasoline. Developed countries will develop domestic new materials to avoid the shortage of certain strategic materials and thereby enhance their national security and bargaining power.

These trends will reduce the growth of demand for such traditional materials as copper, zinc, tin, bauxite, and aluminium. Although some low-cost producers may be able to increase their shares in the slowly growing world markets for traditional materials, they will generally face declining real prices. In the production of some new materials such as fibre-reinforced plastics and fibre-reinforced inorganic materials, developing countries may be competitive. This is due to an abundance of the raw materials required and the labour-intensive character of some parts of the production chain. The use of advanced materials on a per capita basis in developing countries is about 100 times less than in developed countries. Some developing countries (such as Argentina, Brazil, Mexico, Republic of Korea, the Philippines, India, and Indonesia) have been carrying out research in the area of low-cost construction and building materials as well as alloys, polymers and composites. The new materials that are recognized to be most promising for developing countries in Asia and the Pacific are advanced ceramics, plastics, composite semi-conductor materials, and rare and rare-earth metals. The development of new materials, such as ceramics, is advantageous to Latin America and the Caribbean region due to the availability of certain mineral resources (viz., copper, iron, carbon, and aluminium). The newly industrialized countries and Brazil are examples of developing countries that have succeeded in the area of microelectronics. They should also enter into production of semi-conductor materials, silicon, and other new materials that are important inputs for microelectronics. For African developing countries, developing materials for roads and for low and middle-income housing in rural and urban areas is essential. Examples of other possibilities of materials development are shown in table 7.4.

The producers of primary materials, especially those of developing countries, should reconsider their policies concerning materials technology development in the longer term. Their objective should be shifting the production of traditional raw materials to more knowledge-intensive materials. One class of new materials called functional materials is expected to be indispensable in the development of sectors such as microelectronics, telecommunications, informatics, and the electrical industry. The potential world market for four major functional materials—fine ceramics, high performance plastics, composites, and high-purity rare and rare-earth metals—is negligible now but is expected to grow to about $110 billion in the year 2000.[6]

Rare and rare-earth metals are essential for scientific-technical advancement, and their applications are continuously expanding. The recent advances and potential commercialization of super-conductors, for example, have stimulated the interest and demand for rare-earth elements (such as yttrium, europium, neodymium, ytterbium, as presented in table 7.5) and alkaline earth elements (such as strontium) that are needed for high-temperature super-conductivity and whose supply is currently restricted. Many developing countries are major producers of rare metals (table 7.6). Brazil, Nigeria, and Zaire accounted for 88 per cent of the total production of niobium in market economies in 1982; Brazil, Malaysia, Thailand, Mozambique, and Nigeria produced 75 per cent of market economies' total output of tantalum. The world demand for rare metals is projected to rise sharply to the year 2000 and even faster by the year 2020 (table 7.7). The potential for developing countries to produce high-purity rare-earth metals available for high-tech industry is abundant and should be fully exploited.

C. BIOTECHNOLOGY

Biotechnology innovations have already been applied in food and agricultural production, renewable energy, waste recycling, pollution control, and medical treatment. A principal advantage of these innovations is their economical use on a small scale, without large infrastructure requirements, which should facilitate their use in developing countries.

The potential of biotechnology for increasing agricultural productivity is high. The United States Office of Technology Assessment expects that by the year 2000, five-sixths of the annual increase in agricultural production in the world will result from new biotechnology and other yield increases, while one sixth will be due to the increase in the area of land used in production. In the early 1990s, the agricultural production of the developing countries may exceed the present level by 30 per cent. Also, by then the developing countries will probably account for 60 per cent of the world crop production, while Asia may produce 3 times more wheat than the U.S.

Biotechnology can be utilized to develop new and more valuable types of fish and thus enhance the fishery industry of coastal states. The demand for fish is projected to grow to 113.5 million tons by the year 2000, possibly leading to an unsustainable ratio between consumption and replenishment of fish reserves. Already many coastal states are reluctant to allow other nations to fish within their Exclusive Economic Zones. Consequently, countries must rely increasingly on fish farms. For instance, Japan, which obtains about 10 per cent of its total catch from its fish farms, has carried out "biotechnology fish" projects, such as the use of cell fusion technology to produce algae that are 350 times more efficient in raising brine shrimp.

Commercial output of biotechnology products, such as biopharmaceuticals and new chemicals with agricultural applications, is expected to grow by 9 per cent per year until the year 2000. World sales are expected to be about $20 billion in 1996–2000, compared with $8.5 billion in 1986–1990 (figure 7.6). According to another projection, world sales of narrowly defined bio-engineering products will increase from $25 million in 1988 to $340 million in 1990, and then to $10.6 billion by the year 2000. In the 12 leading agriculture-based countries, the retail value of biotechnology-derived seed of 10 principal crops is forecast to grow from $165 million in 1990 to $1.5 billion in 1995, and to $5.9 billion by 2001. About 75 per cent of all major seeds in the next century may be developed by genetic engineering or tissue culture. Moreover, markets for biotechnology products may spread in the developing countries by the middle or end of the decade.

Genetic engineering is already being applied in animal husbandry. For instance, bovine growth hormone can increase milk production by 20 per cent at the same feed costs; its world market was established only two years ago and has already reached $1 billion per year. Developing countries can utilize biotechnology to produce fermented foods and beverages; the sales value of three enzymes (amylases, glucamylases, and glucose isomerase) used in starch and flour processing was expected to rise from $140 million in 1980 to $640 million in 1990. Also, the sales value of calf renin produced by genetically engineered bacteria was estimated at $40

WORLD BIOTECHNOLOGY MARKET
(ANNUAL AVERAGE)

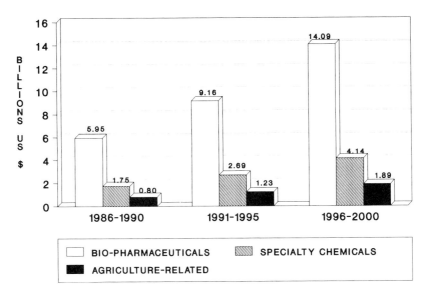

Figure 7.6

million annually in the 1970s, while the combined value of calf and microbial renin is forecasted to reach about $130 million in 1990.

Biotechnology has been efficiently used to produce new pharmaceutical products. Interferon, growth hormone, lymphokines, and tissue plasminogen activators are examples. Their market sales, initiated a few years ago, may reach $55 to 70 billion by the year 2000.[6]

Many developing countries have already applied biotechnology successfully to their production of palm oil and coconut oil plants and to eliminate major disease traits, thereby increasing productivity by about 30 per cent. Tissue culture techniques have been applied to rice, maize, wheat, barley, cabbage, lettuce, tomatoes, peas, onions, potatoes, rape-seed, tobacco, sugar cane, and cotton. Among the purposes of these applications have been gene transfer for disease resistance and salinity tolerance, selection of plants resistant to pathogens, and recovery of immature embryos from defective seeds.

The International Rice Research Institute (IRRI) in the Philippines has succeeded in applying cell culture techniques to produce hybrid rice variations with greater tolerance for soil contents and improved protein contents. IRRI has developed and stored more than 80,000 genetic accessions for future breeding experiments and international co-operation. These genetic accessions offer potential applications such as protein content enhancement, pesticide resistance, disease resistance and elimination, weed and pest control, and biological nitrogen fixation for reduced fertilizer requirements. The Philippines considers its biotechnology programme as the initial step toward an industrialization strategy that will induce biological transformation of biomass into food, fuel, fertilizers, and chemicals. Biotechnology has also been applied to identify and treat diseases in prawns.

Nigeria, Mauritius, Côte d'Ivoire, Thailand, Indonesia, India, Pakistan, the Philippines, Argentina, Brazil, Colombia and Mexico are among several developing countries that have established programmes to incorporate biotechnology in agricultural and industrial activities. Some African scientists have carried out biotechnology research focusing on tissue culture and improved plant and crop varieties. In Nigeria there has been substantial research in biotechnology and genetic resources. This research has led to genetic selection and breeding techniques and to the improvement and production of local varieties of crops with higher yields, greater pest resistance, and earlier maturation. In its effort to promote livestock development and production of food crops, fish, and milk, Mauritius has planned to form a joint venture in gene splicing technology for medical applications, and to develop a niche in the world market for its biotechnology products. India, Indonesia, Malaysia, Colombia, and Côte d'Ivoire have directed their research efforts towards specific traits and have engaged in technical co-operation in information exchange. In Thailand progress has been made in fermentation technology (for production of feed components, single-cell protein, industrial chemicals, etc.) and enzyme technology (for production of antibiotics, sweeteners, etc.) with a potentially large impact on industry.

Various biotechnology products and processes are considered technically and economically feasible for development in Mexico (see table 7.8). Mexico has applied fungi technique to small-scale protein enrichment of cassava flour for animal feed. Furthermore, nitrogen-fixing biotechnology is estimated to increase corn yields in Mexico and Central America by 2 to 4 times.

Plant and animal biotechnologies offer many benefits but may also have some negative impacts for selected aspects of plant biotechnology, as exemplified in table 7.9. The exploitation of tissue culture and other biotechnology may result in the displacement of products that are major exports of some developing countries. For example, the substitution of sugar by biotechnology products may have significant negative impacts on sugar-exporting developing countries.

An assessment of the international transfer of the crop technologies and biotechnologies developed in the U.S. indicates that the transfer potential and the productivity impact depend to a large extent on the research and development capabilities of the importing countries. The study also suggests, however, that the traditional crop production technologies carry a lower rate of transfer from the U.S. than the new biotechnologies.[7]

Potential environmental hazards could be caused by biotechnologies in the alteration of plants and microorganisms, genetic manipulation, and chemical applications. Besides disturbing the ecological balances, the introduction of genetically engineered organisms may engender new plant or animal pests as well as human diseases. Thus, the opportunities offered by biotechnology should be weighed against its environmental risks and the interrelated social and economic implications.

D. DIFFUSION OF NEW TECHNOLOGIES

The diffusion of new technologies depends upon several factors: expected profitability and risk; the required amounts of applied research; development and investment costs; marketing and production capabilities of firms; resource endowments (especially engineering skills); and relative factor prices. The lead time from invention to innovation (first practical use) and to commercial application has been diminishing over time. The lag is generally shorter for consumer products than for industrial products, as well as for inventions requiring relatively small investment. In general, diffusion tends to be more rapid in the United States and Japan than in Western Europe, possibly because of closer links between industry and universities, greater mobility of technologically skilled personnel, and lower barriers to market entry.

The transfer of new technologies has been more rapid among countries with higher levels of technical development and greater financial resources. Japan adapted over 30,000 items of technology from abroad during the years 1950–1986.[8] Developing countries with relatively large domestic markets and more open economies tend to have more rapid diffusion with shorter time lags. The time needed to imitate a product or adopt a process also decreases as more resources are available. Firms with comparable technological capability monitor the changing technology of their competitors closely and imitate them rapidly. Advances made in communication and transportation technology tend to speed up this process. Also, the recent successive and fast incremental innovations capable of diffusing horizontally in various sectors have led to a high rate of product obsolescence. This shortens the product life cycle, but it also makes new investments riskier and may discourage firms from engaging in innovation. For instance, compact disks that have better sonic quality than vinyl records and various tape formats have been used for only a few years, but they will be replaced soon by digital audio tape. This new product embodies a superior technology and will dominate the consumer recording market. An analysis of a sample of 48 product innovations introduced from 1960 to 1976 in the chemical, drug, electronics, and machinery industries in the U.S. showed that about 60 per cent of the patented inventions were imitated within four years. The ratio of imitation time to innovation time averaged about 0.70, and the ratio of imitation cost to innovation cost averaged about 0.65.[9]

The time lag between invention and application appears to vary significantly across industries. Based on a sample of 11 petroleum refining processes and 35 products and processes in other industries, the average time lag was 11 years in the petroleum industry and about 14 years in the others.[10] Mechanical inventions were found to have the shortest time lags in other industries, followed by chemical and pharmaceutical inventions and then electronics. Certain inventions can be applied profitably only after changes occur in tastes, technology, and factor prices. Also, some inventions deviate substantially from prevalent technology, while others are merely improvements.[11]

The diffusion lag also differs among individual countries. The differences depend on policy and institutional environments, technology and organizational capabilities, availability of skilled human resources, and different economic climates. New advances in technology tend to spread more rapidly in the U.S. than in some other developed countries, both through the direct transmission of ideas among universities and industries and through the high mobility of technologically skilled personnel. Lower barriers to entry in U.S. industries are also conducive to this process. In microelectronics, for example, the imitation lag was estimated to be 0.1 year in the U.S., 2.2 years in the United Kingdom, 2.7 years in the Federal Republic of Germany, and 2.5 years in Japan.[12]

The channels for the international transfer of technology take many forms, and they may be either commercial or non-commercial.[13] Non-commercial channels include, for example, technical assistance provided by Governments. Commercial transfer of technology is made through a variety of channels such as foreign direct investment, joint ventures, trade in capital goods, licensing of patents or outright purchase of patent rights, subcontracting, and supply of consultancy services. International transfer of technology has been dominated by private foreign direct investment and inter-firm licensing. Despite its present sluggishness, foreign direct investment is expected to continue its important role in this arena, but joint ventures and licensing are increasingly preferred and are expected to rise more rapidly.[14]

The strategy of transnational corporations (TNCs) will continue to have a dominant impact on the transfer of technology. A major portion of the technology transfer to developing countries in the past has been made through TNCs in the form of foreign direct investment, licensing, and other means. Recently, TNCs have expanded their operations in information-intensive services (banking and finance, in particular), the bulk of them concentrated in developed countries. Transnational banks transfer new and advanced technology to the financial sector of the developing countries by training local employees in using the new financial products and services. The number of technology agreements between TNCs and developing countries has risen significantly. It is increasing at the annual rate of 1,000 technology agreements in Brazil and India, and more than 400 in the Republic of Korea. The global economic activities of TNCs may continue to expand in the 1990s in response to economic growth and opportunities arising from technological innovation and changing market conditions. The trend is increasing for major TNCs to acquire and takeover smaller companies in the same or related fields owing to growing interrelationship between such industries as computers and telecommunications, chemicals, and pharmaceuticals.

The major TNCs have developed and adapted a substantial share of innovative products, processes, and applications in their research laboratories, thus speeding up the international transfer of technologies. In the 1960s the share of new technologies less than 5 years old being transferred by U.S.-based TNCs was only 27 per cent, but it increased to 75 per cent in the 1970s.[15] The diffusion of electronics technologies in developing countries has originated mostly from TNCs' offshore assembly activities. However, it is more difficult to negotiate contracts for new technologies than for mature technologies. The royalty rates in computer software agreements, for instance, may be higher than 3 to 5 per cent of net sales. This is the royalty rate usually provided for more mature technologies to developing countries.

Several of the more advanced developing countries (in particular, India, Brazil, Argentina, Republic of Korea, and Taiwan, Province of China) have emerged as important exporters of capital goods and new sources of technology in the past decade. Fast technology development and emergence of new technology transfer may help developing countries to import technology at lower prices and with greater choice for a specific technology package. Creation of a domestic technological capacity is done through appropriate skill formation and enhancement of R&D capabilities and technologies for monitoring and disseminating information on new technologies. It is an important though costly policy pursued by an increasing number of developing countries.

NOTES

1. For a discussion of the impact of science and technology on long-term economic development in the context of ECE member States, see United Nations Economic Commission for Europe, *Overall Economic Perspective to the Year* 2000 (United Nations publication, Sales No. E.88.II.E.4), chap. VI.

2. OECD, *New Technologies in the* 1990s; *A Socio-economic Strategy*, Paris, 1988.

3. United States Department of Commerce, "Status of Emerging Technologies: An Economic/Technological Assessment to the Year 2000," National Technical Information Service, PB87–195301, June 1987.

4. Commission of the European Communities and UNCSTD, "Distributed Data-Base systems for small and medium enterprises," final report of the seminar held in Beijing, China, May 1989.

5. Reported in UNCSTD, *Update*, No. 38, 1989.

6. E. M. Omeljanovsky, "On the conception of advanced materials for development," UNCSTD, 1988.

7. United Nations Development Programme (UNDP), "Plant biotechnology including tissue culture and cell culture," July 1989.

8. United States General Accounting Office, *World Agriculture: Factors Influencing Trends in World Agricultural Production and Trade*, GAO/RCED-89-7, Washington, D.C., January 1989.

9. Hyung Sup Choi, 1989, "Transition from imitation to creation," *Technological Forecasting and Social Change*, 36, pp. 209–215.

10. E. Mansfield, Schwartz, M., and Wagner, S., 1981, "Imitation Costs and Patents: An Empirical Study," *Economic Journal*, 91 (December), pp. 907–918.

11. J. Enos, "Invention and innovation in the petroleum refining industry," *The rate and direction of inventive activity*, Princeton, N.J., 1962.

12. Edwin Mansfield, *The economics of technological change*, W. W. Norton & Company, Inc., New York, 1968, p. 101.

13. Gert Lorenz, "The diffusion of emerging technologies among industrial countries," in Giersch, Herbert, ed., *The Diffusion of Emerging Technology among Industrial Countries: Symposium*, 1981.

14. UNCTAD, *Trade and Development Report*, 1987, (United Nations publication, Sales No. E.87.II.D.7), pp. 85–100.

15. These channels are not mutually exclusive. The total flow of foreign direct investment to developing countries decreased from $15 billion in 1981 to $10 billion in 1983 and $11.5 billion in 1985. The share in world total foreign direct investment decreased from 26 per cent in 1975 to 23 per cent in 1985. Foreign direct investment inflows are also very unevenly distributed among the developing countries. Flows of foreign direct investment tend to be concentrated in those countries that are rich in natural resources, have large domestic markets or an abundant supply of skilled but low-cost labour. In 1980–1985, 18 countries and territories accounted for 86 per cent of the flows of foreign direct investment to developing countries as a whole. United Nations Centre on Transnational Corporations (UNCTC), *Transnational corporations in world development: Trends and prospects.* (United Nations publication, Sales No. E.88.II.A.7), 1988. The selective technology import policy of developing countries (especially by those that have some technology base) tends to induce unpackaging of the technology components and thus licensing and other more specific technology contracts are expected to rise along with the industrialization of developing countries.

16. E. Mansfield & Romeo, A., 1980, "Technology Transfer to Overseas Subsidiaries by U.S.-based firms," *Quarterly Journal of Economics*, December.

TABLE 7.1 *Market Shares and growth rates of developing countries' exports of manufactures to developed market economies by R&D intensity category, 1970–1987*[a]

R&D intensity category/product group	Market Share (percentage)			Value ($US, billions)	Growth rate (percentage)		
	1970	1980	1987	1987	1970–75	1975–80	1980–87
High R&D intensity category	2.6	9.5	13.1	33.6	43.1	30.6	15.4
Electronic components	12.0	29.9	27.7	7.5	40.0	31.5	10.5
Telecommunication equipment	4.9	19.0	22.0	5.1	44.6	33.4	13.9
Electrical machinery	1.9	8.5	16.0	4.6	46.2	30.5	19.5
Office machines and components	1.3	3.8	14.1	5.9	67.6	7.3	41.8
Non-electrical machinery	1.6	5.8	13.8	4.1	38.2	28.2	24.9
Scientific instruments	1.3	9.9	9.4	3.4	59.5	34.9	7.3
Chemicals	0.4	3.9	4.8	1.7	30.5	85.9	10.2
Drugs and medicines	6.9	6.9	4.0	0.3	24.2	9.8	-0.2
Aerospace	1.4	3.9	3.8	1.0	30.6	28.6	7.2
Medium & R&D intensity category	4.5	6.5	9.6	60.3	19.7	27.3	14.8
Non-ferrous metals	31.8	43.6	35.3	1.6	10.7	24.4	-8.7
Other manufacturing industries	20.9	19.8	29.2	17.1	15.3	30.1	12.7
Other electrical machinery	5.5	15.9	23.0	13.7	35.8	27.9	10.6
Rubber, plastics	6.1	8.2	13.3	3.8	22.4	26.3	16.9
Other scientific instruments	0.7	4.8	7.7	1.1	46.0	40.7	16.4
Other non-electrical machinery	0.7	2.3	6.4	9.2	34.2	31.5	24.7
Other chemicals	4.5	4.3	5.4	6.6	16.9	21.3	10.0
Motor vehicles	0.2	0.9	3.6	7.1	45.9	28.9	35.1
Low R&D intensity category	15.8	21.2	23.6	130.4	23.6	19.4	6.3
Petroleum refineries	37.1	39.6	38.7	22.2	31.4	24.0	-3.1

continued

TABLE 7.1 *Market Shares and growth rates of developing countries' exports of manufactures to developed market economies by R&D intensity category, 1970–1987*[a] *(continued)*

R&D intensity category/product group	Market Share (percentage)			Value (US $ bill)	Growth rate (percentage)		
	1970	1980	1987	1987	1970–75	1975–80	1980–87
Textiles, clothing, footwear, leather	19.1	30.7	38.7	61.4	26.3	22.8	12.1
Ship building	4.0	13.7	28.5	1.5	23.1	27.6	12.8
Wood, cork, furniture	14.6	17.0	21.4	9.3	17.0	25.0	9.4
Food, drink, tobacco	26.0	20.8	17.3	19.3	18.0	8.4	1.6
Stone, clay, glass	2.8	5.6	11.6	3.0	23.4	29.7	18.3
Ferrous metals	2.9	6.1	11.1	5.4	21.0	25.7	10.8
Fabricated metal products	2.5	7.7	14.0	5.9	31.0	33.9	15.9
Paper & printing	0.9	3.0	4.1	2.4	29.1	33.1	11.9

Source: UNCTAD, "Impact of technological change on patterns of international trade," 8 March 1989 (ID/B/(XXXV)SC.I/CRP.2), pp. 8–10.

[a] The classification of R&D intensity categories is based on the methodology described in Selected Science & Technology Indicators: Recent Results, 1979–1986 (Paris: OECD, Sept. 1986) and OECD "Commerce des produits de haute technologie première contribution a l'analyse statistique des échanges de produits de haute technologie" (DSTI/IND/84.60), Paris, 31 Jan. 1985.

TABLE 7.2 *Occupational employment trends in the United States, 1960–2000*
(In percentages)

Occupation	1960	1980	1995[a]	Moderate economic growth scenario[a] 2000	Moderate technological diffusion scenario[b]
Clerical	15	19	19	20	11
Professional and technical	11	16	17	17	20
Service	12	13	16	17	15
Craft and related	13	13	12	12	15
Managerial and related	11	11	10	10	7
Operatives	18	14	12	9	16
Sales	6	6	7	9	7
Labourers	6	5	5	3	6
Farm	8	3	2	3	3
Total	100	100	100	100	100

Sources: (a) 1960–1995: cited in R. W. Rumberger and H. M. Levin, "Forecasting the impact of new technologies on the future job market", Technological Forecasting and Social Change, *vol. 27, 1985, p. 409; (b) 2000: United Nations Secretariat, Department of International Economic and Social Affairs, based on projections by United States Department of Labor, Bureau of Labor Statistics,* Monthly Labor Review, *vol. 110 (No. 9), Sept. 1987, p. 47, and W. Leontief and F. Duchin,* The Future Impacts of Automation on Workers, 1963–2000, *Oxford University Press, New York, 1986.*

[a] *Based on moderate-trend projections in United States Bureau of Labor Statistics,* Monthly Labor Review, *1987, op. cit.*

[b] *Based on moderate technological diffusion rate scenario in W. Leontief and F. Duchin, op. cit.*

TABLE 7.3 *Market for materials in the United States, 1970–2000
(In billions of dollars)*[a]

Products	1970		1980		1990		2000		Annual growth rate 1990–2000
	%		%		%		%		%
Metals	120	(49)	132	(46)	135	(41)	141	(38)	0.4
Polymers	36	(15)	53	(19)	76	(23)	96	(26)	2.4
Inorganic materials (ceramics, glass)	38	(16)	45	(16)	53	(16)	63	(17)	1.7
Other materials (including wood)	49	(20)	55	(19)	66	(20)	70	(19)	0.6
Total	243	(100)	285	(100)	330	(100)	370	(100)	1.2

*Source: H. Czichos, "International trends in new materials research and development:
current status and sectors affected", United Nations Centre for Science and Technology for
Development (UNCSTD), 1988.*
[a] *The figures in parentheses represent the percentage share of the sum total of the four
classes of products.*

TABLE 7.4 *Possible scenarios for materials development in Africa*

1. Use of coconut pith as filler in furane plastics to replace petroleum-based plastics and metals, especially the rare metals, to reduce the cost and amount of energy used in metal extraction and recycling.
2. Increased research and development work in the application of such abundant metals as iron, aluminium and silicon in place of such metals as copper, nickel, lead, tin, zinc, tungsten, vanadium and silver.
3. Replacement of today's structural steel skeleton construction techniques in all major buildings with composite materials construction techniques which could provide equally strong but lighter structures.
4. Substitution of steel, glass, wood and concrete by aluminium.
5. Development of new devices for in-depth exploitation of ocean resources.
6. Massive replacement of steel and concrete by wood and aluminium for primary structural support members in bridges, low- and high-rise buildings, commercial aircraft, transportation, furniture, automobiles and ships.
7. Use of ceramic coatings such as graphite, glass, silicon, nitride, zirconium oxide, chromium oxide and a few borides.
8. Increased importance of alumina, beryllia, zirconia and magnesia in ceramics.
9. Production of possible commercial porcelain coatings.

*Source: A. M. Goka, "Materials technology forcasting", ATAS Bulletin, No. 5, Ma-
terial Technology and Development, UNCSTD, 1988, p. 107.*

TABLE 7.5 *Current and potential uses of rare earth elements*

Element	Uses
Yttrium	High-temperature alloys, metallurgy, red phosphor, optical glasses, ceramics, catalysts, lasers, microwave devices
Lanthanum	Misch metal,[a] high-refraction low-dispersion glasses, arc light carbons, petroleum-cracking catalysts
Cerium	Polishing powders, opacifier for porcelain coatings, glass decolourizer and melting accelerator, photographic materials, textiles, arc lamps, ferrous and non-ferrous alloys including high-temperature magnesium alloys, automotive catalytic converters, misch metal[a]
Praseodymium	Alloys, didymium glass (for protective goggles), yellow ceramic pigments, cryogenic refrigerant, misch metal[a]
Neodymium	Electronics, steel manufacture, glazes and coloured glass (including didymium glass), lasers, magnets, petroleum-cracking catalysts, misch metal[a]
Promethium	(All isotopes are radioactive and synthetically prepared.) Miniature batteries for harsh environments
Samarium	Reactor control and neutron shielding magnets, luminescent and infra-red absorbing glasses, catalysts, ceramics, electronic devices, magnetostrictive alloys, misch metal[a]
Europium	Phosphor activator, electronic materials, neutron absorber
Gadolinium	Electronic materials, high-temperature refractories, alloys, cryogenic refrigerant, thermal neutron absorber, superconductor, magnetic materials, bubble memory substrates
Terbium	Lasers, electronic materials, erasable optical memory substrate magnetostrictive alloys
Dysprosium	Catalysts, electronic materials, phosphor activators, magnetic refrigeration, magnetostrictive alloys
Holmium	Electronic devices, catalysts, refractories, magnetic materials, magnetostrictive alloys
Erbium	Infrared-absorbing glasses, phosphor activator
Thulium	Portable X-ray units
Ytterbium	Research applications
Lutetium	Research applications

Source: A. McCullock, Materials Australasia, *May 1987, p. 5.*

[a] Misch metal is an alloy of about 50 per cent cerium, 25 per cent lanthanum, 15 per cent neodymium and 10 per cent other rare earth metals. It is used to manufacture pyrophoric alloy with iron and deoxidizer in metallurgical applications, and to remove oxygen from vacuum tubes, high-strength magnesium alloys, etc.

TABLE 7.6 *The share of developing countries in total output of rare metals in market economies, 1982[a]*
(In percentages)

Rare metals	Share	Main producing countries
Lithium	8.5	Zimbabwe, Brazil, Namibia
Berythllium	16	Brazil, India, Argentina, Uganda, Zimbabwe, Rwanda
Strontium	55	Mexico, Algeria, Iran (Islamic Republic of)
Rare earths	14	Brazil, India, Malaysia, Thailand
(including monazite concentrates)	33	Brazil, India, Malaysia, Thailand
Yttrium	37	Brazil, India, Malaysia, Thailand
Zirconium	4	Brazil, India, Sri Lanka
Niobium	88	Brazil, Nigeria, Zaire
Tantalum	75[b]	Brazil, Malaysia, Thailand, Mozambique, Nigeria
Cadmium	14[c]	Mexico, Peru, Zaire
Bismuth	32[c]	Mexico, Peru, Bolivia
Selenium	10[c]	Mexico, Peru, Chile, Zambia
Rhenium	49[c]	Peru, Chile

Source: B. I. Kogan, "Basic trends and particularly important results in activities related to the study and use of rare metals", paper presented to the eighth session of the Committee on Natural Resources.

[a] *Since no information is available on the United States outputs of bismuth, yttrium and rhenium, the share of developing countries regarding these metals is approximately estimated. Their share in caesium, germanium, tellurium and indium output cannot be assessed.*

[b] *Including residue slags from tin-smelting plants.*

[c] *The real share is significantly larger, since the metal is not taken into account in exported sulphide and other concentrates, as well as in crude heavy non-ferrous metals.*

TABLE 7.7 *World demand for rare metals, 2000–2020*
(In thousands of tons)[a]

Metals	2000	2020
Lithium	80–100	120–150
Caesium	0.5–0.6	1–2
Berythllium	0.6–1	3–5
Strontium	100–125	250–300
Rare earths (aggregate)	100–125	250–350
Zirconium	200–300	450–550
Vanadium	75–100	200–250
Niobium	60–80	200–250
Tantalum	3.5–5	7.5–10
Cadmium	30–35	45–50
Bismuth	6–7	10–12
Germanium	0.35–0.4	0.6–0.8
Selenium	5–6	8–10
Tellurium	0.6–0.7	2–3
Gallium	0.1–0.5	3–4
Rhenium	0.02–0.03	0.1–0.2

Source: Ibid.
[a] *Projections based on the contents of each of the metals in all types of base raw materials.*

TABLE 7.8 *Estimates of the technical and economic feasibility of development of selected biotechnology products and processes in Mexico, 1984–2000*

Products and processes	Estimates of technical and economic feasibility		
	1984	1990	2000
Utilization of marine algae spirulina	T,[a] E,[b]	T,E	
Reutilization of excretions	T,E		
Increased digestibility of farm produce and agro-industrial byproducts	T,E	T	
Vitamins	T,E	T,E	T,E
Foliar protein and other concentrates	T	T,E	T,E
Single-cell proteins:			
Agro-industrial byproducts (solids and liquids)	T,E	T,E	T
Molasses	T,E	T,E	T
Methanol	T,E	T,E	T
Others	T,E	T,E	T
Mushroom and fungus production	T,E		
Bone meal and dried blood, meat, and/or fish	T,E		

continued

TABLE 7.8 *Estimates of the technical and economic feasibility of development of selected biotechnology products and processes in Mexico, 1984–2000 (continued)*

Products and processes	Estimates of technical and economic feasibility		
	1984	1990	2000
Enzymes (a-amylases, gluco-amylase, lactose, invertase, proteases, pertinase, glucose isomerase, penicillinase, cellulases)	T,E	T,E	T
Proteolytic enzmyes of plant origin	T,E		T
Amino acids (lysine, glutamic acid, methionine, tryptophan and all other essential amino acids)	T,E	T,E	T,E
Protein enrichment of various substances	T		
Biopolymers	T,E		
Production of micro-algae	T		
Production of essential oils		T,E	
Mononucleotides		T	
Processes based on improved and/or genetically constructed rootstalks		T	
Improved production of vitamins, single-cell proteins, biopolymers, fungi, powders, protein concentrates		T,E	
Pigment production		T,E	
Production of alternative feedstock (fermentation of solid base)	T,E	T,E	
Lactic acid		T,E	
Sweeteners (fructose)		E	
Microbe oil		E	
Unconventional new food sources		E	
Immobilized enzymes		T,E	
Synthetic protein			E
Anaerobic digestors for biogas production	T,E		
Biogas reactors		T,E	
Methane production from:			
Sanitary landfills		T,E	
Industrial waste		T,E	
Animal waste	T,E		
Hydrogen production			E
Ethanol production from:			
Sucrose	T,E		
Starch and other unconventional bases		T,E	
Cellulose and agricultural byproducts			T,E
Hydrocarbon production from:			
Rapid-growth plant species		E	T,E
Biochemical combustible cells		E	T

Source: R. Quintero Ramerez, ed. Perspectiva de la biotechnologéa en Mexico, *Mexico, Javier Barros Sierra Foundation and CONACYT, 1985, pp. 474–475.*

[a] *T = Development estimated to be technically feasible.*
[b] *E = Development estimated to be economically feasible.*

TABLE 7.9 *Impact of selected aspects of plant biotechnology*

Aspects	Positive impact	Negative impact
Genetic diversity	Quick means of germplasm transfer; broader breeding base; genetic base for new production; reduction in losses	Increase in uniformity and vulnerability; genetic erosion
Germplasm identification	Elimination of undesirable characteristics; acceleration in new cultivar development	Ignorance of local conditions such as local pests
Cultivar dissemination	Production of broad variety of new plants; replanting of crop feasible within a growing season	Reduced long-term biological potentials of crops
Production	Most productive significant increase in yield	Overproduction; market instability; reduced export income
Pest problems	New and fast ways to combat pest epidemics	Alteration of natural composition of organisms with unknown consequences
Mechanization	Amenability to harvest, process and package	Unemployment; reduced product varieties
Germplasm	Viable means for long-term storage	Storage concentrated in a few countries with potentials for discriminatory exploitation
Land use	Reduction in land area needed for production gives room for other national purposes and redistribution of land to small farmers	Global overproduction; depressed economies unable to take advantage of potential benefits
Environment	Development of organisms likely to survive in difficult natural environments	Upsetting balance of nature through release of genetically altered micro-organisms

Source: UNCSTD, "End of Decade Review: Implementation of the Vienna Programme of Action, State of science and technology for development: options for the future", (Background document prepared for the Intergovernmental Committee of Science and Technology for Development, tenth session, 21 August–1 September 1989 (mimeo)).

8.
Structural Changes in Production and Trade

THE STRUCTURAL CHANGE of an economy as it develops and matures is reflected in the differential growth rates of its branches of production. Many factors contribute to this change: different rates of growth of productivity among sectors; changes in the factor proportions of capital and labour; and the explosive character of new technologies. The most obvious consequence of growth and development is the shift in output composition and resource allocation from agriculture to industry and from industry to services.

A. PROJECTIONS OF OUTPUT BY MAJOR SECTORS

To capture the effects of all these factors in the baseline projections of GDP by sector, several regression equations were specified and estimated based on time series data for individual countries and regions. More weight was given to the more recent developments unless they contradicted long-term patterns of change in the productive structure of individual economies. Since separate projections for different sectors do not necessarily add up to the total for projected GDP, the sectoral detail of projected GDP was computed on the basis of shares in the sum for the projected individual sectors.

The composition of output by major producing sector, measured at constant 1980 prices, has changed considerably from the 1970s.[1] For market economies, shares of agriculture and industry, including mining in GDP, have declined, but that of services has increased by about 5 per cent between 1970 and 1985. The share of agriculture is expected to decline to 5.6 per cent in the year 2000 compared with 7.4 per cent in 1970 and 6.3 per cent in 1985 (table 8.1). The share of manufacturing has fluctuated slightly but has remained at about 24 per cent at the end of the period. These trends are projected to continue in the 1990s.

These shifts reflect not only evolving patterns of demand and productivity but also the relocation of a significant portion of manufacturing capacity from developed to developing economies. The figures for the world market economies as a whole, therefore, conceal opposing trends between developed and developing economies. In the former the shares of agriculture, manufacturing, and other industry all decline, while that of services increase more than the average for the world economy. In the developing countries, on the other hand, the shares of agriculture and services are projected to fall while those of industry and especially of manufacturing are projected to rise.[2]

Within developing countries, as projected under the baseline scenario, marked differences in the structures of production will continue to exist. In the 1970s and 1980s, manufacturing output and exports have been growing rapidly in the newly industrialized economies (NIES) of South and East Asia. This has led to a corresponding increased proportion of GDP originating in the manufacturing sector. Further increases in the manufacturing share in the global production are expected in the major manufacturing exporters, a group that includes large economies such as Brazil and India as well as the newly industrializing economies of Asia. In 1985 the four Asian newly industrializing economies accounted for only about 14 per cent of total developing country manufacturing production. The baseline scenario indicates, however, that even if world economic growth continues at the modest rates now expected, this group of countries will have a share of manufacturing in their GDP significantly greater than that projected for the developed market economies, that is, 43 per cent as compared to 24 per cent. A similar shift, but at a slower pace and often towards domestic sales rather than exports, may be expected in other manufacturing-oriented developing countries.

The low income and least developed economies present a picture of slow structural change with a pattern of production still heavily reliant on agriculture.

Past and projected baseline distributions of developing countries output by different types of economic activities are summarized in table 8.2. The nature and extent of change in the origin of production in these economies varies from group to group, but certain trends stand out. Taken as a group, the developing countries increased their share of world market manufacturing output from 11.9 per cent in 1970 to 16.1 per cent in 1985. Their share is projected to be over 22 per cent in the year 2000. This increase in the weight of developing countries as a group, however, masks divergent trends. For example, the newly industrializing economies of South and East Asia, although they still account for only a small part of gross world output, increased their share of developing country output in all sectors and are projected to continue to do so.

The weight of petroleum exporting economies is expected to taper off in all sectors. The primary commodity exporters, which consist mainly of mineral product exporters, are projected to return to about their 1970 shares. The low income and least developed economies as well as the other manufacturing oriented economies, shares of which have tended to decline or stagnate in the 1980s as compared to the 1970s, are projected to continue in this trend under the baseline scenario.

Many of the developing economies that grew slowly during the historical period experienced little positive structural change. Baseline trends projected to the year 2000 indicate that agriculture will continue to be the predominant source of income and employment in many of these countries. The slow growth of this sector may expect to be translated into slow growth for the economy as a whole. Consequently, the share of these economies in world production may decline or at best remain stable during the world period to the end of the century.

The geographic distribution of the developing countries sectoral output and labour force also shows a mixture of trends (table 8.3). Historically the Latin American economies have had the largest share of total developing country GDP. In the late 1980s they were almost replaced by the South and East Asian economies. This region, including the newly industrialized Asian economies, has exhibited an increasing share of every sector of production, together with a slightly declining share of labour force and thus of increasing efficiency. Under the baseline scenario this region's share of industrial output will be triple its 1970 level, while both services and GDP as a whole double their 1970 share by the end of the century.

The North African economies will maintain their share in all sectors for the year 2000 except for a slight decline projected in industry. Similarly, under the baseline scenario the developing economies of Cyprus, Malta, Turkey, and Yugoslavia are projected to maintain their historical share of production, and labour force. The petroleum exporting economies of Western Asia are projected to continue their declining trend, as is the larger part of Africa, the sub-Saharan region. The most noticeable decline in this region has been its agricultural output share between 1970 and 1985. Under the baseline scenario, this region will more or less maintain its mid–1980 share of developing countries output in all sectors by the year 2000.

World trade has been greatly influenced by structural change. The resulting changes in export shares reflect changes in final demand patterns within the developed economies, technology changes that have reduced raw material and energy-intensity requirements, and shifts in the location of industrial production from developed to developing countries.

For the past 30 years trade has increased in importance relative to GDP in all regions, but trade concentration ratios have fallen and the variety of products exported by developing countries has increased. However, for developing countries the trends of their share of world trade are mixed. Developing countries' total share rose in the 1970s from 18.2 per cent to a high of 21.4 per cent in 1980, then declined to almost their 1970 level (18.7 per cent) in 1986.

The share of developing countries in world exports of food declined slightly in the early 1970s. It recovered in the middle to late 1970s, but in the 1980s it stagnated around 28 per cent, as compared to more than 30 per cent in the second half of the 1960s.

For most of the historical period the trend of developing countries exports of manufactured goods is one of rising shares. The share of the newly industrializing economies in Asia in world exports has risen steadily from 2.2 per cent in 1970 to 5.2 per cent in 1980 to 6.7 per cent in 1986. The share of the other major manufacturers also rose, from 3.5 per cent in 1970 to 9.3 per cent in 1984 but recently seems to have begun to decline (8.4 per cent in 1986).

The share of fuel exports by oil exporting developing countries rose from 50 per cent in 1970 to 60 per cent in 1975 but has since steadily declined to 35 per cent in 1986. On the other hand, developing countries' share of the ores and metals and raw materials category has remained around 27–28 per cent since 1970.

B. STRUCTURAL CHANGE IN WORLD MANUFACTURING

There have been substantial structural changes in world manufacturing in the recent past, and the changes will continue in the coming years. The present projections are based on an examination of the growth patterns of 29 categories of manufactures in 75 countries over the period 1965–1986, and on plausible assumptions about future developments. The patterns of structural change in manufacturing vary considerably among countries and over time. At this level of aggregation, however, some general trends are associated with growth of per capita GDP, country size, and characteristics of export orientation and trade policies.

Given the expected rate of growth of world trade at 4.5 per cent per annum and changes in major proportions under the baseline scenario, the share of manufacturing value-added (MVA) in total GDP of the developing countries, which has increased substantially during the past two decades, is expected to increase further, from 18.8 per cent in 1985 to 23 per cent by the year 2000 (table 8.1). For the developed market economies, on the other hand, the share is expected to decline by 1 percentage point.

The relative weights of manufacturing activities in developing countries depend mainly on degree of industrialization and their export orientation.

Regional differences in shares of manufacturing in economic activities are expected to increase by the year 2000. Given the expected rate of growth of manufacturing varying from about 5–6 per cent of manufacturing oriented developing countries to 1.5 per cent of the least developed countries, the relative weight of manufacturing in the year 2000 measured by the MVA/GDP share would range from less than 9 per cent for the least developed countries to 24–25 per cent for the manufacturing oriented countries. Among manufacturing oriented countries, Asian NIES are expected to sustain their high growth of manufacturing output and their MVA/GDP shares are expected to increase further to about 25 per cent in the 1990s. Other manufacturing oriented countries, especially in Latin America, are expected to reverse in the 1990s the declining trend of the 1970s and 1980s. The share of manufacturing will be almost the same as that of major exporters of manufactures.

In the process of industrialization and modernization, demand for investment goods embodying particular technologies becomes more widespread. There are strong links between growth of manufacturing industries and growth of trade in investment goods. The recent investment boom associated with technological restructuring in developed countries has been a major force sustaining the expansion of trade and production in these economies, and also of the world trade at around 7 per cent annually. As developing countries have limited capabilities for producing investment goods and depend mostly on imported capital investment goods, their economic growth tends to promote trade between the North and the South.

The developing countries are expected to increase their share in world industrial output, mostly at the expense of the developed market economies (figure 8.1). The increase is a result of both increasing share of manufacturing in their economies and the expected higher rate of growth of GDP. Their manufacturing output in the year 2000 will be about 27 per cent of that of the developed market economies, compared with 12 per cent in 1965.

A limited number of developing countries, however, are expected to account for the major portion of industrial activities in the developing countries. In particular, seven economies, namely Brazil, Hong Kong, India, the Republic of Korea, Singapore, Taiwan, Province of China, and Yugoslavia should make up about half of the total manufacturing output of the developing countries in the year 2000.

For every broad category of manufacturing (consumer goods, capital goods, and intermediate goods) the share of the developing countries as a whole in the respective world sectoral output is expected to increase. The capital goods output of the developing countries in the year 2000, however, will still be about one fifth of that in the developed countries. The output of both consumer goods and intermediate goods in the developing countries will be about 40 per cent of those in the developed countries.

Despite the stable share of manufacturing output in GDP in the developed market economies, the industrial structure is also expected to change, although less than in the developing countries. The main thrust in changing their industrial structures and trade patterns is expected to come from the high-tech industries and the enhancement of the high-tech content of the traditional industries. Intra-branch specialization in particular, based on technological innovators, is expected to dominate changes in their manufacturing. For the United States the share of high-tech prod-

SHARES OF MAJOR COUNTRY GROUPS IN VALUE-ADDED OF MANUFACTURING

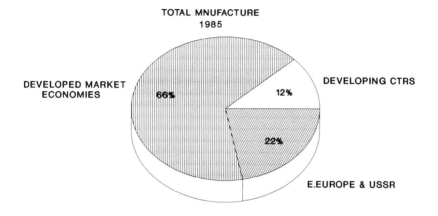

TOTAL MNUFACTURE
1985

DEVELOPED MARKET ECONOMIES 66%

DEVELOPING CTRS 12%

22%

E.EUROPE & USSR

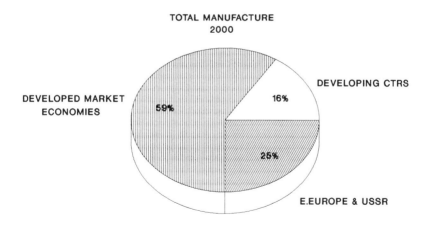

TOTAL MANUFACTURE
2000

DEVELOPED MARKET ECONOMIES 59%

DEVELOPING CTRS 16%

25%

E.EUROPE & USSR

Figure 8.1

ucts in exports of manufactured goods is already about one third. There will be some shift of relative weights, however, from the United States to other developed countries, Japan and EEC in particular.[3]

One notable feature of their current industrial transformation is the advances of information technologies. Flexible manufacturing systems based on computerization of all stages of production (design, control, and manufacturing) are expected to bring about profound changes in production processes. This process has already contributed to stabilize the share of manufacturing in GDP and is expected to transform this sector into a more information intensive one.

The capital goods industries of developed market economies, which contain a high percentage of high-tech items, are projected to grow more rapidly than other industries and to sustain a predominant position in their manufacturing sector. The share of this sector in manufacturing output is expected to increase from 49 per cent in 1981–1985 to 54 per cent in the year 2000 (figure 8.2). Sustained economic growth and continuing restructuring efforts in the 1990s are likely to require more investment activities and thus create additional demand for capital goods in general and for high-tech goods in particular.

With the narrowing gap in technology and income, the share of the capital goods sector in Japan and the Federal Republic of Germany has already surpassed that of the United States. A general tendency under growing product differentiation is to increase production of more sophisticated machineries and other precision equipment that depend heavily on research and development, technology innovation, and diffusion.

The consumer goods industries produce mostly traditional labor intensive items and are nearing a saturation point of demand in many product lines. For these industries a decline to 29 per cent is expected in the 1990s compared with 33 per cent in 1981–1985. The intermediate goods industries are expected to maintain the average pace of the manufacturing output, and thus their share will remain at 18 per cent. Some segments of this subsector that are affected by the development of substitutes and input conser-

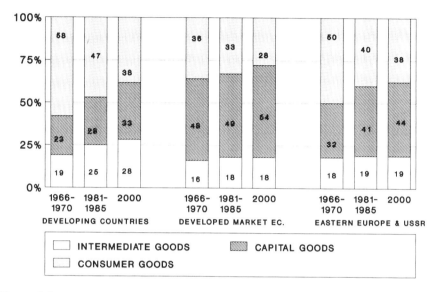

Figure 8.2

vation technologies, however, or those which are environmentally hazardous, are expected to decline.

The sectoral composition of manufacturing in the developing countries is changing more than in the developed countries. The share of consumer goods industries is steadily declining as in the developed countries, but will continue to account for the largest share in their total manufacturing output, 38 per cent in the year 2000 (table 8.4).

Production of capital goods as a share of total value added in the manufacturing sector of the developing countries is expected to increase from 28 per cent on average in 1981–1985 to 33 per cent in the year 2000, reflecting increasing production capacities in the process of development. Advanced developing countries are beginning to produce more technology intensive goods that are expected to substitute for increasingly large segments of capital goods imports. The slight increase in the share of intermediate goods in the developing countries reflects mainly the rapid increase in chemicals and petroleum refinery products.

Among developing countries, changes in industrial structure of major exporters of manufactures, especially the Asian newly industrializing economies, have been most pronounced in the past two decades and are expected to account for the largest portion of the changes. Their capital goods industries, in particular, are projected to grow on average more than 7.2 per cent during the 1990s, and the share of these industries in total MVA is expected to increase by 7 percentage points in the year 2000 from already high level of 35 per cent in 1981–1985 (table 8.4). The share of their consumer goods industries, on the other hand, is expected to fall by more than 10 percentage points to 32 per cent in the year 2000 from 43 per cent in 1981–1985.

As for other developing countries with relatively large manufacturing sectors, their industrial structure has already shown significant change during the past two decades but less than that of the major exporters of manufactures (table 8.6). In contrast with major exporters of manufactures, the share of their intermediate goods industries is projected to remain virtually constant, at 26 per cent in the year 2000. Their consumer goods industries and capital goods industries will follow more or less the general trend of the developing countries. There are, however, significant variances in structural change among countries within this subgroup. Malaysia, Pakistan, and Thailand have shown much more dynamism in their industrialization, while Colombia, Guatemala, Nicaragua, and Zambia have shown very minor structural changes or suffered reverses. These divergent trends should continue through the year 2000. The industrial structures of the least developed countries are expected to change little in the 1990s.

Long-term trends in the composition of MVA in different groups of countries traced at a more detailed sectoral level show some regularities that may continue in the 1990s. In the developed market economies, the MVA shares of high-tech and knowledge-intensive branches such as non-electrical machinery, electrical machinery, and professional and scientific equipment are expected to be sustained or increased (table 8.5). Progress in microelectronics should play a key role through their contribution to the development of information technologies and their widespread application to the whole range of production processes and products. Reflecting this key role, electrical machinery is projected to grow fast, and its share in manufacturing to increase from 10 per cent in 1981–1985 to 18 per cent in the year 2000. As the developed market economies sustain comparative advantage in high-tech industries, the shift of their trade towards these products is also expected to continue.

The MVA shares of traditional consumer goods industries such as food, leather and footwear, textiles and wearing apparel, which are mostly labour-intensive or less skill-and technology-intensive, are expected to decline further in the developed countries. Food processing, however, will retain a share of 8 per cent in the year 2000 compared with 9 per cent in 1981–1985. The developed market economies are also expected to lose more competitiveness in segments of mature and high-tech industries such as iron and steel, metal products, general purpose machinery, shipbuilding, automobiles, home electronics, small computers, some types of semiconductors, as well as some intermediate goods industries whose substitutes are being developed.

In the case of the U.S., its share in the world semiconductor market decreased from 50 per cent in 1984 to 37 per cent in 1988. Part of the lost market share, however, was taken by other developed countries. The U.S. lead in high-tech products is lessening relative to other major developed countries and is increasingly squeezed to the upper part in the scale of the technological sophistication.

Efforts of the developed countries to revive certain segments of "sunset" industries through new technologies (labor saving in particular) have been met with limited success in the past. In textiles, for example, automation, based on new technologies such as open-end spinning and shuttelless looms, has contributed to keeping the productivity growth of textile industries at 4 per cent. This is above the manufacturing average. In the apparel industry it has been less successful.[4] Despite the attenuation of the declining tendency of their "sunset" industries by the introduction of cost saving or quality enhancing technologies, overall growth in these industries in the developed market economies is expected to be slow, leading to additional decline in their relative shares.

In the developing countries the shares of textile and wearing apparel in their MVA have been falling and are expected to continue to do so while the shares of chemicals, oil products, iron and steel, and electrical machinery will increase (table 8.6). Food, textiles, and wearing apparel, however, would continue to be the two largest industrial branches, accounting for 13 and 11 per cent respectively of the manufacturing sector.

Differences in the structure of manufacturing among developing countries have increased in the process of successive catch-up cycles by countries at different development stages. A group of more advanced developing countries has already established some industrial base and is more dynamic than other developing countries. Thus this group continues to account for the major part of the changes in the developing countries.

Structural change proceeds rapidly in the major exporters of manufactures. Post export-led development strategies and increasing sources of technology available to the Asian newly industrialized economies resulted in technological capability in these countries sufficient to compete with developed countries in a wide range of products. Although their specific patterns vary, they are gaining competitiveness in segments of mature technologically-advanced industries such as petrochemicals, segments of microchemicals, automobiles, general purpose machinery, electrical machinery, home electronics, and precision tools and equipment. They are also in the process of entering the lower spectrum of high–tech capital intensive industries: semiconductors, small computers, automated office equipment, optic fibres, telecommunications, and pharmaceuticals. Reflecting the shift in comparative advantage, the shares of technology intensive products in their exports have increased rapidly. On the other hand, the share of labor intensive goods in the total exports of Hong Kong and the Republic of Korea decreased from 76 and 53 per cent in 1970 to 63 and 46 per cent in 1979, respectively, and will continue to fall.[5]

Shares of the developing countries and China in world trade in machinery and transport equipment increased from 1 per cent in 1970 to 10 per cent in 1987, but the major share was concentrated in about 10 countries.[6] Some of these developing countries have entered into the design and manufacture of complex capital goods.[7]

These strong trends become more uncertain because of the significantly shortened life cycles of products and increasing competition from other developing countries ("next tiers," in particular). Major exporters of manufactures are striving to shift towards technologically more advanced industries or higher quality segments of the traditional industries such as high-quality and fashion textiles, specialized ships, micro-chemicals, specialty steels, industrial electronics, and electrical machinery.

For major exporters of manufactures, industrial chemicals, electrical machinery, and transport equipment are projected to grow faster in the baseline than total manufacturing output and show markedly increased shares in their total MVA by the year 2000 (table 8.5). As their technology and industrial base deepen, their dependency on imports for intermediary products may be relatively reduced. They are also expected to achieve self-sufficiency in a considerable portion of mature products and be able to export more capital goods. In the case of the metal products and machinery industry in Korea, the ratio of imports to the domestic output decreased from 50.5 per cent in 1970 to 35.8 per cent in 1980.[8]

The shares of labour-intensive goods such as food, textiles, and wearing apparel, on the other hand, are projected to decrease from 11 and 14 per cent respectively on average in 1981–1985 to 9 and 11 per cent in the year 2000. Recently, Asian newly industrialized economies have begun to redeploy segments of their labour-intensive industries to other developing countries such as Thailand, Malaysia, and the Caribbean countries, and at the same time, orient their industries towards their domestic markets. They also are intensifying their efforts further to diversify exports. By the year 2000, their industrial structures are expected to resemble closely those of developed market economies.

Other developing countries with relatively large manufacturing sectors are projected to improve their comparative advantage in traditional consumer-goods industries. For example, textiles and apparel, footwear, and rubber products. The same is true for segments of mature industries such as ship-building, iron and steel, metal products, and petrochemicals, which are based on standard technologies and benefit from low labour cost. The share of labour intensive goods in the total exports of the Philippines and Thailand increased from 1.4 and 1.6 per cent in 1970 to 12.4 and 12.1 per cent in 1979 respectively.[9] Many countries in this group will soon be able to develop more industries requiring large economies of scale. Taking advantage of the wage increases in most of the major exporters of manufactures, the "catch-up behavior" of many of these countries (Thailand and Malaysia, in particular) has been accelerating recently. Some of them are expected to achieve the degree of success of the major exporters of manufactures by the year 2000.

The majority of developing countries other than the above mentioned two groups, however, have benefited less from technology diffusion so far. This is due to weak industrial and technological base. They are specialized in products at the lower end of technological sophistication such as processed food, textiles and wearing apparel, leather and footwear. Most of them, having abundant cheap labour, will continue to have a comparative advantage in labour intensive goods. Their export share of these items in the world market is expected to increase.

In the least developed countries in particular, industrialization has not progressed markedly in the recent past. Their manufacturing sector still remains small relative to their agricultural sector and is projected to grow at an annual rate of 1.5 per cent on average in 1991–2000, compared with 5.6 per cent in the developing countries as a whole (table 8.6). Their manufacturing activities are mostly based on resources and labour intensive industries such as food processing, beverages, tobacco, textiles and wearing apparel. The shares in MVA of textiles and wearing apparel and footwear in 1981–1985 were more than twice as large as those in the major exporters of manufacturing. The agricultural sector performance will continue to affect their manufacturing industries, both as a market for manufacturing goods and as a supplier of raw materials.

Slow growth in MVA has been recorded since the mid–1970s in the sub-Saharan countries. During the first half of the 1980s aggregate demand was adversely affected by a number of factors, including severe droughts. Many countries in the region are attempting to reorient their industrial base to emphasize small and medium scale industries to meet the domestic demand for necessities. The share of consumer goods industries in total MVA is expected to increase somewhat during the 1990s.

In such a transitory period when adjustment to rapidly changing comparative advantage is inevitable, competition and some frictions between the North and the South and within each group are possible. On the other hand, the increasing overlapped segments of technology scale among countries offer more room for both horizontal and vertical division of labour among them. Multilateral coordination and trade liberalization are certainly required to reduce the negative impacts of the evolving competition in world markets. Japan and the EEC countries are expected to play a greater role as regional gravity centers in the next decade. Their established strong industrial base is almost at par with that of the United States in most of their industries. More regionalization of trade is expected as they harmonize their trade by better exploiting complementarities within the region where countries are at different stages of development.

C. WORLD TRADE IN NON–FUEL PRIMARY COMMODITIES

Despite the considerable diversification in the exports of developing countries, many of them continue to depend on a relatively small number of primary commodities. The long-term prospects for some of these primary commodities, such as food and tropical

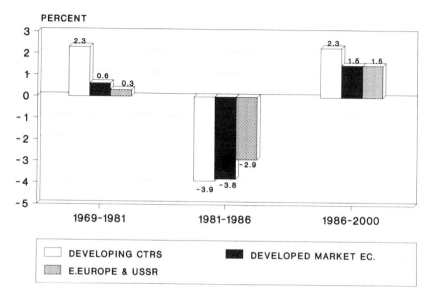

GROUTH RATES OF NON-FUEL PRIMARY COMMODITY PRODUCTION

Figure 8.3

beverages, are determined mainly by the evolution of final demand but also by the development of substitutes (e.g., artificial sweeteners and imitation cocoa butter) and by agricultural protectionism. The shift in demand towards services in the developed market economies has reduced the use of raw materials relative to GDP. New technologies tend to reduce the raw material intensity of production and to develop synthetic substitutes, as was discussed in section B above.

Combined with the prospect of generally slow GDP growth for the developed market economies, these factors imply relatively slow growth of world consumption for most primary commodities. The World Bank has projected an average growth rate for world consumption of non-fuel primary commodities to the year 2000 of only about 2 per cent (figure 8.3).

An increasing share of total consumption, however, is expected to be provided by imports. Growth in the volume of world exports of non-fuel primary commodities thus should be about 4 per cent. Growth of world exports for food, especially cereals and fats and oils, is projected to be somewhat greater than 4 per cent, but demand for sugar and tropical beverages is expected to grow by less than 1.5 per cent per year. Export volume growth of textile fibres and most metals and minerals is anticipated to be only about 1 per cent per annum, but rubber and copper may experience export growth of about 2 per cent per annum.

During the 1970s and the first half of the 1980s, the growth rate of production of non-fuel primary commodities in the developing countries was much higher than that in the industrialized countries. Some reduction in the growth rate of production in all regions is expected during the 1990s. Developing countries are expected, however, to continue to achieve substantially higher growth than other world regions.

One consequence of these differential production rates is that developing countries would continue to increase their share in world production of non-fuel primary commodities. Their share increased from an average of 49 per cent during the period 1969–1971 to 53 per cent during the period 1984–1986 and is projected to reach about 56 per cent by the year 2000 (see figure 8.4).

Competition for increased shares in the world market by developing countries with debt-servicing problems is expected to be intensive and is likely to result in much greater growth in export volume than in export earnings. A shift in market shares is highly probable in the absence of increased protectionism, but this can be expected to occur only as falling prices eliminate higher cost producers, mainly in the developed market economy countries. Thus, the purchasing power of most primary commodity exports of the developing countries almost certainly will grow more slowly than export volumes.

STRUCTURE OF NON-FUEL PRIMARY
COMMODITY PRODUCTION

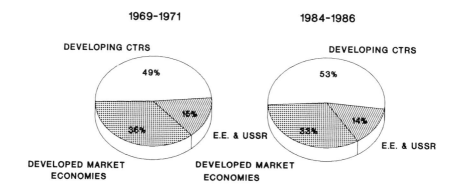

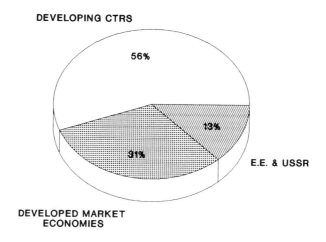

Figure 8.4

NOTES

1. Constant price data are useful in gauging the extent of shifts in the structure of output from the standpoint of the end-user. Because relative prices and sectoral productivity change over time, however, these figures tend to understate the true extent of structural change. In the United States, for example, the proportion of the labour force employed in manufacturing declined from 24 per cent in 1970 to 21 per cent in 1975, and 18 per cent in 1985.

2. For a discussion of the prospect of world agriculture for the year 2000, see 2000 (C/87/27), July 1987. FAO considers that rates of growth of agricultural production from 1983 to 1985 to the year 2000 under a somewhat optimistic assumption could be about 0.9 per cent per annum in the developed market economies, 1.5 per cent per annum in Eastern Europe and the U.S.S.R., and 2.8 per cent per year in the developing countries, or 3.0, including China.

3. Lester Davis, "Technology intensity of U.S. output and trade," United States Department of Commerce, Office of Trade and Investment Analysis, July 1982, appendix tables 3 and 4.

4. See William R. Cline, "The future of world trade in textiles and apparel," Institute of International Economics, Washington, D.C., 1987.

5. Lawrence B. Krause, "The structure of trade in manufactures goods in the East and Southeast Asian Region", Colin I. Bradford, Jr., and William H. Branson, ed., Trade and Structural Change in Pacific Asia, National Bureau of Economics, 1987.

6. United Nations Monthly Bulletin of Statistics, May 1989, special table C.

7. UNCTAD, the capital goods sector in developing countries, United Nations Sales No. E.85.II.D.4, pp. 22–29.

8. Bank of Korea, "An input-output analysis of Korean industrial structure in 1980," December 1982.

9. Lawrence B. Krause, *op. cit.*

TABLE 8.1. *Sectoral origin of world market economy production:
historical and projected under a baseline scenario, 1970–2000
(Percentage shares in GDP)*[a]

| Year and country group | Agri-culture | Composition of GDP | | Services |
| | | Industry | | |
		Total	Manufactures	
1970				
World market	7.4	40.8	23.7	51.8
Developed market	4.4	40.6	25.7	55.0
Developing countries	20.7	41.3	15.1	38.0
Petroleum exporters	15.0	61.0	5.6	24.0
Major mfg. exporters	26.6	31.0	21.8	42.4
Other mfg.-oriented	16.6	32.6	21.8	50.8
Primary commodities exporters	26.3	30.7	11.4	43.0
Least developed	57.3	14.4	8.7	28.3
1985				
World market	6.3	36.3	24.0	57.4
Developed market	3.6	36.9	25.3	59.5
Developing countries	16.9	36.1	18.8	47.0
Petroleum exporters	13.6	44.6	9.4	41.8
Major mfg. exporters	17.3	36.0	25.8	46.8
Other mfg.-oriented	15.2	32.3	21.5	52.5
Primary commodities exporters	23.8	24.9	10.9	36.1
Least developed	48.4	15.5	8.3	36.1
2000				
World market	5.6	36.0	23.7	58.4
Developed market	3.1	34.8	24.0	62.1
Developing countries	13.8	39.8	23.0	46.4
Petroleum exporters	12.5	45.0	9.8	42.5
Major mfg. exporters	11.5	43.0	32.0	45.4
Other mfg.-oriented	13.8	34.8	23.4	51.4
Primary commodities exporters	19.1	34.2	20.6	46.7
Least developed	41.3	18.3	9.6	40.4

*Source: United Nations Secretariat, Department of International Economic and Social
Affairs.*

[a] *Measured at 1980 prices and exchange rates.*

TABLE 8.2. *Distribution of developing market economy production: historical and projected under a baseline scenario, 1970–2000 (Percentage shares in GDP)*[a]

Year and country group	Agricul- ture	Industry total	Manufact- ures	Services	GDP
1970					
Developing countries	100	100	100	100	100
Petroleum exporters	25.7	51.9	12.9	22.2	35.3
Major mfg. exporters	31.4	18.3	35.3	27.2	24.4
Other mfg.-oriented	25.7	25.3	46.3	42.8	32.0
Least developed	12.1	1.5	2.5	3.3	4.3
Primary commodity exporters	5.1	3.0	3.0	4.5	4.0
1985					
Developing countries	100	100	100	100	100
Petroleum exporters	22.3	34.3	13.9	24.7	27.8
Major mfg. exporters	33.9	33.1	45.7	33.1	33.2
Other mfg.-oriented	29.0	28.8	38.9	35.9	32.2
Least developed	10.2	1.5	1.6	2.7	3.6
Primary commodities exporters	4.7	2.3	1.9	3.6	3.3
2000					
Developing countries	100	100	100	100	100
Petroleum exporters	21.5	26.6	10.0	21.5	23.5
Major mfg. exporters	32.6	41.9	54.1	38.0	38.8
Other mfg.-oriented	30.6	26.5	31.0	33.6	30.4
Least developed	9.9	1.5	1.4	2.9	3.3
Primary commodities exporters	5.5	3.4	3.5	4.0	4.0

Source: Ibid.
[a] *Measured at 1980 prices and exchange rates.*

TABLE 8.3. *Geographic distribution of developing economy production: historical and projected under a baseline scenario, 1970–2000 (Percentage shares in GDP)[a]*

Year and country group	Share in gross world market sectoral product			
	Agri-culture	Industry	Services	Domestic product
1970				
Developing countries	100	100	100	100
North Africa	4	11	4	7
Sub-Saharan Africa	25	8	10	12
Latin America and the Caribbean	20	36	52	38
Western Asia	6	26	7	15
South and East Asia	38	14	21	22
Mediterranean	6	5	6	6
1985				
Developing countries	100	100	100	100
North Africa	4	9	5	7
Sub-Saharan Africa	16	6	7	8
Latin America and the Caribbean	23	35	41	36
Western Asia	8	15	11	12
South and East Asia	43	27	29	31
Mediterranean	6	7	7	7
2000				
Developing countries	100	100	100	100
North Africa	5	8	5	6
Sub-Saharan Africa	14	5	6	7
Latin America and the Caribbean	20	27	35	29
Western Asia	7	11	9	10
South and East Asia	47	43	40	42
Mediterranean	6	6	5	6

Source: Ibid.

[a] *Measured at 1980 prices and exchange rates.*

TABLE 8.4. *Structure of MVA by broad economic categories, subgroups of developing countries, 1966–2000*[a]
(In percentages)

Country group and branch	1966–1970	1976–1980	1981–1985	2000
Major exporters of manufactures				
Consumer goods	59	46	43	32
Capital goods	26	34	35	42
Intermediate goods	15	20	22	26
Other countries with relatively large manufacturing sectors				
Consumer goods	58	50	50	47
Capital goods	23	27	26	27
Intermediate goods	19	23	24	26
Oil exporters[b]				
Consumer goods	50	46	46	40
Capital goods	15	19	18	18
Intermediate goods	35	35	36	42
Least developed countries				
Consumer goods	76	69	68	63
Capital goods	11	14	13	15
Intermediate goods	14	16	19	22

Source: Ibid.

[a] *Shares may not add to 100 per cent because of rounding.*

[b] *Excluding high-income oil exporters (see explanatory notes) for lack of comprehensive data.*

TABLE 8.5. *Shares of selected industries in MVA in the developing countries and their subgroups, and the developed market economies, 1966–2000[a]*
(In percentages)

Industry	Developing countries			
	1966–1970	1976–1980	1981–1985	2000
Food (311)	18	15	16	13
Textile and wearing apparel (321, 322)	20	15	14	11
Footwear (324)	2	1	1	1
Industrial and other chemical products (351, 352)	6	9	9	12
Petroleum refineries and rubber products (353, 355)	6	7	7	8
Iron, steel and non-ferrous metals (371, 372)	7	7	7	8
Metal products (381)	5	5	5	4
Non-electrical machinery (382)	3	5	5	5
Electrical machinery (383)	3	5	6	9
Transport equipment (384)	5	6	6	6

Industry	Major exporters of manufacturing			
	1966–1970	1976–1980	1981–1985	2000
Food (311)	12	12	11	9
Textile and wearing apparel (321, 322)	24	17	14	11
Footwear (324)	2	1	1	1
Industrial and other chemical products (351, 352)	5	8	10	13
Petroleum refineries and rubber products (353, 355)	3	4	4	3
Iron and steel (371)	5	6	6	7
Non-ferrous metals (372)	1	1	1	2
Metal products (381)	5	5	5	5
Non-electrical machinery (382)	5	8	7	7
Electrical machinery (383)	5	7	8	13
Transport equipment (384)	5	6	6	7

continued

TABLE 8.5. *Shares of selected industries in MVA in the developing countries and their subgroups, and the developed market economies, 1966–2000ᵃ (continued)*
(In percentages)

Industry	Other countries with relatively large manufacturing sectors			
	1966–1970	1976–1980	1981–1985	2000
Food (311)	21	19	21	21
Textile, footwear and wearing apparel (321, 324, 322)	18	11	13	11
Industrial and other chemical products (351, 352)	7	9	11	13
Petroleum refineries (353)	3	3	4	4
Rubber products (355)	2	2	2	2
Iron and steel (371)	4	5	5	6
Non-ferrous metals (372)	2	2	2	3
Metal products (381)	5	5	5	4
Non-electrical machinery (382)	3	4	4	3
Electrical machinery (383)	3	4	4	5
Transport equipment (384)	5	6	6	6

Industry	Oil exporters			
	1966–1970	1976–1980	1981–1985	2000
Food (311)	17	14	14	10
Textile, footwear and wearing apparel (321, 324, 322)	17	16	15	14
Industrial and other chemical products (351, 352)	5	6	6	6
Petroleum refineries (353)	19	19	20	24
Rubber products (355)	2	1	1	1
Iron and steel (371)	3	3	3	3
Non-ferrous metals (372)	3	1	1	1
Metal products (381)	3	4	4	3
Non-electrical machinery (382)	1	2	2	2
Electrical machinery (383)	1	3	3	5
Transport equipment (384)	3	6	5	4

continued

TABLE 8.5. *Shares of selected industries in MVA in the developing countries and their subgroups, and the developed market economies, 1966–2000ᵃ (continued) (In percentages)*

Industry	Least developed countries			
	1966–1970	1976–1980	1981–1985	2000
Food (311)	12	13	13	12
Textile, footwear and wearing apparel (321, 324, 322)	41	35	33	24
Industrial and other chemical products (351, 352)	9	11	13	12
Iron, steel and metal products (371, 381)	7	9	8	4

Industry	Developed market economies			
	1966–1970	1976–1980	1981–1985	2000
Food (311)	9	9	9	8
Textile, footwear and wearing apparel (321, 324, 322)	7	8	7	4
Industrial and other chemical products (351, 352)	7	9	9	4
Petroleum refineries and rubber products (353, 355)	3	3	3	1
Iron, steel and non-ferrous metals (371, 372)	10	9	8	2
Metal products (381)	7	7	7	5
Non-electrical machinery (382)	11	11	12	13
Electrical machinery (383)	7	8	10	18
Transport equipment (384)	11	11	11	11

Source: Ibid.

ᵃ *The shares of the selected industries in total manufacturing do not add to 100 per cent because those of other industries are not shown.*

ᵇ *Excluding high-income oil exporters (see explanatory notes) for lack of comprehensive data.*

TABLE 8.6. *Growth rates of MVA and its major categories in subgroups of developing countries, 1966–2000 (In percentages)*

Country group and branch	1965–1970	1970–1975	1975–1980	1980–1986	1986–1990	1990–1995	1995–2000
Developing countries							
Total manufacturing[a]	6.5	6.3	5.2	4.0	5.0	5.4	5.7
Consumer goods	4.8	4.3	3.7	3.1	3.9	4.2	4.4
Capital goods	8.6	9.5	6.5	4.5	6.1	6.4	6.6
Intermediate goods	9.1	7.2	6.8	4.9	5.7	6.1	6.5
Major exporters of manufactures							
Total manufacturing[a]	6.4	8.2	6.4	5.4	6.1	6.1	6.2
Consumer goods	4.8	5.6	4.2	3.8	4.7	4.4	4.4
Capital goods	9.3	11.9	8.1	6.9	6.9	7.1	7.2
Intermediate goods	11.0	9.0	8.6	6.2	7.1	7.1	7.0
Other countries with relatively large manufacturing sectors							
Total manufacturing[a]	6.0	4.4	3.8	2.0	3.8	4.2	4.7
Consumer goods	4.2	2.8	2.9	2.1	3.1	3.6	4.0
Capital goods	7.9	6.6	4.7	0.7	4.9	5.0	5.5
Intermediate goods	8.7	5.9	4.5	3.0	4.3	4.6	5.1
Oil exporters[b]							
Total manufacturing[a]	7.5	8.2	7.2	5.6	4.8	6.0	6.4
Consumer goods	7.8	6.7	6.6	5.2	4.2	5.3	5.4
Capital goods	8.9	14.1	5.6	5.5	5.2	6.0	6.0
Intermediate goods	6.5	7.6	8.8	6.1	5.4	6.9	7.7
Least developed countries							
Total manufacturing[a]	5.5	3.7	3.2	−0.1	1.2	1.4	1.5
Consumer goods	5.2	2.0	3.0	−1.6	1.4	1.5	1.6
Capital goods	6.2	7.8	5.6	0.4	1.3	1.6	2.1
Intermediate goods	6.5	8.6	2.1	4.6	0.8	0.9	1.1

Source: Ibid.

[a] *Total manufacturing comprises consumer, capital and intermediate goods defined by ISIC categories as defined in table IV.4, footnote a.*

[b] *Excluding high-income oil exporters (see explanatory notes) for lack of comprehensive data.*

9.
Population: Demographic and Labour Force Trends and Issues

DEMOGRAPHIC TRENDS are fairly predictable and provide a good basis for the analysis of structural economic change and the associated economic and social policy issues of the next decade. Against a background of generally slower population growth, which will result in a world population of 6 billion just before the turn of the century, there will be considerable regional diversity. The fastest growth (an annual rate of 3 per cent) will occur in Africa, where the task of economic recovery and restoration of self-sustained growth will be particularly difficult. There will be less dispersion, however, in labour force growth rates in the developing world. The rate will average 2.5 to 3 per cent. In contrast, labour force growth rates in developed countries will be less than 1 per cent. Employment is likely to grow more slowly than the labour force in most countries, and unemployment will be a concern for all groups of countries.

For the world as a whole, the dependency ratio* is expected to fall, but this is the result of opposing trends in major world

---

* The ratio of the number of people aged 0–14 and 65 or more to the number aged 15–64; see table 9.3 and discussion in Section A.5, below.

regions. In the developing countries, the total dependency ratio should fall as fertility declines. In the developed countries it is expected to rise, mainly as a result of the increase in the elderly population. This increase will raise the level of the real and financial resources needed for health care and other support of the elderly.

The pressure for international migration should accelerate in the 1990s as income differentials increase and the cost of transportation declines relative to incomes. Urban population will continue to grow faster than rural population in all regions of the world, due principally to rural-urban migration, and the number and size of "megacities" is expected to increase rapidly in developing countries.

A. POPULATION TRENDS AND STRUCTURE

1. New growth trends

The world's population surpassed 5 billion in the middle of 1987 and is projected to grow to 6 billion just before the turn of the century. In the previous 13 years, it grew from 4 to 5 billion. The quarter century from 1975 to 2000 will have witnessed the greatest absolute expansion of the global population in such a short time. From 1980 to 1985 the annual rate of population growth was 1.7 per cent, compared with the peak rate of 2.0 per cent in the period from 1965 to 1970. It is expected to continue to decline slowly in the future. Only in the next century, however, will there be a significant decline in the size of the net annual increments to the world total.[1]

There was a clear dichotomy in the 1960s between slow growth of population in the developed countries (the average annual rate was 1.1 per cent) and rapid growth in the developing countries (the average annual rate was about 2.5 per cent). The major developing regions showed little diversity, ranging from 2.4 per cent in Asia (excluding Japan) to 2.7 per cent in Latin America (see table 9.1). Since the 1960s, however, the rates of population increase have become more diverse among the developing regions and their constituent countries, and the divergence is expected to increase in the 1990s. Population growth in Africa began to accelerate in the 1950s and continued to do so through the 1980s, while in most of the other developing regions it began to decelerate in the 1970s. The drop in the growth rate was particularly notable in China and the Asian planned economies; the drop is expected to continue in the 1990s, falling to little more than half the rate of the 1960s. Projected population growth rates for the 1990s are now about 3 per cent in Africa and Western Asia, 2 per cent in South and East Asia (excluding Japan and the Asian planned economies), 1.9 per cent in Latin America, and 1.3 per cent in China together with the Asian planned economies. The growth rate in the developed countries as a whole has fallen to 0.6 per cent in the 1980s and is projected to be only 0.5 per cent in the 1990s (0.8 per cent or less in North America and Eastern Europe and 0.3 to 0.5 per cent in the European market economies and Japan). These differential growth rates will result in quite different age structures that, in turn, will affect many aspects of development.

The shift in the regional shares of global population is dominated by the growth of developing Africa and West Asia. Their combined share was 10 per cent in 1960 and 12 per cent in 1980. It is projected to reach 16 per cent in 2000. In contrast, the proportion of world population accounted for by the developed countries declined from 31.4 per cent in 1960 to 25.8 per cent in 1980, and is projected to be only 20.6 per cent in 2000.

Population growth in the least developed countries has accelerated from an average rate of 2.4 per cent in the 1960s to 2.6 per cent in the 1980s.[2] This is in contrast to a dramatic drop in China together with the Asian planned economies, from 2.4 per cent to 1.3 per cent, and a slight decline in the other developing countries as a whole. The difference is expected to be even greater in the 1990s—2.9 per cent in the least developed countries versus 1.3

per cent in China and the Asian planned economies and 2.3 per cent in the developing countries as a whole.

2. Mortality and life expectancy

Population growth rates are affected by trends in mortality and fertility. Mortality has declined unevenly in most countries during recent decades. Although it remains high in most of the developing countries, the mortality rate has declined very rapidly in some and has reached levels as low, or nearly as low, as those in developed countries. In the past decade, there have been decreases in infant mortality rates in nearly all countries, but more than one quarter, representing 29 per cent of world population, still have rates above 100 per 1,000 live births. Between 1985 and 1990, the average in the least developed countries is estimated at 123 per 1,000. In Africa as a whole it is 106, while the average in the developed countries (excluding South Africa) is about 15.

Mortality levels and trends are influenced by many social, economic, and cultural factors, including policies and programmes outside the health sector. Economic development is usually associated with mortality decline, since improved economic conditions imply higher living standards and increased financial resources for health services. But low mortality levels have also been achieved in some low-income countries where Governments are committed to reducing mortality; China, Cuba, Sri Lanka, and the state of Kerala in India are well-known examples, as is Costa Rica among middle-income countries.

Deaths of young children in developing countries constitute a large share of all deaths, and children are considered the major target in efforts to reduce overall mortality. The factors having the greatest effect on the mortality of children are those related to parental education, especially of mothers. Analysis of data from the World Fertility Surveys show that infant and child mortality generally decreases as the average number of years of the mother's education increases.[3] Survey results suggest that the effect of parental education may be greater than that of income-related factors and access to health facilities combined.[4]

One of the most important findings from the World Fertility Surveys concerns the exceptionally high mortality among children born after a short birth interval.[5] This suggests that family planning programmes aimed at spacing births and avoiding high-risk pregnancies could help to reduce infant, child, and also maternal mortality. Other interventions that can lower mortality in developing countries include efforts to improve the nutritional level of the population, immunization programmes, and other health measures.

The mortality assumptions underlying the population projections shown in table 10 are given in the form of life expectancy at birth and age and sex patterns of survival probabilities. In general, mortality trends followed the assumption of a quinquennial gain of 2.5 years in the expectation of life at birth until life expectancy reaches 62.5 years, followed by a slow-down in the gain thereafter. For some developing countries, however, recent evidence has indicated a retardation or an acceleration in the improvement of mortality levels. For them the assumed future quinquennial gains were adjusted accordingly. The anticipated quinquennial gain in life expectancy, for example, was lowered from 2.5 years to two years or less for some sub-Saharan African countries. In those countries where life expectancy at birth has already reached a high level, the maximum level of expectancy was assumed to be 82.5 years for males and 87.5 for females.[6] Mortality may be increased significantly in the future by the increasing incidence of AIDS, though sufficient data are not yet available to predict the specific impact in individual countries.

In the developed countries, life expectancy at birth has increased from 66 years in the early 1950s to 73 years in the late 1980s, while in the developing countries as a whole (including China), it has increased from 41 to 60. There was a dramatic increase in China, from 41 years in the early 1950s to 69 in the late 1980s; in Africa, it increased from 35 years to 49. The average life expectancy in the least developed countries in the period from

1985 to 1990 is also about 49 years. The low life expectancy and high infant mortality in the least developed countries reflect their unfavourable living conditions and imply that their population may increase even more rapidly in the future if mortality conditions improve and fertility remains unchanged.

Life expectancy at birth is generally several years longer for women than for men, especially in the developed countries: 77 years for women versus 70 years for men in the late 1980s. In the developing countries (including China), it is about 61 years for women and 59 years for men. The region where average expectancy for women is the same as for men is South Asia, although improvements in female life expectancy in Sri Lanka in the past two decades have resulted in a more normal pattern in that country. By the year 2000, the difference is projected to increase to three years in the developing countries as a whole, and to remain constant in the developed countries.

3. Factors affecting fertility trends

The level of fertility in the 1950s and 1960s provided a generally reliable means of distinguishing the developed from the developing countries. In the last two or three decades, the distribution has become less prominently bimodal. With substantial fertility declines in a number of developing countries of Latin America and Asia and persisting high fertility in most of Africa and Western Asia, the fertility differentials currently observed within the developing world are now as wide as those formerly found between the developing and the developed countries.[7]

The most rapid fertility declines have occurred in developing countries with a combination of profound improvements in child survival, increases in educational levels, and strong family planning programmes. Since the late 1950s, total fertility rates have declined by 2 to 3 children per woman in China, the Republic of Korea, Thailand, Malaysia, Sri Lanka, Brazil, Mexico, and Colombia. The proportion of married women of childbearing age currently using contraception in all these countries grew rapidly since at least the mid–1960s, gaining 2 to 3 percentage points a year. In the 1980s, it reached levels of 50 to 70 per cent. Simultaneously, under-five mortality (i.e., the combined mortality of infants and children under age 5) declined in China from 240 per thousand to 55, and from a range of 120 to 190 per thousand in the other seven countries to a range of 40 to 90. Gross enrolment ratios of females for the second level of education rose from less than 15 per cent in all these countries to between 30 and 35 per cent in Thailand, Brazil, and China. It rose to about 50 per cent in Sri Lanka, Malaysia, Mexico, and Colombia and to 90 per cent in the Republic of Korea.

Conversely, low rates of child survival, low levels of education, and insufficient access to birth control methods impede the transformation to lower fertility in most countries of sub-Saharan Africa, as well as in such Asian countries as Pakistan, Bangladesh, Nepal, and Afghanistan. Total fertility rates in many of these countries average 6 or 7 children per woman. They show few signs of decline[8] despite significant government initiatives in immunization and family planning. Under-five mortality is still well above 150 per 1000 in most of them and often exceeds 250; the female gross enrolment ratio for the second level of education and the proportion of married women currently using contraception are typically below 10 per cent and rarely above 20 per cent.

Recent studies confirm the strong negative relationship between development and fertility. They also show that, within groups of countries at similar levels of development, fertility decline generally has been greatest in countries with strong family planning programmes.[9] Without deliberate government fertility intervention, the diffusion of development is likely to induce fertility decline first among the more economically advanced population groups; at a later stage, declines are observed across all groups. Variations among countries at similar levels of development are also likely to be related to differences between social settings in household organization and institutional arrangements for the rearing of children.

Improvements in child survival increase the predictability of the family's life cycle and thus create an appropriate environment for the adoption of family planning practices.[10] The "insurance effect" operates at a later point in the demographic transition when family size desires are clearly formulated. Because family planning methods other than sterilization are not yet widely accessible in many countries, there still is considerable potential for large reductions in fertility.[11]

Education may affect fertility through acquired skills and knowledge, including the ability to provide safe child care and to use contraception effectively. Advanced education usually delays marriage and thus reduces the length of the childbearing lifespan. In the developing countries, women with seven or more years of schooling marry, on average, nearly four years later than women with no education. Educational status may also convey the influence of residence, income, or socio-economic status on marriage age and fertility. In addition, women's education is often positively associated with the opportunity costs of childbearing.

Although fertility decline due to education tends to be quite large in relatively advanced developing countries, in the least developed countries women with just a few years of education bear more children than those with no education. This may be due to the effect of reduced breast-feeding on the part of the more educated women, which outweighs the effect of possible initial efforts by those women to use contraception.

Fertility decline may be assisted by changes in marriage patterns or by maintenance of lengthy breast-feeding, but efficient practice of birth control is essential to achieve and sustain low levels of reproduction. Most of the inter-country variation in current national fertility levels is explained by differences in contraceptive use. Though contraceptive use varies according to the level of development, population policies have a strong independent effect, as seen in the high levels of contraceptive use achieved by some poor countries with strong family planning programmes.

In preparing the population projections shown in table 9.1, past and current fertility trends for each country are evaluated and placed within the social, economic, and political context of each country. Trends and anticipated changes in the socio-economic structure and cultural values of the society, as well as policies and programmes directed towards family planning, are considered *vis-à-vis* expected trends in fertility. For many low-fertility countries, fertility levels are assumed to decline or to remain below replacement level until about the end of the century. Then they are expected to be close to replacement level. For high-fertility and moderate-fertility countries, the level is expected to decline as countries advance in their social and economic development, which is generally assumed to progress as time passes. For those countries existing or anticipated governmental policies and programmes for family planning and related-governmental activities are assumed to accelerate or expedite the process of fertility decline. Once the decline in fertility starts, it is expected to begin slowly, gain momentum, and then slow down.[12]

4. Changing population structure

The population age structure and the pattern of changes in it differ greatly among major regions of the world. Children under the age of 15 made up only 22 per cent of total population in the developed regions in 1985, but 37 per cent in the developing regions (including China); 45 per cent in Africa. The elderly population (aged 60 years and older) comprised 16 per cent of the total population of the developed regions, but only 7 per cent in the developing regions; in Africa they comprised only 5 per cent. In the middle range of the age distribution, the developed regions had a relatively small proportion (16 per cent) of youth aged 15 to 24, and a relatively large proportion of adults aged 25 to 59 (46 per cent). Youth comprised 20 per cent of the total population in the developing regions, while those in the 25 to 59-year-old group were only 36 per cent of the total.[13]

Changes in fertility and mortality in the past 40 years have introduced bulges and troughs in the age structure, with predictable time lags. Especially noteworthy are the baby booms that occurred shortly after the Second World War in many developed countries, and the drop of fertility rates with varying speed and timing among many developed countries in the past 30 years. Significant reductions of infant and child mortality rates, or increases in fertility rates, resulted in a sharp increase in the child and school-age populations during the 1950s and 1960s. Forty to fifty per cent of the world's population increase in those decades consisted of children under 15 years of age. With a time lag, these inflated population cohorts moved to the youth category. As they reached adulthood, the main working-age population, aged 25 to 59, has begun to increase rapidly in the 1980s and will continue to accelerate in the 1990s.

The primary and secondary school-age populations are defined by the United Nations Educational, Scientific and Cultural Organization (UNESCO) for statistical purposes as children aged 6 to 11 and 12 to 17, respectively. In the developed countries plus China and several other countries in East Asia, the school-age population has declined in the 1980s as a result of the fertility decline in the 1970s. As a result of the gradual fertility decline in recent years, the school-age population in Latin America and southern Asia will increase more slowly in the 1990s than before. In Africa, however, it will continue to grow rapidly, at about the same rate as the total population.

5. Aging of populations

Recent demographic trends suggest that from 1985 to 2000 the populations of both the developed and the developing regions will grow older. This is so in the sense that the median age and the proportion of elderly (60 and over) will increase. Between 1985 and 2000, the median age is projected to increase by 3.8 years in the developed regions and by 2.8 years in the developing regions as a whole. But in Africa it is expected to remain virtually constant. There will be very large increases in the number of the elderly in all regions, reflecting growth rates considerably greater than the growth rates of the total population. The world's elderly population will grow by 2.45 per cent annually between 1985 and 2000, compared with 1.68 per cent annually for the total population. The annual rate of growth of the number of elderly in the developing countries will be about 3 per cent, almost twice as high as in the developed countries. Nonetheless, the share of the elderly in the total population will not increase very much between 1985 and 2000. In the developed countries, it will rise from 16 to 19 per cent; in the developing countries, from 7 to 8 per cent (in Africa it will remain at 5 per cent). For the world as a whole, it will rise from 9 to 10 per cent.[14]

Dependency ratios seek to capture the changes in the relative proportions of the economically active population, which is conventionally defined as the age group between 15 and 64, and those which are younger or older. This is obviously a gross simplification. In many countries, most of the young contribute to production before the age of 15 and in others, much later. Similarly, some adults retire from active economic life before the age of 65 and others, only later. Minor differences between the ratios in different countries should not be regarded as significant, therefore, but major changes will reflect economically important aspects of a changing population structure.

For the world as a whole, the old-age dependency ratio (the ratio of those over 65 to those between the age of 15 and 64) will not change much between 1985 and 2000, rising from 10 to 11 per cent. This will be more than offset by a 5 percentage point decline in the child dependency ratio, and the total dependency ratio is projected to fall from 65 to 61 per cent. The decline corresponds closely to the overall trend in the developing countries (including China), where the average old-age dependency ratio is expected to rise by 1 percentage point and the child dependency ratio to fall by 8 points. The total dependency ratio would fall from 71 to 64 per cent. In the developed countries, however, the old-age dependency ratio is expected to rise by 3 percentage points and the child dependency ratio to fall by that amount, so that the total dependency ratio would remain constant at 51 per cent (figure 9.1).

There is little likelihood of the projected changes in age struc-

Figure 9.1   Child and Old-age Dependency Ratios *

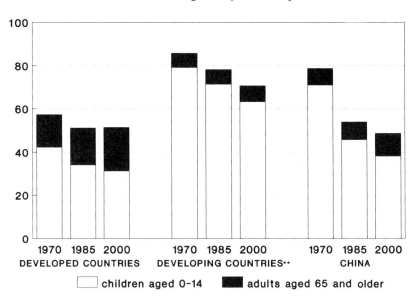

children aged 0-14   adults aged 65 and older

* Number of dependents per 100 people   ** excluding China
aged 15-64

ture being nullified, either by unforeseen events or by policy-induced changes in fertility or mortality patterns. As the twenty-first century approaches, the aging of the world's population is a virtual certainty. Thus it provides a firm foundation for long-range planning.[15] Projections for the long period from 1985 to 2025 indicate that, in the more developed regions, the elderly proportion would increase by 9.2 percentage points. In the less developed regions, the proportion is projected to increase by 5.5 percentage points.[16]

In the process of modernization, increased life expectancy and lower fertility tend to be accompanied by a weakening of the extended family. This weakening raises new demands for the support of the older age group. Until recently, this has been an issue primarily in industrialized countries. Now it is a world-wide concern. Policies of mandatory ages of retirement were regarded as socially progressive when work was regarded as painful and retirement could be appropriately financed. Now they have to be rethought in countries where rising health standards have pro- longed potential working life. In many developing countries, there will be a need to develop social institutions to compensate for the declining role of the extended family. Developed countries face growing tax burdens on the economically active population, com- petition for resources to provide for the needs of children and the elderly, and a need to allocate costs and responsibilities of caring for the elderly between Governments, individuals, and families. These challenges may be magnified by declines in the productivity and mobility of the labour force.

6. Labour force—quantitative outlook

Labour force growth trends are determined by changes in pop- ulation structure and participation rates. The growth of the labour force in the 1990s is projected to slow significantly in the devel- oped regions and China but remain fairly stable in the developing regions. For the world as a whole, the average annual rate of labour force increase will decline dramatically to 1.5 per cent during the period from 1990 to 2000. This compares with 2.1 per cent during the period from 1970 to 1980 and 1.9 per cent between 1980 and 1990 (see table 9.2). The average annual increase will decline slightly from 41 million in the 1980s to 39 million in the 1990s; more than 35 million of the increase will occur in the developing countries. An important policy question for the 1990s will be whether growth in the demand for labour will be able to absorb this increasing supply.

About 58 per cent of the world's population aged 10 and over in 1980 were members of the labour force, including those without jobs who were looking for employment; overall, the participation rate was 73 per cent among males and 43 per cent among females. The rates varied significantly among regions, especially for fe- males, ranging from about 60 per cent in the centrally planned economies to about 10 per cent in North Africa and Western Asia

Figure 9.2   Labour force participation rates, 1990

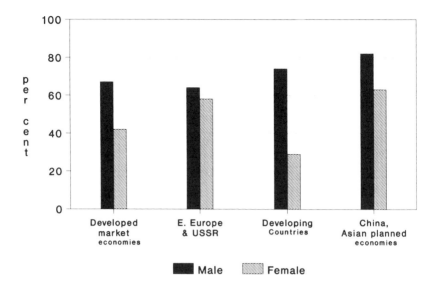

Labour force as percentage of population
aged 10 and over

(figure 9.2). The apparent diversity between the high female participation rate in sub-Saharan Africa (51 per cent) and the lower
rates in Latin America and South Asia (25 per cent) may reflect
cultural differences in the definitions of female work and labour
force participation.

Persons aged 25 to 59 comprised 65 per cent of the world
labour force in 1985 and will account for virtually all of the labour
force increase in the 1990s. That group is projected to increase in
the 1990s at the same rate or higher than in the 1980s in most
regions, except for Latin America where the annual growth rate
is projected to decline from 3.2 to 2.9 per cent. The projected
annual rates of increase for other regions are between 2.7 for the
developing countries in Asia and 3.0 per cent for Africa. The
increased concentration of the labour force in the group will tend
to increase overall labour productivity, because this group is more

experienced, on average, than the labour force under 25 years of age.

The proportion of the labour force in the 10 to 14 age group is negligible for the developed regions but averages 5 per cent in the developing regions, reaching 7.9 per cent in Africa. This proportion is in sharp decline in every region of the world except for Africa, and the trend is projected to continue through the 1990s.

Decelerating growth of the number of youth (aged 15 to 24) in the labour force will be a new phenomenon in the 1990s in several regions of the world. There will be absolute declines in some countries. These changes will be caused primarily by declines in the size of the youth population and also by its declining rate of labour force participation. Based on the projections of labour force participation made by the International Labour Office,[17] the number of youth in the labour force in East Asia (including Japan and China) will decline at an annual rate of 3 per cent in the 1990s; there was a positive growth rate of 2.3 per cent in the 1980s. In southern Asia (including Western Asia and South-eastern Asia), the annual growth rate will fall from 2 per cent in the 1980s to 1.1 per cent in the 1990s. The youth labour force in the more developed regions will decline 0.2 per cent per year in the 1990s, compared with an annual increase of 1.0 per cent in the 1980s. Overall, the total number of youth in the world labour force will grow much more slowly in the 1990s (at an average rate of 0.5 per cent) than the 1.1 per cent rate of the 1980s.

The elderly labour force, aged 60 years or older, comprises 5.4 and 5.0 per cent of the total labour force in the developed and the developing regions respectively. Its projected rates of annual increase in the 1990s are relatively modest: 1.2 per cent for Latin America, 1.5 per cent for the developed regions, 1.7 per cent for Asia, and 2.1 per cent for Africa.

In both developed and developing regions, the percentage of women in the economically active population has increased since 1950; women represented 36.5 per cent of the world's labour force in 1985. Relatively little change is expected in women's average labour force participation rate in most regions in the 1990s (see figure 9.2). Moderate increases in participation by middle-aged

and older women in some regions will be offset by lower participation by younger women, as they spend more years in full-time
education. However, the projected trends do not take into account
possible policy changes. Some changes with a large potential impact are already visible in 1988: legal equality has been achieved
in many countries, and more affirmative actions favouring wom-
en's participation are being implemented. If encouraged by further
policy initiatives, women's overall economic participation in the
year 2000 may well be greater than currently projected.

B. INTERNATIONAL MIGRATION

International migration has been motivated by economic considerations throughout history. In recent times migration for reset-
tlement, labour migration, and flows of undocumented migrants
have been associated with significant economic disparities between
sending and receiving countries. Although the forces giving rise
to the movement of refugees are often non-economic in nature,
the presence of refugees has economic repercussions.

During the past 30 years, the two main destinations of labour
migration have been the industrialized countries of Western
Europe and the oil-producing countries of the Middle East. Migration was promoted by the Governments of receiving countries
in both regions to satisfy the labour needs of their growing economies. The labour-importing countries of Western Europe and
the Middle East have at different times experienced a period of
expansion followed by a recession. Inflows of foreign labour
served to fuel or maintain the expansion, but during the recessions
some migrants departed, often as a result of measures taken by
the receiving country, while others remained.

Labour migration to Western Europe was officially stopped
around 1974, but migration to the Middle East increased rapidly
at that time and peaked by about 1983. The discontinuation of
labour immigration in Western Europe did not, however, stop
migration completely. The adoption of policies favouring family

reunion fueled the continued growth of the foreign population in most receiving countries, except Switzerland. By 1982 there were nearly 13.2 million foreign residents estimated to be in the main receiving countries of Western Europe (Federal Republic of Germany, France, the United Kingdom of Great Britain and Northern Ireland, Switzerland, Belgium, the Netherlands, Sweden, Austria, and Luxembourg).[18] By 1980, there were approximately 2.8 million foreign workers in the Middle East.[19] Lack of reliable data makes that estimate a tentative one and precludes definite assertions about the evolution of migration during the early 1980s. Data on work permits issued by the United Arab Emirates, Bahrain, Kuwait, and Qatar indicate a decline as of 1983 and 1984.[20] Although the inflow of migrant workers may be declining, an increasing proportion of them appear to be remaining after the completion of their initial contracts.[21] Thus, as in Europe, the total foreign population in the Middle East may not decline even if the inflow of foreign labour is stopped.

In addition to the benefits accruing to the workers themselves, employers in the receiving countries during the period of expansion benefited from the importation of labour that tended to prevent sharp rises in domestic wages. Unemployment in the receiving countries was mitigated, however, by the departure of foreign workers in periods of contraction. Their return tended to reduce wages, increase unemployment and underemployment, and reduce foreign exchange earnings in their home countries.

The selectivity of migration has had undesirable effects in some sending countries whose emigrants have tended to be better educated and to possess higher skills than the average population.[22] In those countries the depletion of the pool of local skilled labour has been a serious impediment to the expansion of modern economic activities. Opportunities for migration have encouraged some people in other countries to invest in their own education. Although returning migrants tend to bring back some of their foreign earnings, other benefits that might be expected from the return of migrants have not always materialized. Migrants have generally experienced negligible occupational upgrading while abroad,[23] and those choosing to return seem to be negatively selected in terms of skills, age, or health status. In addition, some sending countries often lack the open and flexible socio-economic environment that stimulates the success of the innovating individual.

Among the factors responsible for immigration to the United States, satisfying the need of the economy for workers plays only a minor role. It is interesting to note, nonetheless, that the number of foreign-born persons living in the United States in 1980, 14.1 million, is of the order of magnitude of the number of foreigners in the former labour-importing countries of Europe. This foreign-born population in the United States included the survivors of permanent immigrants (about 9.2 million from 1956 to 1980), a small number of temporary workers and trainees (approximately 300,000 of whom were admitted since 1971), and an estimated 2 million undocumented immigrants. From 1981 to 1987, the United States admitted 4.1 million permanent immigrants and about 500,000 temporary workers and trainees. In addition, some 1.7 million people have applied for legal residential status under an amnesty programme for certain groups of undocumented immigrants.[24]

Predicting likely trends in international migration is a precarious task, because it is greatly affected by unpredictable political, economic, and social circumstances in both countries of origin and destination. International migration can change dramatically, even reversing direction, in a comparatively short time. For some countries, net migration is relatively small. Consequently, in the preparation of estimates and projections at the national level, no migration was assumed. For those countries that have a long history of international migration, a simple constant net migration flow was assumed. For other countries it was generally assumed that the current migration flows would decline and reach zero at around the year 2000. For countries in which migration has been of a temporary nature resulting from either civil conflicts, sudden change in the national economy, or specific governmental policies, migration was assumed only for the period from 1985 to 1990.[25]

Refugee movements form a most dramatic type of international migration. Conventional refugees are those who have crossed an international border to avoid being persecuted or to escape war-like conditions in their home countries. *De facto* refugees include those who have left their country under normal departure procedures but are prohibited from returning home without risking their lives owing to intervening events there.

The current global refugee population is estimated to be about 12 million. Some four-fifths are found in developing countries, including somewhat less than one third in Africa.[26] During the past few years some Western countries have tended to restrict the granting of asylum. There is reason to believe that the proportion of refugees accommodated in the developing countries will be increased in coming years, even though developing countries have experienced serious socio-economic problems with hosting large refugee populations.

Approximately half of the global refugee population is currently assisted through official schemes. Examples are reception centres, holding centres, camps, or designated land settlements and villages. The remainder have found a place to stay on their own, sometimes illegally or in consultation with local people and authorities, often in areas bordering their home countries. In addition to relief supplies, these schemes to aid refugees often include social infrastructure, such as schools and health centres, to which local people may also have access. But distribution of food and other relief items is limited to refugees, even in areas with groups of destitute local people. With the exception of land settlements where refugees are given plots to cultivate, income-generating activities have been developed for only a small percentage of refugees in most official schemes. In some cases, refugees in official schemes do not receive their entitlements; distributions are irregular, and they must find supplementary sources of income. Thus they often provide labour and services for surrounding host populations. Barter systems involving the exchange of donated relief items for items of local production between refugees and their hosts have developed in some areas. A recent large-scale survey of the socio-economic conditions of refugees in Pakistan, host to about one fifth of the estimated global refugee population, found that new arrivals have less means at their disposal per household member than those who arrived earlier. They are also most frequently subject to irregular food distributions. Some refugees have experienced conflict with local citizens when seeking employment or agricultural land, or when collecting firewood and other natural resources.[27] Similar friction has been reported in other countries as well.

In areas with relatively abundant resources and a buoyant local economy, refugees are often well received. They are willing to engage in menial tasks despised by others, including unskilled manual work for local farmers. Refugees will search for vacant land and develop their own agriculture, or supply unskilled and semi-skilled labour to local building contractors and manufacturers. Some take up crafts and trade and increase the varieties and quantity of locally available goods. But because more of the casual and unskilled work is undertaken by the refugees, their activities may indirectly worsen the conditions of some members of local vulnerable groups such as female heads of households, the disabled, and the elderly who all depend on this work for their incomes. Over time, friction between refugees and these groups may materialize, and some refugees or local destitute groups may leave the area. On balance, the refugee inflow contributes positively, however, to the general development of areas with adequate resources and economic growth.

In poorer areas, refugees are resented by many. As they flood the labour market, wages drop for casual labour and even for semi-skilled and skilled jobs. Local prices for food, fuel, medical supplies, and commodities often rise. Refugees may collect firewood for fuel in neighbouring areas and further afield, contribute to deforestation in some areas, and impede the access of local people to common property resources. Although employers benefit from the ready labour supply provided by refugees, many workers and destitute groups do not. The resentment may lead to violence, with the result that a part of the refugee population may be relocated and have to start again in a new setting.

It is impossible, of course, to predict whether the size of the world refugee population will tend to increase over time because of the unpredictability of conflicts that give rise to them. Nonetheless, in countries that currently host large numbers of refugees, budgetary provisions will have to be made to provide assistance during the foreseeable future.

C. URBAN AND RURAL POPULATION AND INTERNAL MIGRATION

Forty-one percent of the world's population resided in urban areas in 1985: 72 per cent in the developed regions, 69 per cent in Latin America, and about 30 per cent in Africa and Asia.[28] The definition of urban areas differs from one country to another. The smallest places that are classified as urban range between 200 and 30,000 people. The process of urbanization, defined as an increase in the proportion of population living in urban areas, is largely a one-way process leading to a concentration in the pattern of population distribution.

The dynamics of population growth, industrialization, and agricultural modernization are expected to keep urban population growth rates above the rural growth rates in all regions. The urban population of developed countries is expected to rise from 71.5 per cent in 1985 to 74.8 per cent by the year 2000. In Africa, it is expected to increase from 31 to 41 per cent; in Asia (including Japan), from 28 to 35 per cent; and in Latin America, from 69 to 77 per cent. The number and size of "megacities" will increase rapidly in developing countries.

Despite the continuing exodus to urban areas, the population residing in rural areas still comprises a majority in most developing countries. Approximately one third of the total population increase in the developing countries in the 1990s will occur in rural areas. In the developed countries, the rural population accounted for less than 28 per cent of the total population in 1985, and it is projected that the share will fall to 25 per cent in the year 2000.

The total rural population of the developing countries (including China) is expected to increase at an average annual rate of 1.24 per cent during the period from 1990 to 1995 and at 0.96 per cent per year between 1995 and 2000. In Latin America, the growth of the rural population nearly halted after 1980. The size of its rural population (125 million in 1985) is projected to be practically unchanged through the year 2000. Rural population growth in Africa, however, was about 2.1 per cent per year in the period from 1980 to 1985, and in Asia it was about 1.45 per cent per year. By the year 2000, the rural growth rate is projected to fall slightly in Africa, to about 1.8 per cent, and substantially in Asia, to about 0.8 per cent, due to migration and declining rates of natural increase. Nevertheless, the rural population will still comprise a large majority in these regions: Africa, 59 per cent; East Asia (including Japan), 67 per cent; and southern Asia (including Southeastern and Western Asia), 63 per cent.

Rural-to-urban migration is only one type of population movement within a country. There are movements from urban to rural areas, among urban areas and among rural areas. All types of migration are intimately related to social and economic changes and have significant policy implications. However, it is difficult to assess the situation, due to lack of statistical data.

An analysis of data from 57 countries, both developed and developing, indicates that the annual rate of net in-migration in urban areas (the number of in-migrants net of out-migrants divided by the urban population) ranged between 0.9 and 4.6 per cent in the developing countries and between 0.03 and 2.9 per cent among the developed countries.[29] In Latin American countries and in the developed countries, there is a tendency for female rural-to-urban migrants to outnumber their male counterparts. Male migrants are relatively more numerous in Africa and Asia. Among the 57 countries surveyed, 24 had sex ratios of the migrants (number of males per 100 females) smaller than 80, while migrants in 10 countries had sex ratios over 110. These migrants tend to be young. In the developing countries, around 25 per cent of the migrants were aged 15 to 24, and in the developed countries more than 20 per cent were in that age bracket; in some countries, the proportion was much higher. Another 20 to 40 per cent were children under the age of five.

NOTES

1. *World Population Prospects 1988* (United Nations publication, Sales No. E.88.XIII.7), table 2.4.

2. The figures apply to 35 of the larger least developed countries, with 328 million people in 1980; seven others had a total of 889,000.

3. Hobcraft, J., J. McDonald, and S. Rutstein (1984), "Socio-Economic Factors in Infant and Child Mortality: A Cross-National Comparison," in *Population Studies*, vol. 38, No. 2.

4. Based on multivariate analysis of an index of child mortality (ratio of the number of child deaths to the "expected" number of dead children), as reported in Caldwell, J. C., and P. F. McDonald (1981), "Influence of Maternal Education on Infant and Child Mortality: Levels and Causes," in *International Population Conference, Manila, 1981: Solicited Papers*, Liége, International Union for the Scientific Study of Population, vol. 2., pp. 79–96, and in *Socio-Economic Differentials in Child Mortality in Developing Countries* (United Nations publication, Sales No. E.85.XIII.7).

5. Hobcraft, J., J. McDonald and S. Rutstein (1983), "Child-Spacing Effects on Infant and Early Child Mortality," in *Population Index*, vol. 49, No. 4.

6. *World Population Prospects 1988, op. cit.*, pp. 15–17.

7. *World Population Monitoring 1989* (United Nations publication, forthcoming, ST/ESA/SER.A/113).

8. *Ibid.*

9. Department of International Economic and Social Affairs. *Fertility Behaviour in the Context of Development: Evidence from the World Fertility Survey* (United Nations publication, Sales No. E.86.XIII.5).

10. Improvements in child survival generate various distinct but closely interdependent types of changes in patterns of reproduction, which typically result in lower fertility levels. Several of these, in particular, "the physiological effect," which links a child's death with a shortening of birth intervals through its effect on lactational amenorrhea and the "replacement effect," which links a child's death to birth spacing and fertility through the interrupting of family planning, are rather modest in magnitude, resulting in a maximum in 300 to 500 fewer births for every 1,000 fewer child deaths.

11. *Family Building by Fate or Design: A Study of Relationships between Child Survival and Fertility* (United Nations publication, ST/ESA/SER.R/74).

12. *World Population Prospects 1988, op. cit.*, pp. 20–22.

13. *Ibid.*, pp. 54–62.

14. *Ibid.*, p. 60.

15. "Global trends and prospects of aging population structures," in *Economic and Social Implications of Population Aging* Proceedings of the Tokyo Symposium on Population Structure, (United Nations publication, ST/ESA/SER.R/85).

16. *World Population Prospects 1988, op. cit.*, p. 60.

17. International Labour Office, *Economically Active Population 1950–2025*, vol. V, Geneva, 1986.

18. Denis Maillat, "Long-term aspects of international migration flows. The experience of European receiving countries" in *The Future of Migration*, Organisation for Economic Co-operation and Development (Paris), p. 40.

19. *World Population Trends, Population and Development Interrelations and Population Policies, 1983 Monitoring Report* (United Nations publication, Sales No. E.84.XIII.10), vol. I, p. 220.

20. J. S. Birks, I. J. Seccombe and C. A. Sinclair, "Migrant Workers in the Arab Gulf: The Impact of Declining Oil Revenues," in *International Migration Review*, vol. 20, winter 1986, pp. 799–814.

21. *Ibid.*, p. 813.

22. See, for instance, W. R. Bohning, *Studies in International Labour Migration* (London, 1984) and E. MacLean Petras, "Economic consequences of migration and return" in D. Kubat (ed.), *The Politics of Return. International Return Migration in Europe*, Center for Migration Studies (New York); and J. S. Birks and C. A. Sinclair, "Egypt: frustrated labor exporter?", *The Middle East Journal*, vol. 33, No. 3 (Summer, 1979), pp. 288–303.

23. See Entzinger, H. (1978), "Return migration from West European to Mediterranean countries," World Employment Programme Research Working Papers, No. 23, ILO (Geneva) and Papademetriou, D. G. (1984), "Return to the Mediterranean Littoral: Policy Agendas" in Kubat, D. (ed.), *The Politics of Return. International Return Migration in Europe*, Center for Migration Studies (New York).

24. United States, Department of Justice, *Statistical Yearbook of the Immigration and Naturalization Service 1987*, and earlier volumes.

25. *World Population Prospects 1988, op. cit.*, p. 25.

26.   The estimated number of the global refugee population is based on figures provided by Governments according to their own records and methods of estimation. See *Refugees*, No. 35, November, Office of the United Nations High Commissioner for Refugees, Geneva, and *World Population Monitoring 1989, op. cit.*

27.   United Nations Research Institute for Social Development, "Survey of the Social and Economic Conditions of Afghan Refugees in Pakistan," by Hanne Christensen and Wolf Scott, working paper edition, Geneva, 1987.

28.   *Prospect.*

29.   *World.*

TABLE 9.1 *Total population (in millions) and average annual growth rates (percentage) by decade, 1960–2000*

Country groups[a]	1960	1960–1970	1970	1970–1980	1980	1980–1990	1990	1990–2000	2000
Developing countries									
North Africa	54	2.53	69	2.55	89	2.80	117	2.32	148
Sub-Saharan Africa	210	2.60	271	2.98	364	3.13	495	3.25	681
South and East Asia	794	2.41	1,008	2.27	1,262	2.23	1,573	2.05	1,928
West Asia	46	3.23	63	3.41	88	3.67	126	3.15	171
Mediterranean	47	1.92	57	1.81	68	1.75	81	1.43	93
Western hemisphere	217	2.74	284	2.41	361	2.16	447	1.88	538
Subtotal, developing countries	1,367	2.51	1,752	2.45	2,230	2.44	2,838	2.29	3,558
China and Asian planned economies	704	2.36	889	1.87	1,070	1.39	1,229	1.32	1,400
Developed market economies	633	1.10	705	0.85	768	0.60	816	0.49	857
Eastern Europe and USSR	313	1.08	348	0.81	378	0.70	495	0.57	429
Total, 151 countries	3,016	2.05	3,694	1.87	4,445	1.75	5,286	1.68	6,244
World total[b]	3,019		3,698		4,450		5,292		6,251
Least developed countries	200	2.43	254	2.58	328	2.59	424	2.90	564

Source: Department of International Economic and Social Affairs of the United Nations Secretariat. Calculated from country data in World Population Prospects—1988, *United Nations publication, Sales No. E.88.XIII.7. The projections for 1990 and 2000 are based on the "medium variant" projection for each country.*

[a] *Definitions of the country groups are given in the "Explanatory notes," preceding the Introduction.*

[b] *Includes a number of small countries and territories, which had a combined population of about 5 million in 1980 and are projected to have 7 million in the year 2000.*

TABLE 9.2 *Total labour force, in millions, and average annual growth rates by decade 1970–2000*
(In percentages)

Country groups	1970	1970–1980	1980	1980–1990	1990	1990–2000	2000
Developing countries							
North Africa	18.0	2.79	23.7	3.02	31.9	3.01	42.9
Sub-Saharan Africa	121.1	2.55	155.8	2.44	198.2	2.70	258.7
South and East Asia	390.8	1.99	475.9	2.19	591.0	1.99	719.6
South Asia	277.8	1.82	332.8	2.14	411.1	2.00	501.1
East Asian newly industrializing economies	13.8	2.92	18.4	2.30	23.1	1.68	27.3
Others	99.2	2.31	124.7	2.32	156.8	2.00	191.2
Western Asia	17.3	3.54	24.5	3.48	34.5	3.44	48.4
Mediterranean	25.6	1.43	29.5	1.72	35.0	1.57	40.9
Latin America and the Caribbean	90.4	3.12	122.9	2.52	157.6	2.37	199.1
Subtotal, developing countries	663.3	2.30	832.3	2.33	1,048.1	2.25	1,309.6
China and Asian planned economies	455.1	2.47	580.6	2.24	724.3	1.23	818.4
Developed market economies	304.4	1.34	347.9	0.91	380.9	0.52	401.3
Eastern Europe & the USSR	172.4	1.21	194.5	0.65	207.6	0.58	219.9
World total, 150 countries	1,595.2	2.06	1,955.3	1.90	2,360.9	1.53	2,749.3
Least developed countries	103.9	2.09	127.8	2.39	161.9	2.54	208.1

Source: United Nations Secretariat, Department of International Economic and Social Affairs, based on country population in World Population Prospects—Estimates and Projections as Assessed in 1984 *(United Nations publication, Sales No. E.86.XIII.3), and labour force participation rates from the International Labour Organisation (ILO),* Economically Active Population, 1950–2025, *Geneva, 1986. The projections for 1990 and 2000 are based on the "medium variant" population projection for each country.*

10.

Human Settlements

SOCIAL PROGRESS and sustainable economic growth require an efficient spatial and administrative system of human settlements, a system that provides the concentration of infrastructure and buildings where people can live and work with some degree of safety, comfort, and efficiency.

Increased investment in shelter, infrastructure, and related services can be a major source of economic growth. Construction accounted for 62 per cent of gross fixed capital formation in 1985 in the 53 developing market economies for which data were available, and for 57 per cent in 25 developed market economies. Approximately one third of the construction was devoted to housing and two thirds to non-residential buildings and other construction (see table 10.1).

For most developing countries, construction based on appropriate technologies and standards uses mostly domestic material. Using inputs that are primarily domestic, including semi-skilled and non-skilled labour, it can provide a degree of insulation from external economic shocks and be used as a macro-economic policy instrument to stabilize economic growth. Although most human settlements investments do not generate foreign exchange directly, they can contribute to the overall productivity of the economy, including the export sectors. They should not be ranked so low, as they have been in most developing countries, relative to conventional import-substitution or export-promotion programmes. Transforming the rural economy from one of traditional subsistence agriculture to a diversified rural sector that produces for national and international markets requires a supporting system of human settlements. Intermediate-sized towns can efficiently provide services for a modernized rural economy and process some agricultural commodities, with increased employment opportunities for rural emigrants.[1]

A. TRENDS IN THE GROWTH AND FUNCTION OF URBAN AREAS

Urban population has been growing faster than total population in all parts of the world, especially in the developing countries, and this trend is expected to continue through the 1990s and beyond. Although the very large "megacities" in developing countries show some signs of decrease in their growth rates, their populations are rapidly passing the levels of many of the largest urban areas in the developed countries. The rate of population growth in large cities (i.e., those with a population of 2 million or more) in the developing countries is on the average 3 times the rate in the developed countries, due to higher rates of natural increase and immigration. In 1985, there were 100 cities or urban areas in the world with over 2 million residents; 30 had a population of 5 million or more and 11 had 10 million or more. By the year 2000, the number of urban areas in the world with over 5 million inhabitants is expected to reach 45, and 34 will be in the developing regions (see figure 10.1). There is little evidence to indicate that the largest projected "megacities" will be technically unmanageable, despite fears to the contrary. Nevertheless, revised policies and administrative mechanisms for urban expansion and operation are badly needed to improve their efficiency and livability, or at least to maintain the present levels.

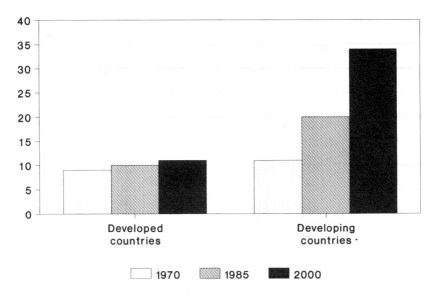

Figure 10.1 **Number of cities (urban areas) with more than 5 million people, 1970 - 2000**

□ 1970 ▨ 1985 ■ 2000

* including China

The rate of urban population increase in both developed and developing countries appears to decline slightly as the population of an urban area increases. While the growth rate of urban areas with more than 2 million inhabitants generally exceeds that of the total population, it tends to be lower than that of the total urban population. Taken together, the four agglomerations with 10 million or more people in the developed countries, namely, Tokyo/Yokohama, New York, London, and Los Angeles, had an average annual growth rate of 0.73 per cent from 1980 to 1985 and an expected growth rate of 0.72 per cent between 1985 and 1990. The growth rates of the total urban population in their countries (Japan, the United States, and the United Kingdom) are 0.85 and 0.67 per cent for the two periods respectively. In the developed countries as a whole, the total urban growth rate was 1.0 per cent from 1980 to 1985 and is estimated at 0.87 per cent from 1985 to 1990.

The seven agglomerations with 10 million or more people in 1985 in the developing countries—namely Mexico City, Sao Paulo, Shanghai, Calcutta, Buenos Aires, Rio de Janeiro, and Seoul—had an average annual growth rate of 2.8 per cent between 1980 and 1985; a growth rate of 2.4 per cent from 1985 to 1990 is expected. The total urban population in the six countries containing these seven cities grew at 2.9 per cent annually from 1980 to 1985 and was expected to grow at 3.0 per cent between 1985 to 1990. These rates are compared with 3.6 per cent in both periods for the developing countries as a whole. The same pattern holds for the agglomerations with 5 to 9.9 million inhabitants (6 in the developed countries and 13 in the developing countries).

The demographic trends associated with urbanization and rural-urban migration should be interpreted as propelled by changing economic forces. Most developing countries are rapidly changing from a predominantly agrarian economy to an economy in which urban centres play a predominant role. About 70 per cent of the GDP on the average in developing countries is already generated by towns and cities, and this figure is expected to increase somewhat by the end of the century.[2] At the same time, the agrarian economy is shifting to more market-oriented production using modern technologies, and the growing presence of foreign firms generates direct and indirect demand for urban services that meet international standards.

The decline of traditional sectors of industry in the predominantly urban economies of many developed countries has affected the fiscal base and the social and physical environment in many of their older cities. Fiscal incentives and new communication and information technologies have reduced the traditional advantages of large cities as locations for economic activity. Large numbers of affluent workers and retired people have moved to smaller urban centres that offer advantages of climate and amenity. Thus, the shift towards a service and high-technology economy has been accompanied by the location of new economic activity in the suburbs and small and medium-sized cities. This is producing large shifts in the geographic structure of the population and in the age structure of the urban population.

Continuation of the trend towards dispersal of settlements seems likely, and this trend will not necessarily be restricted to industrialized countries. The infrastructure is not likely to be in place for this to have a dramatic influence in the developing countries by the year 2000. But if renewable-energy technologies become more practical, they could allow the development of new settlement patterns to accommodate the rapidly increasing urban population in the developing countries, and the decay of older urban centres could become a preoccupying policy issue in the future.

B. HOUSING CONDITIONS[3]

1. Developed market economies

The quantity and quality of housing is generally satisfactory in most of the developed market economies, where a rough degree of parity has been attained between households and the number of dwellings. Housing conditions have markedly improved in all of the developed market economies since the end of the Second World War. The rate of housing construction has been higher than population growth and household formation. The result is that the scarcity of dwellings that existed after the War has been almost completely eliminated. Most of the developed market economies had over 400 dwellings per 1,000 inhabitants by 1985. As housing shortages became less of a problem, countries shifted gradually from quantity to quality objectives in housing policy.[4] In some countries, virtually the entire population is adequately housed, and social-mix objectives have been largely attained. In other countries, some families are "overhoused" while others are in desperate need. Distortions created by restrictive legislation and certain tax relief measures have aggravated the situation.

In countries where there are still shortages of good quality housing, as in some large cities of the Mediterranean region and in Japan, new construction accounts for the bulk of housing investment. In others where there is an adequate supply of standard housing, in particular several of the Nordic countries, investment in the maintenance and modernization of the existing stock exceeds that of new construction. Infrastructure needs have also gained more attention in recent years, for example the improvement and repair of aging systems in much of Europe and the expansion of insufficient networks in Japan. An acute shortage of inexpensive rental accommodations has also emerged in some large cities.

During most of the post-war period, per capita incomes rose more rapidly than housing costs. Income-maintenance schemes helped to assure most households of a steady disposable income over their lifetime. Access to home ownership was made easier through housing finance innovations, tax relief measures and, in some countries, the large-scale production of homogeneous, moderate-cost, suburban housing. In the 1970s and 1980s, however, costs of housing and financing have outpaced the rise in household incomes in some countries. High unemployment levels in many countries have made growing numbers of people dependent on government assistance to ensure that they are adequately housed. Post-war prosperity and welfare support mechanisms have encouraged the formation of smaller households, such as those consisting of elderly persons and single-parent families who had not previously been prone to living alone. More recently, however, many of these households have had lower incomes relative to housing costs, increasing the number of people with affordability problems in some countries. Such changes in household composition and incomes have increased the demand and need for a greater supply of inexpensive accommodation in a number of countries.

The construction of new dwellings is expected to continue outpacing the formation of new households in the developed market economies in the 1990s (see table 10.3). But many low-income and even moderate-income households will face increasing difficulty in finding affordable housing. This is particularly the case in large metropolitan centres with high costs for land and construction and in cities of various sizes where rent controls and other development restrictions discourage the production of new, moderate-priced housing. Rent control and home-owner tax relief measures could be largely replaced by direct subsidies to low-income households for a more efficient and equitable use of public funds and the housing stock. Tax allowances might be limited to first-time buyers for the first several years only. The revenues obtained by limiting tax relief for homeowners could pay for the direct subsidies given to needy occupants of rent-deregulated premises. Such reforms might slow the rate of growth in housing prices and reduce distortions in housing investment by placing the returns on investment on a more even footing with owner-occupied housing. This could induce an increased supply of rental premises. Some tenants would move to accommodations that better suited their current needs and circumstances, activating the filtering-down of the older, formerly regulated rental stock. This would facilitate labour mobility and help to meet the residential needs of low-income households and some of the homeless.

2. Eastern Europe and the USSR

Housing conditions in most of Eastern Europe and the Soviet Union are much better than they used to be. Since the end of the Second World War, these countries have invested up to 5 or 6 per cent of their net material product in housing. This was done to meet the needs of rapid urbanization and industrialization, to replace substandard housing, and to replace residential stock destroyed during the War. As a result, over 85 per cent of the population of the Soviet Union and two thirds of the population of Hungary, to take two examples, live in accommodations built after the War. By 1985, all but two of these countries had reached a level of 300 dwellings or more per thousand inhabitants. A few countries, in particular, the German Democratic Republic, have nearly achieved their goal of housing all of their population adequately, whereas others have waiting lists of various lengths for State-supplied dwellings and housing co-operative units.

Despite this progress, insufficient housing is still considered to be one of the most pressing social problems in those countries where housing has chronically been in short supply. The shortage of sufficient residential accommodation manifests itself in overcrowding and the intergenerational sharing of premises, which in turn are believed to contribute to lower birth rates and to the rise in divorce among young couples. As the disposable incomes of households increase and their expectations grow, complaints about the scarcity of housing have been more frequent.

The improvements in housing construction, amenities, and floor space per capita achieved over the past several decades in part reflect the evolution of government policies and the growing diversification in housing supply. The supply includes public rental apartments, co-operative housing, and individually owned dwelling units. The options thereby provided have enlarged the financial base of housing through increased use of family savings, in accordance with the income levels of different population strata.

During the past few years, these countries have tried to encourage residential construction by enterprises, co-operatives, and individuals, but housing production has nonetheless declined sharply in a number of countries during the 1980s. The burden of economic adjustment that has resulted from stagnating growth, shifting terms of trade, external debt servicing, and higher energy costs has fallen largely on investment targets in housing and other sectors. With the exception of the German Democratic Republic, all of these countries have been lagging in the construction of new dwelling units compared to the number of households formed annually through marriages and divorces. The situation is even more critical when the backlog of accumulated demand is taken into account. The time spent on waiting lists for an apartment, according to national sources, is about five years in Czechoslovakia, 4 to 10 years in Hungary, and 15 to 30 years in Poland. Waiting lists may overstate the demand for new construction, to the extent that they contain small households occupying large premises and big families in small flats. Single adults wishing to split off from extended families or commuters living at the edge of major cities who would like to obtain accommodations closer to the centre, generally may not place their names on waiting lists. In Bulgaria, the German Democratic Republic, and Hungary, among others, preferential housing allocation is made to young families with children, partly as an inducement to reverse falling birth rates. Other groups with special needs, such as the handi-capped, are also often placed on shorter lists.

Despite large allocations of resources to the housing sector, housing deficits have not been eliminated. In fact, the gap appears to be widening in most of these countries. Approaches to housing policy that supply housing at greatly subsidized rentals appear to be at the root of much of the problem. Some countries have introduced options recognizing the capacity and willingness of households to save and to supply self-help labour to obtain hous-ing. Many households are willing to pay more for housing and even to participate in its construction if they can obtain accom-modations more rapidly. The relatively successful implementation of these and other policies suggests that their wider use over a number of years could greatly reduce housing shortages.[5]

3. Developing countries

The nature and scale of the housing problems in developing coun-tries are poorly understood. A lack of basic data on the number of existing dwelling units, or on housing quality, tenure, and the number of units added to or retired annually from the stock, makes it difficult to assess whether housing conditions have improved or worsened in many of these countries. The limited available evidence suggests a decline in average shelter conditions since the 1970s. In many cities, 40 to 50 per cent of the people live in slums or squatter settlements. Some of these settlements have been growing at rates up to 20 per cent per year. An estimated 1 billion people were living in very poor quality housing in the early 1980s, and this number may well double by the year 2000. Past commitments by Governments to provide affordable housing have been eroded by economic and financial difficulties in many countries, with resulting reductions in public expenditure for shelter, and by policies that led to inefficient forms of both public and private expenditure.

The construction of new permanent dwellings, in relation to the increase in the number of households in a sample of 45 developing countries, has been highly correlated with their levels of per capita income and investment.[6] During the early 1980s, the ratio in the low-income countries was less than one new permanent dwelling for every 10 additional households; the ratio in the middle-income countries was four new dwellings for 10 households, and in the higher-income countries it was 9 for 10. Thus, about 90 per cent of the additional households in the low-income countries had to double up in existing shelter or find new, temporary shelter, typically in squatter settlements lacking adequate water supply and sanitation. Although the situation in the higher-income countries was more satisfactory, their construction of permanent dwellings was not enough to accommodate all of the additional households, nor to allow for replacement of the oldest stock or for rural-urban migration.

In recent years, rented housing has accounted for one quarter to two thirds of the housing market of large cities in the developing market economies. It has increased in response to increases in land values that prevent squatting and inexpensive owner-occupancy. In the worst cases, mostly in inner-city tenements, several households share a single room, or alternate with one another in day and night shifts. Local authorities are partly responsible for overcrowded conditions, especially where they forbid informal construction yet enforce rent controls that discourage new construction. Many housing banks and other public and private financial institutions have been unwilling to devise new policies and programmes adapted to the real needs and opportunities in the potential markets for low-cost housing.

If present policies on informal housing construction continue along with low investment and economic growth, little increase in the ratio of new permanent authorized dwellings to new house-holds is expected for the low-income developing countries. Only moderate improvements (one new unit for every two additional households) is projected for the middle-income countries by the late 1990s (see table 10.3). With higher investment and economic growth rates, the supply of permanent housing could improve for both groups of countries, compared to the baseline projection, but still leave about 90 per cent of the new households in the low-income countries without access to permanent dwellings. The outlook is much better in the high-income developing countries, even with slow economic growth.

In view of the shortage and high cost of officially authorized permanent housing, developing countries have to make better use of the informal housing sector. Informal subdivisions have already gained a large share of the housing markets in many developing countries. They are typically supplied by developers who illegally purchase and subdivide unserviced land at the urban periphery. Infrastructure and service usually are not supplied until well after many of the dwellings have been built. Despite the interim hard-ship, the delay enables households to phase their expenditures in a more affordable way. Compared to their previous living con-ditions, informal subdivisions provide more space and privacy to both owner-occupants and tenants, and more infrastructure and services. The quality of housing (shelter and related services) pro-duced in the informal sector varies with per capita income and government policies. Where policies are supportive of the estab-lishment and upgrading of informal housing, the quality difference between authorized and informal housing is often small. Increased security of tenure and public supply of water and other services have catalysed substantial investment in informal land develop-ment and shelter. However, lack of maintenance of infrastructure is a serious failing of many government-sponsored upgrading programmes.

As a general rule, owners spend more on housing than renters at given income levels. For many low-income home-owners, housing is less important as a source of shelter than as a productive investment for supplementary income. Opportunities to install a small business or rent auxiliary units and expectations of growing house and land prices and values give a substantial premium to owner-occupancy. Since rapidly rising land prices and falling incomes make the transition from renting to ownership far more difficult than it used to be, owner-occupant landlords have a useful role in accommodating the rapidly growing numbers of urban poor. Whereas large-scale absentee landlords sometimes exploit their tenants, owner-occupants tend to have close social ties with the tenants who share their house. They are usually more concerned with minimizing tenant turnover than with maximizing rents.

In the upgrading of informal settlements, if standards are set high and full legal title is given, many of the poorest occupants sell out or subdivide their plot and sell part of it. Poor tenants may be forced out by higher rents, and replaced by households with higher incomes. The growing presence of middle-class households in informal settlements and subdivisions is likely to induce government officials to take more initiative in supplying and regularizing services. Where service standards are low and a title or lease is not provided, the cost of housing does not increase very much, nor is the area improved enough to attract the middle class. Instead, limited upgrading induces the residents to remain and to improve their dwellings to earn rental income.

4. China

As in Eastern Europe and the Soviet Union, most of China's urban housing stock is supplied by the Government, either directly or through government-owned enterprises. More than 96 per cent of urban housing units have piped water and electricity and 34 per cent have toilets, according to a survey conducted in 1985. Typical shelter consists of one or two rooms per family, often with shared kitchen and bathroom facilities. Faced with an estimated shortage of 14 million dwellings in urban areas in 1982, China increased the share of housing from about 10 per cent of total State investment in the 1970s to more than 20 per cent in the early 1980s. Funds invested by enterprises accounted for 60 per cent of the total investment in urban housing.

Rents and utility charges have been gradually increased in conjunction with price reforms, especially for households occupying more space than deemed necessary. Revised policies seek to encourage households to invest in new dwelling units, with payment responsibility typically divided about equally between the State, the individual buyer, and the employer. The high cost of energy has led China to allow the use of light, weight-bearing clay bricks to supply the large volume of building materials needed. Reinforced concrete materials are also produced on a large scale, since they are easy to use and less expensive than steel or wood.

C. POLICIES FOR SETTLEMENTS DEVELOPMENT AND MANAGEMENT IN DEVELOPING COUNTRIES IN THE 1990s

Because so much urban growth in the developing countries is still to come and because community patterns are evolving rapidly, their Governments have a great opportunity to revise their policies so as to promote more flexible and efficient urban forms and functions. There is a noticeable trend towards decentralization of central-government powers and functions to lower-level administrative units. The effectiveness of such arrangements requires adequate financial resources and trained personnel for these units. In some developed countries, many municipal services might be provided more cheaply and efficiently by the private sector, and government perhaps should not be a direct producer of shelter. In developed and developing countries, Governments are reconsidering their roles in the light of the potential contributions of the formal and informal private sectors, community groups, cooperatives, and non-governmental organizations.

In the past, training programmes concerned with settlements

in the developing countries were aimed at public agencies that wanted conventionally trained administrators, architects, engineers, and public health personnel. The programmes were based on often inappropriate models from the industrialized countries. In many cases, this situation continues. Training programmes in the 1960s and 1970s began to advocate that planners focus more on the intended beneficiaries of settlements development and target their efforts so as to reduce inequities. In the 1980s, budgetary constraints and growing concern with optimization of resource use have led to increased attention to cost-effectiveness. As settlements development has gained increasing importance in national economic policies, the need to reconcile national and regional policies with local planning and local initiatives has become more urgent. The potential roles of self-help and the informal sector call for related modifications in training.

The Global Strategy for Shelter to the Year 2000 was adopted by the United Nations General Assembly in 1988 (resolution 43/181, para. 1). It emphasizes that Governments can indirectly improve housing conditions and can use the housing sector to renew economic growth by encouraging rather than hindering informal housing investments, by providing basic infrastructure and security of land tenure to informal subdivisions, and by removing rent restrictions from owner-occupied housing. Such an approach could create work for the underemployed, stimulate greater production of building materials, reduce housing capital-output ratios, lead to more efficient use of land and infrastructure, and be paid for by the residents themselves. By tapping the potential entrepreneurship, savings, and other underused resources of the informal sector, revised policies on shelter could reduce the pressure to draw on formal-sector resources needed for other parts of the economy.

NOTES

1. For a more extensive discussion of a number of the issues reviewed in this section, see *Global Report on Human Settlements, 1986*, published by Oxford Uni-

versity Press for the United Nations Centre for Human Settlements (Habitat), 1987.

2.   In 1985 about 19 per cent of GDP was in manufacturing and 47 per cent in services in the developing countries; cities also would account for a large share of the 8 per cent in construction and utilities. The percentages projected for the year 2000 are about 23 in manufacturing, 46 in services and 9 in construction and utilities.

3.   For a more detailed discussion of the issues reviewed in this section, see United Nations, *Housing and Economic Adjustment*, Taylor and Francis, New York and Philadelphia, 1989. (ISBN 0-8448-1564-0).

4.   By 1980, nearly all dwellings had a kitchen; more than 9 dwellings in 10 had piped water; more than 8 in 10 had a flush toilet; and more than 7 in 10 had a fixed bath or shower. Partly as a result of the cultural and demographic trend towards smaller-sized households, the average number of persons per room fell by 11 per cent, from 0.74 to 0.66, between 1970 and 1980.

5.   For a more detailed discussion of policy options in the centrally planned economies, see *Housing and Economic Adjustment, op. cit.*, pp. 37–49.

6.   Permanent housing is defined by the United Nations Statistical Office as dwellings constructed well enough to last for 10 years. Although they do not necessarily have safe water supply or adequate sanitation, in most developing countries the only data collected on a systematic basis are limited to authorized dwelling units that have clear title and comply with zoning regulations and building code standards. Such data tend to exaggerate estimates of housing "deficits" based on the arbitrary distinction between authorized and informal dwellings. The data can provide a limited indication of varying housing conditions and trends in different groups of countries.

TABLE 10.1 *Construction and other investment as percentage of gross fixed capital formation*[a]

Country group	Residential buildings			Non-residential buildings and others[b]			Total construction			Producer durables, etc.[c]		
	1970	1980	1985	1970	1980	1985	1970	1980	1985	1970	1980	1985
Developing countries												
North Africa	15	12	15	48	55	55	56	52	55	44	47	45
Sub-Saharan Africa	20	12	20	53	50	60	71	62	55	29	38	45
South and East Asia	14	15	18	43	37	37	57	52	55	43	48	45
South Asia	13	16	18	50	37	34	63	52	53	37	47	47
East Asian newly industrializing economies	14	16	19	37	34	38	51	49	57	48	51	43
Others	15	13	15	31	40	39	46	53	55	54	47	45
Western Asia	30	28	27	38	45	44	64	73	70	36	27	30
Mediterranean	20	26	15	46	41	38	65	67	52	34	33	47
Latin America and the Caribbean	23	20	22	37	37	36	60	61	64	44	39	40
Total, developing countries	20	20	22	43	41	41	60	60	62	40	40	38
Least developed countries	26	16	22	32	48	46	50	62	62	50	38	38
Developed market economies	23	25	23	36	35	33	59	60	57	41	40	43

Source: United Nations Secretariat, Department of International Economic and Social Affairs, *based on country data compiled by the Statistical Office of the Department.*

[a] Country group percentages are weighted by gross fixed capital formation in the individual countries.
[b] Including infrastructure and land improvement.
[c] Equals total gross fixed capital formation (100 per cent) minus total construction.

TABLE 10.2 *Urban areas with more than 5 million inhabitants,*
1970–2000

Year	Number of urban areas with more than 5 million inhabitants			Percentage of total urban population in such areas		
	World	Developed countries	Developing countries[a]	World	Developed countries	Developing countries[a]
1970	20	9	11	12.2	12.2	12.2
1985	30	10	20	14.0	12.1	15.3
2000	45	11	34	16.2	12.3	18.1

Source: United Nations Secretariat, Department of International Economic and Social Affairs, based on Prospects of World Urbanization 1988, *New York, 1989 (United Nations publication, ST/ESA/SER.A/112), tables A.9 and A.1.*

[a] *Including China.*

TABLE 10.3 *Housing construction in relation to the increase in the number of households, 1970–1999*[a]

Country group	1970–1974	1975–1979	1980–1984	1985–1989	1990–1994	1995–1999	Number of countries	1980 population (millions)
Developing countries								
North Africa	0.26	0.56	0.78	0.78	0.80	0.85	3	67
Sub-Saharan Africa	0.15	0.11	0.10	0.08	0.07	0.07	8	159
South and East Asia								
East Asian newly industrializing economies	0.72	0.79	0.63	0.84	1.17	1.59	3	46
Others	0.14	0.37	0.09	0.07	0.09	0.09	4	67
Western Asia	0.58	0.85	0.81	0.71	0.67	0.62	5	65
Mediterranean	1.11	1.06	0.95	0.91	0.99	1.10	4	68
Latin America and the Caribbean	0.26	0.25	0.28	0.24	0.26	0.32	18	221
Total, developing countries	0.42	0.53	0.41	0.38	0.41	0.45	45	693
Least developed countries	0.17	0.04	0.05	0.05	0.04	0.05	3	45
Developed market economies, total	2.44	1.45	1.21	1.43	1.75	2.23	25	768
South Africa	0.37	0.24	0.26	0.19	0.19	0.20	1	29
Eastern Europe & the USSR	1.77	1.37	1.31	1.49	1.70	1.83	7	375

Source: United Nations Secretariat, Department of International Economic and Social Affairs, Construction Statistics Yearbook 1984, *New York, 1986 (United Nations publication, Sales No. E.86.XVII.20) and earlier volumes, and United Nations Secretariat, Department of International Economic and Social Affairs, "Estimates and projections of the number of households by country, 1975–2000" (ESA/P/WP.73), annex tables 1 and 5.*

[a] *Calculated as the ratio of the sum of permanent new dwelling units reported during the calendar years indicated, divided by the projected net increase in the total number of households in those years.*

11.

Education

EDUCATION, especially primary schooling for literacy, is a major goal of development. It is also a means for achieving the inter-related goals of health, higher labour productivity, more rapid GDP growth, and the broader goal of social integration, including participation in cultural and political affairs.[1]

The proportion of illiterates among the adult population has steadily decreased, but the absolute number has grown. There is increasing concern about the functional quality of literacy in both developed and developing countries. A population with a high proportion of illiterates is poorly prepared to cope with modern technology. In addition to basic literacy and numeracy, schools should also teach some of the knowledge and methods essential for participation in a modern economy, including the agricultural sector.[2] The more advanced levels of education are increasingly important to enable individuals and countries to understand and participate in the technological and administrative processes of the modern global economy. In practice most Governments have not given education top priority as a development objective. Some countries have made great efforts, however, and have reduced illiteracy very quickly. Great uncertainty prevails about the economic prospects of many specific investment projects, but the role of education and human capital formation in development stands out more clearly than ever.[3]

A. RETURNS ON INVESTMENT

The private rate of return on the investment cost of all levels of education is generally high, especially in developing countries, reflecting in part government subsidization of education. This has stimulated the demand for access to education. The social rate of return to education, although consistently lower than the corresponding private return, is generally no less than average rates of return on fixed capital investments. Using this criterion, developing countries underinvest in education.

But estimates of both private and social rates of return, the majority based on cross-section estimates of private earnings streams, have to be treated with caution. Earnings differences between people with different educational levels may be attributable to other individual characteristics, such as intelligence, determination, and social or political status, rather than or in addition to their level of education. On the other hand, such estimates may understate the external effects of education. Examples are the beneficial effects of educated people on the productivity of those around them or on the health of their families and the power of education to enrich people's lives.

Country studies carried out mostly in the 1970s and earlier suggest that the rate of return on primary education in the developing countries has been higher than the return to second-level and third-level education, at least in the past (table 11.1). A more recent analysis[4] of two countries in Africa, however, suggests that as average education levels increase over time, the marginal rates of return to the different levels (i.e., the lifetime rates of return for new entrants into the labour force) tend to converge rapidly towards the narrower and lower range observed for the second and third levels in the developed countries. Two or three decades ago, workers with only a primary education were still quite scarce in many developing countries and were able to obtain a large share of the relatively high-paying jobs in the industrial and government sectors. Now, however, most of these jobs require replacement workers with a second-level or even a third-level education.

A related question is the relative value of completing all or just part of primary education. A case study of agriculture in three regions of Peru in the early 1980s found that the impact of a full six years of primary education varied greatly according to the region's level of development. After allowing for other factors, such as access to extension service, credit, and improved seeds, completion of six years increased the productivity of the farmers in the most advanced region by about one third. In the intermediate region, completion of at least four years implied "an increase of about 15 per cent in output as compared to farmers with less than four years of education," but completion of all six years did not show any greater effect than just four or five years. Completion of at least one year in the most traditional region was helpful, compared with having no schooling at all, but there was no further advantage from completing all six years.[5]

The social return to expansion of primary education in agrarian societies depends largely on its effects on the productivity of peasant farmers. The evidence suggests that this in turn depends on whether farmers are operating in a traditional or a modernizing environment, i.e., one in which change is rapid. Education assists farmers to obtain and evaluate information about improved technology and new economic opportunities and thus to innovate. The level of education required depends on the levels of technology currently in use and potentially suitable. Education being complementary to other inputs, its value cannot be assessed in isolation. It depends on the degree of access to credit, extension services, new seeds, and other inputs. The greatest impact on rural development can thus be made where education is part of a package of measures.[6]

B. LITERACY, SCHOOL ENROLMENT AND PER CAPITA INCOME

Illiteracy is largely a result of inadequate enrolment in school, as well as the absence of large-scale adult literacy programmes. In 1985 about 135 million children aged 6–11 were not enrolled in school in the developing countries, including China. The number is expected to increase in Africa and the least developed countries by the year 2000, while falling in Asia and Latin America (see table 11.2). The proportion not enrolled should fall from 26 per cent in 1985 to 18 per cent in 2000, and the total number is projected to remain well over 100 million. For the 12–17 age group, the number of out-of-school was almost 290 million in the developing countries in 1985, and is projected to remain above 260 million in the year 2000. The number is expected to increase in Africa and the least developed countries but to fall in Asia and Latin America. The proportion not enrolled would decline from 56 per cent in 1985 to 44 per cent in the year 2000 in the developing countries.

In the developed countries, the number of out-of-school youth would continue to decrease. Moreover, the enrolment figures exclude part-time vocational education, which is important in some industrialized countries. Also, at these ages most of the out-of-school youth in the developed countries have completed primary and part of secondary education as well.

Children may be out of school (not enrolled) because there are not enough places in nearby schools or adequate transport to more distant ones, especially in rural areas or because their families cannot afford the fees or the forgone income that the children can earn.[7] Some traditional cultures still discourage school attendance, especially by girls. Drop-outs include children rejected by the school as failures or withdrawn by their parents, and children who drift from absence into drop-out. Some children do not go beyond primary school because their parents regard basic literacy and numeracy as sufficient school-based skills. For others, places in second level education are not available; this group in many countries is growing rapidly. Some children have not yet entered school but will enter later (e.g., six-year-olds in a system where the starting age is seven).

Out-of-school youth in many countries, both developing and developed, face a lack of early employment possibilities. In Argentina, Brazil, Ecuador, Honduras, and Panama, computations drawn from census samples show a sharp increase in the proportion of young adults aged 24–34 with post-primary education in the labour force. Although Colombia had enrolment rates below the Latin American median during the years 1960–1985 for the 6–11 age group and around the median for the 12–17 group, by the year 2000 more than half of its total labour force—including the rural component—are expected to have secondary or post-secondary education.[8]

Poorer countries generally have lower rates of school enrolment and literacy. Public funds to provide teachers and schools are lacking. Many children drop out early, usually to work in low-skilled jobs where they tend to lose whatever literacy they have attained because it is not used in their work or at home or reinforced by any kind of literacy maintenance programme.

Literacy rates have risen considerably since 1970, but the number of illiterate adults (persons aged 15 years and over) in the world increased from 760 million in 1970 to more than 960 million in 1985, of which 910 million were in the developing countries. Nine countries accounted for three quarters of the total and India and China for well over half (see table 11.3). UNESCO projects that there will be about 920 million illiterates in the developing countries in the year 2000, even though the literacy rate for the group as a whole will increase from 61 per cent in 1985 to 72 per cent in the year 2000.[9]

The relation between per capita income and literacy is quite obvious. By 1985 the higher-income developing countries had reached literacy rates of 85 per cent or more for adult males and

70 per cent or more for females. In the lower income groups less than 65 per cent of the adult males and less than 40 per cent of the adult females were literate. In the least developed group only 47 per cent of adult males and 27 per cent of adult females were literate (see table 11.4).

In 1985, the literacy rate was lowest in South Asia followed by North and sub-Saharan Africa and Western Asia. Females had lower rates of literacy than males in all developing regions: the difference was at least 20 percentage points in Africa and 26 in South Asia. It was smaller in the East Asian newly industrializing countries and in Latin America and the Caribbean and was only 1 (one) percentage point in the developed regions. Literacy rates in the developing countries were higher for the 15–24 age group (79 per cent for males and 67 per cent for females in 1985) than for the entire adult population, but still low enough to indicate that adult illiteracy is likely to remain a major problem in the 1990s and beyond. This is especially so in the least developed countries, where the 15–24 age group literacy rate was estimated to be only 36 per cent for females and 58 per cent for males.[10] In Bangladesh, only 20 per cent of the pupils entering primary education emerge literate.[11]

Most of the developed countries have literacy rates above 95 per cent, after several decades of universal primary education, and can be considered as having eradicated illiteracy. However, modern life is demanding ever higher levels of skills in all countries and many of the developed countries are concerned with the pervasive problem of functional illiteracy.

In the few low-income areas where universal primary education was started several decades ago as in Sri Lanka, literacy rates are high. But higher per capita income levels in other areas have allowed greater expenditures for education and, as a result, generally large increases in enrolment and literacy rates. Many of the higher-income developing countries reached gross enrolment rates of 100 per cent or more[12] for primary school during the 1970s, and several regions have had gross rates above 100 per cent for males and 90 per cent for females since 1980 or before (see table 11.5).

   Dramatic increases in primary enrolment in lower-income regions were achieved in the 1970s. In the 1980s, the gross enrolment
rate in South Asia continued to improve, although the rate for
girls remained far below the rate for boys. The average rates for
both sexes fell back in sub-Saharan Africa: among the 41 sub-
Saharan countries for which data were available, from 1980 to
1985 the enrolment rate for boys fell in 22 countries and the rate
for girls fell in 18, while remaining stable or increasing in the
others. In the 31 sub-Saharan countries for which more recent
data are available, after 1985, the enrolment rate for boys has fallen
in 13 of them and for girls in 15 of them.

C. SECOND-LEVEL AND THIRD-LEVEL
ENROLMENT

The number of students enrolled in all types of second-level education, in relation to the official second-level school-age population, typically ages 12 to 17, increased from about 35 per cent
for the world as a whole in 1970 to 45 per cent in 1985, responding
to the high rates of private and social return noted above. Second-
level gross enrolment rates increased by at least 10 percentage
points in most regions from 1970 to 1985 for both males and
females. The largest increases (more than 20 percentage points)
were for females in North Africa, Western Asia, and Latin America and the Caribbean; and for males in Africa and Western Asia.
In sub-Saharan Africa, however, the average rates for both males
and females fell back in a number of countries after 1985. The
second-level gross enrolment rate has increased very little in percentage points in the least developed group, reaching only 10 per
cent for females and 20 per cent for males in 1985, compared with
6 and 15 per cent, respectively, in 1970.[13]
   In contrast, in three of the East Asian newly industrializing
economies, enrolment surged from 33 to 85 per cent for females
and from 49 to 89 per cent for males, almost reaching the average

Figure 11.1 Secondary school gross enrolment rates
in the developing countries and China
1970, 1985 and 2000

Enrolment as % of
population aged 12-17 **

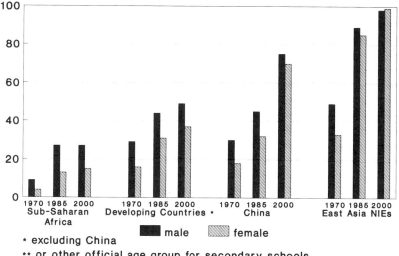

* excluding China

** or other official age group for secondary schools
in some countries

92 per cent rate in the developed market countries. (see figure 11.1).

The third-level gross enrolment rate (defined as gross enrolment divided by population aged 20 to 24) increased from 9.6 per cent to 12.9 per cent in the world as a whole from 1970 to 1985. The largest increases, by sex and type of country, were for males in the East Asian newly industrializing economies—from 11 per cent in 1970 to 41 per cent in 1985, surpassing the rate for males in the developed market economies; and for females in the developed market economies, from 20 to 38 per cent (see figure 11.2). In North America the average rate for females and males combined has been above 50 per cent since the middle of the 1970s, reaching 57 per cent by 1985. This compares with about 30 per cent in the other developed market economies and the East Asian newly industrializing economies, 20 per cent in the developed planned economies, 16 per cent in Latin America and the

Figure 11.2 **Third-level (college/university) gross enrolment rates, 1970-2000**

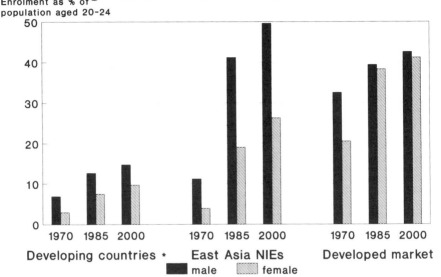

Enrolment as % of population aged 20-24

* excluding China

Caribbean, less than 10 per cent in South and Western Asia and less than 3 per cent in sub-Saharan Africa and the least developed countries. The disparity between the male and female enrolment rates increased in Africa and Asia from 1970 to 1985; in Latin America and the Caribbean, it narrowed slightly. In most of the developed countries approximate equality was achieved by 1985, and in North America the female enrolment ratio was 7 points higher than that for males.

Despite relatively large increases since 1970, third-level enrolment rates remain extremely low for both males and females in sub-Saharan Africa and the least developed countries. This suggests that the poorer regions will continue to lack people with higher skills needed to absorb new technologies from the developed regions and generate appropriate new ones suitable to their needs. Low domestic enrolment is supplemented to some extent by enrolment in foreign universities. Around 1985 there were about 650,000 third-level students from developing countries, including China, in 50 host countries, including 167,000 students from Africa, about 67,000 from Latin America and the Caribbean, and 410,000 from Asia. The developed countries attracted the large majority of these students.[14] For comparison, domestic third level enrolment in the developing countries (including China) was about 27 million in 1986: 18 million in Asia, 7 million in Latin America and the Caribbean, and 2 million in Africa.[15]

D. ENROLMENT IN PRIVATE SCHOOLS

Children in private schools (defined as schools not operated by a public authority) accounted for about 7 per cent of primary enrolment and 12 per cent of secondary general enrolment during 1975–1985. These enrolments were in over 130 countries and territories with about 75 per cent of the world's total enrolment at these levels. The private share of primary enrolment was about the same in the developed market economies and the developing countries (11.4 versus 9.6 per cent) and zero in all the planned economies. At the secondary level the private share in the developing countries was about 29 per cent, far above the 14 per cent share in the developed countries, although it has declined from about 35 per cent in 1975. For both levels of education, the share of private enrolment varies greatly among countries. No private enrolment was reported at the primary level by 28 of the countries and none at the secondary level by 31 countries.[16]

Private schooling has maintained a significant share of total enrolment for several reasons. In some countries it is a response to excess demand, as tight budgetary constraints have prevented Governments from providing enough schools or teachers. With limited public provision, those who can afford it purchase education for their children. Strong demand for vocational training in some developed countries has led to initiatives by private providers. Various social groups wish to use education to maintain their sub-culture. As a result of such pressures, separate religious school systems, operating in parallel with the public, can be found in the Netherlands and Indonesia, for example. In a number of pluralist or multicultural societies, ethnic communities have begun to establish their own schools and to request subsidies from their Governments. Other causes of expansion of the private sector in some countries are policies favouring non-government schools in order to allow parents to exercise greater choice in the selection of schools for their children, or beliefs that a mixed economy of public and private schools, or even private schools alone, would be more effective (and less costly) than a public system.

E. EXPENDITURE ON EDUCATION

Education is financed and provided predominantly by government agencies in most countries. In recent years, adverse macroeconomic conditions and intensified competition for public funds have reduced the ability of many Governments to finance continued expansion of education, especially in the developing countries, while the willingness of households to pay direct fees for education has not been widely tapped. In some countries where the population is growing rapidly, enrolment ratios in primary schools have declined and might decline further. Despite the recent difficulties, many countries have managed to sustain the increase in enrolment. But primary school enrolment rates in many of the poorer developing countries are still low, and it has become more expensive to provide wider access to education and to combat illiteracy.[17]

In the world as a whole (124 countries), public expenditure on education represented 5.6 per cent of gross national product (GNP) in 1980 and 1985, compared to 5.1 per cent in 1970. The percentage spent by the developing countries rose from 3.6 per cent in 1970 to 3.9 per cent in 1980 and to 4.0 per cent in 1985. It increased in all regional groups from 1970 to 1985 except in the developing Mediterranean countries, where there were sharp declines in Turkey and Yugoslavia after 1980. In the least developed countries, it fluctuated from 2.9 per cent in 1970 to 2.6 per cent in 1980 and 2.8 per cent in 1985 (see table 11.6). Of these totals, capital expenditure was about 1 per cent of GNP in the developed countries and about 0.4 per cent in the developing countries.

Substantial absolute reductions in per capita spending from 1980 to 1985 occurred in a number of developing countries, but in most of them the 1985 levels were well above the 1970 levels. In 39 countries in sub-Saharan Africa (excluding Nigeria), the stagnation in GDP after 1980 slightly reduced the average level of public expenditure from $21 per capita in 1980 to $20 in 1985 (in constant 1980 dollars), after an increase from $19 in 1970[18] (see table 11.7). Even with the decline after 1980, however, spending per capita in sub-Saharan Africa in 1985 remained well above the level in South Asia and China, perhaps reflecting greater use of relatively high-salaried expatriate teachers in sub-Saharan Africa, along with greater scarcity of qualified nationals.

Private expenditure on education accounted for another few per cent of GDP in 19 developing countries for which data from the early 1980s are available. The share was above 2 per cent in several countries, and in South Korea it was about 4 per cent in 1985 (5.8 per cent of personal consumption)[19]. While much of this private expenditure is probably incurred by upper-income families, it does indicate a willingness to pay that Governments may wish to consider as they seek additional resources to expand enrolment, particularly in universities and other third-level institutions, and perhaps in secondary schools as well, which now prepare a small minority of the population for relatively high-income jobs.

F. PUBLIC EXPENDITURE PER STUDENT

Public spending per student for education typically is 50 to 100 per cent higher for secondary education than at the primary level and several times higher for third-level education (table 11.8). The differences would be even greater if students enrolled in private schools were excluded; the private share of enrolment is higher at the secondary level than at the primary level, especially in the developing countries. On the other hand, some of the public spending on education is used for partial support of private schooling in some countries, but data on this use are not generally available. In 1985, public spending per student in 1980 dollars was less than $35 for primary education in South Asia and the least developed countries. It averaged only $94 for the developing countries as a whole, compared with $150 for secondary education and $630 for the third level.

Compared with other regions, the spending per student is very high in sub-Saharan Africa in proportion to per capita GDP, especially for the second and third levels (see figure 11.3). Although the spending per third-level student in sub-Saharan Africa dropped from $3,000 in 1980 to $2,100 in 1985, it remained higher there than in all the other developing regions, even Western Asia. Much of this high spending on third-level education is for students' living allowances. In several of the poorest sub-Saharan countries, such allowances were "about one-half of the average salary in the public sector" in 1982, regardless of the students' need.[20] (In eight countries in Latin America and Southeast Asia, the poorest 40 per cent of the population received only 2 to 17 per cent of the total subsidies to higher education.[21]) At the primary and secondary levels, since pupil-teacher ratios are considerably higher in Africa than in the other major regions,[22] the relatively high spending per student implies very high average spending per teacher relative to GDP per capita. This spending is mainly for salaries and other benefits received by the teachers and other personnel in the education system. These categories account for 60 to 90 per cent of the total in most of the developing countries. Two interesting exceptions are the United Republic of Tanzania and Bangladesh, where only about 35 per cent was spent on teachers' salaries and benefits. In the United Republic of Tanzania an unusually large share (30 per cent) was spent on teaching materials and scholarships in 1979; Bangladesh spent less than 1

Figure 11.3 **Public school cost (current expenditure) per student as % of per capita GDP, 1985**

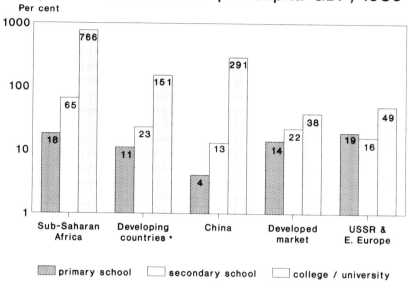

* excluding China

per cent on these categories, but spent 21 per cent on "school meals and board" and other welfare services in 1985.[23]

G. PROJECTION OF ENROLMENT TRENDS

Future enrolment rates will depend on the changing size of the school-age population and on the evolving levels of per capita spending for the different levels of education. Given the relatively poor outlook for economic growth in sub-Saharan Africa and the least developed countries and the high spending per student relative to per capita GDP in many of these countries, it will be necessary to reduce spending per student and/or to increase the share of GDP devoted to education. This is the only feasible way they can reach the goal of universal primary-school enrolment and have adequate second- and third-level enrolment to provide the skills needed for economic and social development.

Projections of first-, second- and third-level enrolment rates for females and males in 1990 and the year 2000 have been based on the trends in enrolment in primary and secondary schools and in universities and other post-secondary training, and on the relation between enrolment rates and GDP per capita from 1970 to 1985. Under the baseline scenario for GDP growth from 1990 to the year 2000, the gross primary enrolment rate (including under-age and over-age children, as noted earlier) would reach 100 per cent or more for boys and over 90 per cent for girls by the year 2000 in almost all regions.[24] But in sub-Saharan Africa the average rate for girls would be only 75 per cent, and the rate for boys would be only 89 per cent. In the least developed countries the rates would be only 66 per cent for girls and 79 per cent for boys. As the net enrolment rates are likely to remain 10 to 20 percentage points lower than the gross rates, large shares and numbers of primary school-age children would remain unenrolled in these groups of countries.

If GDP growth were accelerated to annual rates 1 per cent above those assumed in the baseline scenario, and if a normal proportion of the incremental GDP were allocated to primary education, the gross primary enrolment rates in most of the developing countries in the year 2000 could be 1 to 3 percentage points higher than under the baseline projections. Enrolment rates would then reach about 77 per cent for girls and 91 per cent for boys in sub-Saharan Africa, and 69 per cent for girls and 81 per cent for boys in the least developed countries. To reach the goal of universal primary enrolment (a net enrolment rate of 100 per cent), at current costs per student, would require a significant increase in the allocation of resources to primary education. In sub-Saharan Africa, at least 20 countries would have to raise their spending on primary education. It is projected to be about 1.5 per cent of GDP in the baseline scenario, and it would have to be raised to 2.1 per cent to reach 100 per cent gross enrolment for boys and to 2.4 per cent to reach 100 per cent gross enrolment for girls. Further increases of a similar size would be needed to reach net enrolment rates of 100 per cent and for the costs of additional school capacity and teacher training. Governments will no doubt be under considerable pressure to reduce the cost per student in these countries, as well as to increase private funding for primary education.

In secondary education, most regions would reach gross enrolment rates of 48 per cent or more for males and 42 per cent or more for females in the year 2000 under the baseline scenario. But the average rate for females would be only 15 per cent in the least developed countries and sub-Saharan Africa and 34 per cent in South Asia; the average rate for males would be only 25 per cent in the least developed countries and 27 per cent in sub-Saharan Africa. By contrast, in most of the developed countries and in the East Asian newly industrializing economies, the gross enrolment rates for both males and females would approach 100 per cent. The relatively low rates in Eastern Europe are partly attributable to the exclusion of part-time vocational education from the enrolment statistics. The rapid increases indicated in China for both males and females are largely due to a significant decline in the absolute size of the secondary school-age population (see figure 11.1).

Although there are no internationally agreed targets for second-level enrolment rates, the increasing need in the modern economy for workers with at least second-level education suggests that a goal of 75 per cent for the second-level gross enrolment rate may be useful. (The corresponding net enrolment rates and graduation rates would be significantly lower.) Of the more than 60 developing countries that do not reach 75 per cent enrolment by the year 2000 in the baseline projection, some could do so by spending a few tenths of 1 per cent more of their GDP. But in the least developed countries, an extra 2.1 per cent of GDP would be needed for 75 per cent male enrolment and a further 2.3 per cent to also reach that target for females. To the extent that operating costs per student in these countries are high because of reliance on foreign teachers, some reduction can be expected as an increasing number of nationals qualify as second-level teachers. But the trends in third-level enrolment suggest that such progress will be limited during the 1990s.

The third-level gross enrolment rate (defined as total university and other post-secondary enrolment divided by population aged 20–24) shows a wide range in the baseline scenario in most of the developing regions. For males it ranges from 50 per cent in the East Asian newly industrializing economies to only about 3 per cent in sub-Saharan Africa. The rate for females is substantially lower than for males in most regions except East Asia and Latin America (figure 11.2). A 1 per cent higher rate of GDP growth in the 1990s would raise the enrolment rates by about half a percentage point above the baseline rates in most regions. This would be a relatively large increment in sub-Saharan Africa and the least developed countries as well as China, but it would still leave them with very low enrolment rates compared to the other developing regions.

As noted earlier, spending per student is particularly high in sub-Saharan Africa, and an increase of third-level enrolment rates to, say, 10 per cent there would require the allocation of several per cent of GDP. This suggests that third-level enrolment rates will not increase significantly in these countries unless their relatively high costs per student are reduced. This might be done by making better use of the available teachers and facilities and reducing students' living allowances or by relying more on enrolment in foreign universities, financed by foreign scholarships and part-time employment in the host countries.

H. POLICY ISSUES RELATED TO QUALITY: RELEVANCE, EFFICIENCY, AND EQUITY

The impressive increases in enrolment in recent decades and further increases expected by the year 2000, especially in the developing countries, relate to the input of students into the educational system. But there are also important issues of efficiency, relevance, and equity. All of them are aspects of the quality of education offered by schools and attained by students.

Relevance and efficiency of primary education[25]

In most countries, primary schools have a dual function: to teach essential skills and knowledge and to prepare students for further learning. Almost everywhere priority is given to reading, writing, and basic mathematics. For the last two decades, however, schools in many countries also have been mandated to promote health, nutrition, political orientation, and social equity, usually without additional or sufficient resources to do so. The result often has been poor achievement in these areas as well as in the core curriculum. Emphasis on relevance to the local and immediate environment can take undue precedence over more general competence that students will need during their life time. In deciding on the appropriate balance between immediate and long-term relevance, it may be noted that concurrent and subsequent opportunities for informal learning can supplement formal education.

Although there has been rapid expansion of education in most developing countries, the level of achievement of many students is very low. An international comparative study issued in 1976 found that "educational attainments requiring one year of schooling in an industrialized country tend to require three or four years of schooling in the average school of the developing countries examined. Children in India spent more time in school compared with their counterparts in the industrialized countries, but achieved only 48 per cent as much in reading and about 50 per cent in science."[26] In part this may reflect a lack of early environmental stimulation and the inadequacy of health and nutrition. "Differences in achievement among schools within countries related mainly to the qualities of the students entering the school; factors such as teaching methods or equipment played only a minor part."[27] Better and more equitable early childhood conditions can increase efficiency and equity in achievement at school, as can programmes that support children's health and nutrition while in school.

Low achievement by students also reflects inadequate teacher training and the strain on resources associated with rapid expansion of enrolment, such as overcrowded and ill-equipped facilities, lack of textbooks and other materials, and very high pupil/teacher ratios. The requirements for initial subject mastery are relatively low for teachers in many countries, and recurrent training is needed. In Brazil, the social rate of return to increasing the quality of primary schooling, as measured by teachers' average years of education, was found to exceed the return to increasing its quantity.[28] Teachers recruited from other socio-economic and cultural contexts often have misconceptions about the students. These misconceptions have to be overcome before they can teach effectively. Teacher absenteeism also is a critical concern. Appropriate wages, benefits, rank, and recognition are needed.

Improving teacher quality in the short run is difficult in most countries because of the difficulty of rapidly upgrading their skills or paying for better-qualified replacements. A relatively successful exception was the United Republic of Tanzania's programme to "put new recruits into the schools to teach under the supervision of experienced colleagues and then bring them to the colleges for intensive short bouts of training. Later assessments indicated that the "crash trained" teachers were more effective in the classrooms than their conventionally trained contemporaries. What is more, their training proved considerably cheaper than the usual."[29] Salaries represent a high percentage of the educational budget. Increasing them tends to cause similar wage increases throughout the civil service, which many countries cannot afford. Non-monetary incentives might be used instead to recruit and retain teachers, without extending them to other civil service employees.

The importance of pupil/teacher ratios is unclear. Although research indicates that very small classes (fewer than 15 students) are more effective than large ones, the differences among larger classes are uncertain. By 1985 most developing countries had reduced their average primary class size to a range of 25 to 39 students per teacher, but it is unclear whether this was a cost-effective way to raise quality compared with such alternatives as spending more on learning materials or innovative instructional technologies.

The availability of good educational materials is one of the most powerful and consistent determinants of learning achievement. The complete lack of books in schools and even in teachers' colleges in some African countries is a grave threat to their future. Properly designed materials can help to train unqualified teachers as well as students. In certain situations, programmed instructional materials and electronic educational technologies can enhance learning and efficiency, offsetting the negative effects of multi-grade classrooms, large classes, and inadequately trained teachers. However, in times of fiscal restriction, expenditure on physical inputs is restricted more than salaries.

The importance of the quantity and quality of buildings or equipment is not as clear as that of instructional materials, but overcrowding in primary schools, especially in early grades, is believed to be a major source of poor achievement and attrition. To reduce overcrowding, it may be more cost-effective to have so-called "split shifts," with two or more groups of students using the same school room or other facility during different hours or days, rather than building additional facilities.

Ineffective types of examinations and other systems of incentives limit the quality of learning in many countries. If the first priority of pupils and their teachers is to perform well in stand-ardized examinations in order to secure good jobs, and if the examinations test rote-learning, then repetition and memorization are encouraged rather than the ability to analyse problems. Graduation can become merely an indicator of age and perseverance instead of evidence of learning. Research on learning has found that to be absorbed, information must be disassembled and then reshaped by the learner; then it can be connected with previous knowledge and applied to future situations. In non-compulsory education programmes for youth and adults, motivation to join, to continue, and to succeed is even more critical.

Improvements in quality and efficiency may be possible without raising costs, through reforms in course content and examinations, and less reliance on seniority as the criterion for salary increases. Relatively small increases in expenditures for training in leadership and management for head teachers and the use of fees for additional textbooks may yield high returns.[30] Increased accountability of teachers and administrators to parents and other members of the local community may stimulate greater enthusiasm and support for educational improvements.

Attendance, drop-out, and repetition[31]

To attain literacy and other education goals, children must remain enrolled in school and attend regularly for a sufficient length of time. Learning achievement is proportional to the time spent in learning activities. Because of teacher and pupil absenteeism, holidays, and the needs of agricultural and other employment cycles, the pupils' learning time in many developing nations is less than half of the 800 to 1,000 hours a year that are common in developed nations. Poor attendance often causes pupils to repeat one or more grade levels or to drop out of school entirely.

In 86 developing countries, 18 per cent of the pupils starting school drop out before reaching grade 2, and only 71 per cent reach grade 4. The drop-out rates were particularly high, about 40 per cent before grade 4 in Latin America and the Caribbean and in French-speaking Africa, and extremely high in the Portuguese-speaking African countries (58 per cent). The rate averaged 12 to 16 per cent in the other regions of Africa and 5 to 9 per cent in Asia.[32] The high drop-out rates suggest limited progress in eradicating illiteracy, despite the rapid growth of enrolment during the last 15 years. Although Latin America and the Caribbean had gross primary enrolment ratios well above 100 per cent in 1980 and 1985, the region's production of literate children (as a percentage of their primary-school age groups) may be about the same as in Asia and not much higher than in Africa.

In order to reduce drop-out rates, education authorities must consider to what extent they are caused by failure to pass an end-of-the-year exam, lack of teachers and facilities, school fees or other reasons. High drop-out rates between grades 1 and 2 deserve special attention.

Many pupils repeat one or more grades before dropping out. The percentage of primary school enrolment constituted by repeaters shows wide disparities among the developing countries. In Africa, this percentage ranged from 0 to 50, with a median value of 19 per cent around 1985. The range was somewhat lower in the other developing regions, with median values of 11 per cent in Latin America and the Caribbean and 6 per cent in Asia and Oceania, compared with 2 per cent in Europe and the USSR.[33]

Considering that repeaters use resources that could be made available to children who are not yet enrolled, more attention might usefully be given to this issue. Educators differ in their opinions of the benefit pupils gain from repeating a grade as opposed to being promoted automatically. There is little doubt that a child having serious problems in assimilating the programme in one grade is likely to continue experiencing difficulties if promoted to the next grade without some extra assistance. But it is not clear how repetition will reduce these problems unless special help also is given. Gains from repetition alone are minor, rarely cost-effective, and often promote lower self-esteem and an increased propensity to drop out. Prevention of repetition through improved instruction and in-class remedial work is often less expensive than accepting it as an unavoidable part of the education process. But many schools in the developing countries do not have or use enough resources to remedy initial learning disadvantages or to enable the slower learner to catch up with the other pupils.

To summarize, the current understanding of relationships between inputs and outputs of education systems suggests the following priorities to increase the relevance and efficiency of primary schooling: (a) improving the availability and use of instructional materials; (b) enhancing teacher effectiveness by emphasizing subject mastery, communication skills, and teacher motivation; (c) improving managerial skills, community and institutional structures and individual organizational incentives; and (d) increasing the time actually spent on learning.

Effectiveness of secondary and higher education

High costs per student tend to limit the growth of enrolment for secondary and higher education. These costs are especially high, relative to per capita GDP, in sub-Saharan Africa and the least developed countries. Subsidies are allocated inequitably in several regions, as noted earlier. Greater use of fees, student loans, and need-based rather than general subsidies increases the resources available for secondary and higher education and allocates them more equitably.[34]

The curriculum in many secondary schools is focused mainly on the goal of preparing students for university entrance in conventional academic subjects. Yet in a growing number of developing countries, university graduates in a number of fields are encountering great difficulties in finding employment, even while there are shortages of adequately trained technicians. Many developing countries have adopted systems of secondary and university education from the developed countries. These systems emphasize specialized academic subjects, even in programmes dealing with industry and agriculture, at the expense of more general training adapted to local circumstances.[35]

The cost-effectiveness of sending students abroad for third-level education (more than 600,000 per year from the developing countries in the early 1980s) is an open issue. While it probably is less expensive per student than rapidly building up the necessary physical facilities and importing foreign teachers, at least in small developing countries and highly specialized fields, it contributes to the "brain drain" of many of the developing countries' best secondary-school graduates. It is also costly in foreign exchange to the extent that their expenses are not covered by foreign scholarships or employment in host countries.

In sub-Saharan Africa and the least developed countries, the very low third-level enrolment rates may be explained largely by the small size of the economies. The small economies do not allow for the minimum market size for many subjects requiring third-level training. At the same time, for a majority of the least developed countries, there is a large number of well-educated nationals living outside the country. A desirable alternative way for these countries to acquire high-level skills is to attract more of these nationals back, e.g., through transfer of knowledge through expatriate nationals (TOKTEN) projects sponsored by UNDP.[36]

Equity[37]

Inequities in the availability of education most commonly relate to poverty, location, gender, religious or ethnic identification, and physical or mental disability. Achievement of equity requires specific interventions and acceptance of the reality that compensatory resources and measures are necessary to offset the disadvantages of certain groups. Poor families may require assistance with the costs of school fees, uniforms, and transportation. Equity in rural areas may require flexible scheduling of the school year to minimize conflict with agricultural planting and harvesting.

Although low enrolment of girls often reflects the attitudes of their families and the wider community, schools themselves may reinforce such attitudes. Differences in teacher-pupil interactions and in pupils' use of materials and equipment can create inequities even within a single school or classroom. In some schools females receive less attention from the teacher and experience lower expectations in terms of their school performance. To promote participation and successful academic achievement by girls in communities which disapprove of co-educational classes, the educational system could provide separate schools for girls or even in-home instruction. Where older girls are commonly expected to stay at home to care for their younger siblings, other ways could be used to provide necessary day care.

With regard to youth and adult education programmes, there is a major issue of equity among people of different ages. There also is considerable inequity in the allocation of subsidies for higher education, as noted earlier. Given the low levels of education of much of the adult population, it is not realistic to expect every country to meet immediately even the basic knowledge requirements of all of its adults. Strong arguments exist for giving women highest priority, considering their history of being educationally underserved, their economic contributions to agriculture and industry, and their influential role as mothers and often as head of a single-parent household. Their opportunities should include access to training in non-traditional occupational roles for women, e.g., through agricultural extension services and assistance to small-scale enterprise development.

NOTES

1. For an elaboration of the relevance of human resources development to development strategies, see Committee for Development Planning, *Human Resource Development: A Neglected Dimension of Development Strategy* (United Nations publication, Sales No. E.88.II.A.11), and "Human Development in the 1980s and Beyond", (special issue of) *Journal of Development Planning,* Keith Griffin and John Knight, guest eds., No. 19, 1989.

2. Farmers with four years of education have been shown to have crop yields up to 9 per cent higher than those of farmers with no education. World Bank, *World Development Report 1988*, p. 132.

3. Report of the Administrative Committee on Co-ordination (ACC) Task Force on Long-term Development Objectives on its fifteenth session, New York, 8–10 September 1987 (ACC/1987/14), paras. 67 and 69.

4. J. B. Knight, R. H. Sabot and D. C. Hovey, "Is the rate of return on primary schooling really 26 per cent?", mimeo, June 1989. This analysis is part of a larger study by Knight and Sabot, *Educational Expansion, Productivity and Inequality—The East African Natural Experiment*, World Bank/Oxford University Press, forthcoming (February 1990).

5. Cotlear, Daniel, "The effects of education on farm productivity", *Journal of*

Development Planning (Keith Griffin and John Knight, guest eds.), No. 19, 1989, pp. 86–88.

6.   See *Committee for Development Planning, Report on the Twenty-fourth Session, Official Records of the ECOSOC, 1988*, Supplement No. 6 (E/1988/16).

7.   In rural Mexico, it was found that "the propensity to send children to school corresponded inversely with the use made of children in family businesses", and in Tamil Nadu, India, "even the noonday meal scheme. . .failed to attract the children of the poorest families away from assisting with the family income". Oxenham, John (with Jocelyn Dejong and Steven Treagust), "Improving the Quality of Education in Developing Countries", *Journal of Development Planning*, No. 19, 1989, p. 106.

8.   Inter-American Development Bank, *Economic and Social Progress in Latin America—1987 Report*, p. 109.

9.   UNESCO, "A Summary Statistical Review of Education in the World 1970–1984", ED/BIE/CONFINTED 40/Ref. 1, Paris, July 1986, p. 24, and "Literacy Situation in the World, Preliminary Results of the 1989 Assessment of Illiteracy", November 1989.

10.   UNESCO, October 1982 computer printout.

11.   UNCTAD, *The Least Developed Countries, 1988 Report* (United Nations publication, Sales No. E.89.II.D.3), p. 69.

12.   The gross enrolment rate, or ratio, can be more than 100 per cent because it includes in the numerator children older or younger than those in the denominator, i.e., the number in a country's official age-ranges for different levels of education. Net primary enrolment rates, which exclude under-age or over-age children from the numerator, tend to be 10 to 20 percentage points lower.

13.   A review of enrolment trends and education policies in the least developed countries concluded that "it is clear that, given their other priorities, almost no LDC can afford to press ahead with substantial increases in enrolment at the secondary and tertiary levels of education. [For example] in. . .the policy [of] the Central African Republic. . .in secondary education the essential requirement is to restore its quality and to begin by limiting enrolment [and] Samoa. . .stated that the existing proportion of secondary school places to primary school leavers would be maintained. . ." (UNCTAD, *The Least Developed Countries, 1985 Report*, TD/B/1059, para. 314, p. 107).

14.   UNESCO, *Statistical Yearbook 1988, op. cit.*, table 3.12.

15.   *Ibid.*, tables 2.2 and 3.7.

16. Based on UNESCO, "Development of private enrolment, first and second-level education, 1975–1985", CSR—E—57 (ST-89/WS/4), Paris, May 1989, tables 2 and 5 and annex tables I and II.17.

17. ACC, *op cit.*, para. 66.

18. These figures exclude Nigeria, where per capita expenditure increased from $37 in 1970 to $72 in 1980; the data available after 1981 exclude non-federal public expenditures, which apparently had been much larger than the federal expenditures.

19. United Nations Statistical Office, national accounts data bank.

20. World Bank, *World Development Report 1988*, p. 134.

21. *Ibid.*, pp. 135–136.

22. The ratios in Africa averaged 36 at the primary level and 25 at the secondary level in 1986, versus 30 and 19 respectively in all of the developing countries. UNESCO, "A Review of Education in the World: A Statistical Analysis" (ED/BIE/CONFINTED 41/Ref 1), 1 October 1988, table 13.

23. UNESCO, *Statistical Yearbook 1987*, table 4.2.

24. The projections tend to be a few percentage points lower than those recently prepared by UNESCO (November 1989), which are based on historical trends but are not specifically related to economic trends. The projections shown for China are those prepared by UNESCO.

25. For a more detailed discussion, see "Meeting Basic Learning Needs: A New Vision for the 1990s", background document for the World Conference on Education for All, Thailand, 5–9 March 1990, and Oxenham, John (with Jocelyn Dejong and Steven Treagust), "Improving the Quality of Education in Developing Countries", *Journal of Developing Planning*, No. 19, 1989, pp. 101–125.

26. International Association for the Evaluation of Educational Achievement (IEA), *The IEA Six Subject Survey: An Empirical Study of Education in Twenty-one Countries*, by David A. Walker. Stockholm: Almqvist and Wiksell, 1976, and IEA, *The National Case Study: An Empirical Comparative Study of Twenty-one Educational Systems*. By A. H. Passow, Stockholm: Almqvist and Wiksell, 1976, cited in Oxenham, *op. cit.*, p. 102.

27. IEA (International Association for the Evaluation of Educational Achievement), *The IEA Six Subject Survey: An Empirical Study of Education in Twenty-one Countries*, *op. cit.*, cited in Oxenham, *op. cit.*, p. 104.

28. Behrman, Jere and Nancy Birdsall, "The Quality of Schooling: Quantity Alone

May Be Misleading". *American Economic Review*, Vol. 73, No. 5, pp. 929, 934 and 940.

29. Oxenham, *op. cit.*, p. 110.

30. Committee for Development Planning, *op. cit.*, para. 99.

31. Based on UNESCO, "A Summary Statistical Review of Education in the World 1970–1984", *op. cit.*, pp. 47–48 and UNESCO, "A Review of Education in the World: A Statistical Analysis," *op. cit.* ED/BIE/CONFINTED 41/Ref. 1, *op. cit.* (Oct. 1988).

32. *Ibid.*, pp. 34–35.

33. *Ibid.*, p. 34.

34. See World Bank, *World Development Report 1988*, pp. 136–137, and World Bank, *Financing Education in Developing Countries, An Exploration of Policy Options* (Washington, D.C., 1986).

35. ACC, *op. cit.*, para. 68.

36. UNCTAD, *op. cit.*, para. 315, p. 107.

37. For a more detailed discussion, see "Meeting Basic Learning Needs: A New Vision for the 1990s", background document for the World Conference on Education for All, Thailand, 5–9 March 1990.

TABLE 11.1 *Returns on investment in education, by region,*
type and level
(Annual average, in percentages)

Number of countries	Region	Social			Private		
		Primary	Second-ary	Terti-ary	Primary	Second-ary	Terti-ary
9	North Africa, Middle East and developing Europe	13	10	8	17	13	13
16	Other Africa	28	17	13	45	26	32
10	Asia	27	15	13	31	15	18
10	Latin America	26	18	16	32	23	23
45	Developing countries	24	15	13	31	19	22
15	Developed countries	. . .	11	9	. . .	12	12

Source: World Bank, Financing Education in Developing Countries, an Exploration of Policy Options *(Washington, D.C., 1986), table 3, p. 7.*

TABLE 11.2 *Out-of-school youth*
(In millions)

Region[a]	Ages 6–11			Ages 12–17		
	1970	1985	2000	1970	1985	2000
Developed countries[b]	10	9	10	27	14	8
Developing countries[c]	122[d]	135	118	162[d]	287	263
Africa	34	39	42	35	42	55
Latin America	13	9	7	19	19	14
Asia	75[d]	87	70	106[d]	226	193
Least developed countries	25	35	39	24	38	48

Source: 1970: UNESCO, "A Summary Statistical Review of Education in the World 1970–1984", ED/BIE/CONFINTED 40/Ref. 1, Paris, July 1986, p. 73; 1985 and 2000: United Nations Secretariat, Department of International Economic and Social Affairs, based on enrolment rates by age group for 1985 and 2000 prepared by UNESCO (November 1989) and estimates and projections of the population aged 6–11 and 12–17 in World Population Prospects 1988 *(United Nations publication, Sales No. E.88.XIII.7).*

[a] As defined in World Population Prospects 1988, op. cit. *p. 5.*

[b] More developed regions (see footnote a).

[c] Less developed regions (see footnote a).

[d] Excluding China and the Democratic People's Republic of Korea.

TABLE 11.3 *Countries with 10 million or more illiterates aged 15 or over in 1985*

Country	Illiteracy rate (per cent)	Number (millions)	Percentage of world total
India	56.5	264	29.7
China	30.7	229	25.8
Pakistan	70.4	39	4.4
Bangladesh	66.9	37	4.2
Nigeria	57.6	27	3.0
Indonesia	25.9	26	2.9
Brazil	22.3	19	2.1
Egypt	55.5	16	1.8
Iran (Islamic Republic of)	49.2	12	1.3
Subtotal, nine countries		669	75.2
Other countries		220	24.8
World total		889	100.0

Source: UNESCO, "The Current Literacy Situation in the World" (ST-85/WS-9), Paris, 1985, p. 8.

TABLE 11.4 *Adult literacy rates,[a] 1970–1985*
(Literates as percentage of population aged 15 and over)

Country group	Number of countries	Female			Male		
		1970	1980	1985	1970	1980	1985
Developing countries							
North Africa	5	16	27	31	44	54	57
Sub-Saharan Africa	41	15	25	37	34	46	57
South and East Asia							
South Asia	6	18	25	28	45	52	54
East Asian newly indus-							
trializing economies	3	78	85	89	93	95	97
Others	7	53	66	72	74	81	85
Western Asia	9	18	31	39	42	56	63
Mediterranean	4	52	63	71	79	87	90
Western hemisphere	27	70	78	82	76	82	86
Total, developing countries	102	33	42	47	54	62	67
China and Asian planned							
economies	3	. . .	52	57	. . .	80	83
Least developed countries	28	9	16	27	27	36	47

Source: United Nations Secretariat, Department of International Economic and Social Affairs, based on country rates in UNESCO, "The Current Literacy Situation in the World" (ST-85/WS-9), Paris, July 1985, and Statistical Yearbook 1987 *and earlier editions.*

[a] *Country group rates are weighted by the population aged 15 and over in the individual countries.*

TABLE 11.5 *First-level gross enrolment rates,* [a] *1970–2000*
(*In percentages*)

Country group	Number of countries	Female					Male				
		1970	1980	1985	1990	2000	1970	1980	1985	1990	2000
Developing countries											
North Africa	4	54	70	77	81	93	86	99	99	101	102
Sub-Saharan Africa	41	36	67	65	68	75	56	88	83	83	89
South Asia	5	50	61	71	78	93	84	91	100	99	100
East Asia	10	84	101	106	106	105	93	108	110	109	105
Western Asia	5	49	78	92	99	104	90	106	109	109	107
Mediterranean	4	97	92	107	107	109	119	102	112	112	109
Western hemisphere	24	92	105	106	107	111	95	107	110	111	113
Total, developing countries	93	62	77	82	86	94	84	97	101	100	101
China	1	81	103	114	122	119	97	121	132	136	127
Least developed countries	29	33	49	51	57	66	55	71	69	73	79

Source: United Nations Secretariat, Department of International Economic and Social Affairs, based on country data for the most recent available year around 1985, and for the nearest available year to 1970 and 1980, from UNESCO, Statistical Yearbook 1988, table 3.2, and earlier volumes, and data bank for forthcoming 1989 Yearbook. The projections for 1990 and 2000 for the developing countries are based on the baseline scenario for country GDP growth; those for China were prepared by UNESCO (November 1989).

[a] Country group rates are averages of individual country rates weighted by the population aged 6–11.

TABLE 11.6 *Total public educational expenditure as a percentage[a] of gross product*

Country group	Number of countries	1970	1980	1985
Developing countries				
North Africa	5	5.5	5.7	6.0
Sub-Saharan Africa[b]	39	4.1	4.5	4.6
South Asia	5	2.5	2.7	3.3
East Asian newly industrializing economies	3	3.2	3.3	4.5
Other East Asia	7	3.1	3.1	3.5
Western Asia	6	3.8	5.2	5.5
Mediterranean	4	4.0	3.8	3.0
Western hemisphere	25	3.4	3.6	3.6
Subtotal, developing countries	94	3.6	3.9	4.0
China	1	1.8	2.5	2.7
Developed market economies	24	5.3	6.1	6.0
Eastern Europe & the USSR	5	6.5	6.8	6.7
Total	124	5.1	5.6	5.6
Least developed countries	26	2.9	2.6	2.8

Source: United Nations Secretariat, Department of International Economic and Social Affairs, based on country data from UNESCO, Statistical Yearbook 1988, *table 4.1, and earlier volumes, and from IMF,* Government Finance Statistics Yearbook 1987, *p. 98.*

[a] *Country group percentages are weighted by the gross product of the individual countries.*

[b] *Excludes Nigeria, where 1970 and 1980 percentages were 3.3 and 6.6, including non-federal expenditures, and the 1985 percentage (federal only) was 1.2.*

TABLE 11.7 *Total public educational expenditure per capita,[a] in 1980 dollars*

Country group	Number of countries	1970	1980	1985
Developing countries				
North Africa	5	70	82	85
Sub-Saharan Africa[b]	39	19	21	20
South Asia	5	5	7	10
East Asian newly industrializing economies	3	37	73	130
Other East Asia	7	11	18	22
Western Asia	6	142	217	167
Mediterranean	4	53	74	61
Western hemisphere	25	63	84	77
Subtotal, developing countries	94	27	38	38
China	1	3	7	12
Developed market economies	24	438	635	682
Eastern Europe & the USSR	5	132	206	226
Total	124	112	151	155
Least developed countries	26	7	6	7

Source: United Nations Secretariat, Department of International Economic and Social Affairs, based on country data underlying table VI.8.

[a] *Country group expenditure levels are averages of individual country levels weighted by population.*

[b] *Excluding Nigeria, because available post-1981 data do not include large non-federal expenditures. See table 9.8, footnote b.*

TABLE 11.8 *Public current expenditure per student,[a] by level of education (In 1980 dollars)*

	First level		Second level		Third level	
Country group	1980	1985	1980	1985	1980	1985
Developing countries						
North Africa	169	183	612	423	933	1,008
Sub-Saharan Africa[b]	64	64	264	198	2,992	2,110
South Asia	21	33	42	62	134	231
East Asian newly industrializing						
economies	197	374	210	347	503	503
Other East Asia	69	95	102	126	197	180
Western Asia	378	208	736	451	2,606	1,733
Mediterranean	91	83	157	134	1,365	899
Western hemisphere	190	171	231	176	1,420	1,104
Subtotal, developing countries	97	94	171	152	744	633
China	12	18	33	58	1,124	1,274
Developed market economies	1,253	1,452	2,303	2,466	4,508	4,909
Eastern Europe & the USSR	425	455	350	353	1,518	1,684
Total	181	187	530	545	2,642	2,636
Least developed countries	27	31	93	91	794	363

Source: United Nations Secretariat, Department of International Economic and Social Affairs, based on country data on enrolment, current expenditure as a percentage of GNP and the distribution of current expenditure by level of education from UNESCO, Statistical Yearbook 1988 *and earlier volumes.*

[a] *Includes students enrolled in private as well as public schools (see text). Country group expenditures are averages of the individual country expenditures weighted by the number of students at the respective levels.*

[b] *Excluding Nigeria. See table 9.8, footnote b.*

12.

Health

A. TRENDS IN LIFE EXPECTANCY AND MORTALITY

Health, like education, is an immediate goal of development and a means to achieve the related goals of higher labour productivity and total economic output. Life expectancy and mortality rates are overall indicators of a population's health. Life expectancy is the average number of years a newborn baby can be expected to live if current age-specific mortality rates continue. In developed countries, life expectancy has increased by 7 years, from 66 years in the early 1950s to 73 years in the late 1980s (figure 12.1). In the developing countries as a whole, including China, it has increased much more, from 41 to 60 years. China experienced the most dramatic increase of 29 years, from 41 years in the early 1950s to 70 in the late 1980s. In the least developed countries, the increase was only 13 years, from 36 years to 49. The increases among the developing regions ranged from 13 years in sub-Saharan Africa (from 35 to 48) to 20 years in Western Asia (from 43 to 63 years).

Women's life expectancy at birth is generally several years longer than men's, especially in the developed countries: 77 years

Figure 12.1   # Life expectancy at birth
(average of males and females)
1950 - 2005

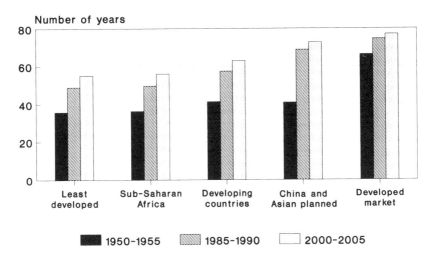

for women versus 70 for men in the late 1980s; in the developing countries, it is about 61 years for women and 59 for men. The only region with virtually equal life expectancy for both sexes is South Asia, where the average is about 57 years for both groups. In Sri Lanka, however, greater improvements in female life expectancy in the past three decades have already resulted in a more normal pattern in that country. In the region as a whole, female life expectancy is projected to be about 63 years in the year 2000, compared with 62 for men.[1]

Maternal mortality rates also reliably indicate the health situation and status of women of child-bearing age. Maternal mortality (death of women caused by pregnancy or child-birth) is the largest cause of death among women of reproductive age in most developing countries. In less developed regions, there were 450 deaths for 100,000 live births around 1983, against 30 in the developed countries.[2] Countries with high maternal mortality rates also have high total mortality. These countries should improve by the year 2000 as they follow the general downward trends of total mortality. But the wide disparities among countries are not likely to disappear, especially as the increase of life expectancy is projected to be slower in Africa, for example, which accounts for 30 per cent of maternal deaths, as against 18 per cent of births.

Five key factors contributing to the high maternal mortality levels in the developing countries are pregnancies in the earliest and latest years of the reproductive period, maternal depletion through too closely spaced pregnancies, high-parity births (i.e., births to women who already have had a high number of pregnancies), lack of access to health services and lack of trained birth attendants. Inadequate nutrition in childhood and adolescence, as well as in adulthood, contributes to many maternal deaths. Complications from poorly performed abortions also cause a significant proportion of total maternal deaths, according to a number of studies. Family planning and good primary health care before and during pregnancy could greatly reduce the number of deaths caused by all these factors. However, because a significant proportion of these potentially fatal complications during pregnancy cannot be predicted or prevented, speedy access to emergency care is also of utmost importance. Not surprisingly then, numerous maternal deaths among rural women in developing countries are due to poor transportation networks.[3]

In the past decade, there have been decreases in the infant mortality rate in nearly all countries, but more than a quarter, representing 29 per cent of world population, still have a rate above 100 per 1,000 live births,[4] while the average in the developed countries is about 18 or 15, excluding South Africa. Continued reductions are projected for the 1990s, but the average for the least developed countries is projected to remain above 100 during the period from 1995 to 2000, falling to 93 between the years 2000 and 2005 (figure 12.2).

Challenges remain to lower worldwide mortality rates and increase life expectancy in the 1990s. Reducing infant mortality rates to below 120 per 1,000 live births by 1990, a goal set forth in the International Development Strategy for the 1980s, will most likely not be met by 21 countries. Rates above the goal of 50 will

Figure 12.2   Infant mortality rates, 1950 - 2005 *

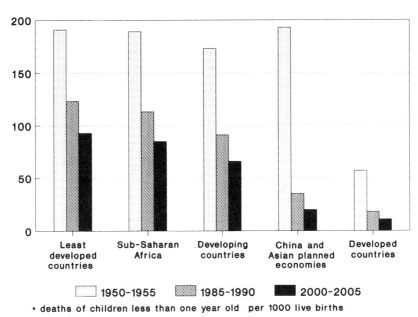

* deaths of children less than one year old   per 1000 live births

still exist in 59 countries in the year 2000, including 41 in sub-Saharan Africa (table 12.1). Similarly, 46 countries are projected not to meet the Strategy's goal of increasing life expectancy to 60 years or more by the year 2000; 36 of these will be in sub-Saharan Africa and 31 will be among the least developed countries.

B. DISEASE AND MORTALITY— PREVALANCE OF MAJOR TYPES OF DISEASE, AND THEIR IMPACT ON MORTALITY[5]

The great majority of deaths, especially of children and older adults, are caused by some type of disease. In the developing countries of Africa and Asia, infectious and parasitic diseases (including certain respiratory diseases) account for about half of all deaths, the majority occurring among infants and young children. By contrast, this group of diseases account for only one tenth of all deaths in the industrialized countries. Instead, 50 per cent of deaths in these countries are from circulatory diseases and 19 per cent from cancer. All developing countries list diarrhea as one of the most serious problems affecting the health of their children and one of the main reasons for contact with the health system. Dehydration from diarrhea can now be treated quite adequately with low-cost oral rehydration therapy, yet some 4 million children still die from it each year.[6] Six major preventable diseases of childhood—diphtheria, pertussis (whooping cough), neonatal tetanus, poliomyelitis, measles, and tuberculosis—together kill some 4 million children each year and cause disability in 4 million more. These diseases have been selected as targets for immunization in most countries, but some still have not allocated the relatively modest resources needed to provide this protection.

Malaria and tuberculosis remain major public health problems, with improvement in some countries offset by deterioration in others. Malaria is an important cause of child mortality, especially in tropical Africa. Efforts to control the disease have been hampered by the emergence of mosquitoes that are resistant to the more readily available insecticides and of forms of the malaria parasite that are resistant to drugs.

Many infectious and parasitic diseases can be overcome by improvements in environmental and living conditions and other preventive action. In India, where 45 per cent of the national health budget is used for the control of malaria by conventional methods, health officials have taken further steps in some communities by enlisting villagers to carry out new, environmentally safer ways to control malaria-bearing mosquitoes.[7]

Communicable and parasitic diseases have been greatly reduced in the developed countries by improvements in sanitary conditions, nutrition and health services, allowing large decreases in premature deaths and relative growth of the older age groups. This larger aging population, together with the changes in lifestyle in industrialized societies, has contributed to the growing incidence of circulatory system diseases, which are also a cause for concern in developing countries. Diseases of the circulatory system are also estimated to account for 20 per cent of total invalidity in the developed countries. These diseases and cancer are difficult and costly to treat. More emphasis is being placed on prevention through modification of individual behaviour. Cigarette smoking, through its relationship to heart disease, lung cancer and chronic respiratory disease, is considered the most important preventable contributor to mortality in developed countries. The rapidly increasing number of older citizens in all countries will pressure health systems to provide a broader variety of care in hospitals, chronic care facilities, communities and homes, with the goal of enabling the elderly to stay healthy and remain at home or nearby.

Viral and bacterial epidemics are still a threat, especially in view of inadequate surveillance and preventive measures and ecological factors, such as the spread of certain parasites through irrigation water and the rapid international transmission of various diseases by airplane passengers. For the present and foreseeable future the AIDS virus is a serious threat, especially in some of the poorer developing countries, as discussed below. Acquired resistance and natural insensitivity of micro-organisms, insects, rodents, and other carriers of disease to available drugs and pesticides have slowed progress in disease reduction and increased the cost of control. Biotechnology is being used to develop a new generation of vaccines and will no doubt be used to develop drugs that target specific organs and cells, reducing unwanted side-effects.

Severe problems associated with cerebral disease or injury affect no less than 2 per cent of most populations, and neurotic and psychosomatic disorders and alcohol- and drug-related problems affect 3 to 7 per cent. More effective methods of prevention and treatment to deal with alcohol and drug abuse may, however, depend as much on the resolution of economic, social and political problems as on progress in medical technology. Severe mental disorders are also increasing with the aging of the population in most industrialized countries, and psycho-geriatric problems are claiming a significant share of resources for health care. World-wide, an estimated 340 to 480 million people are disabled as a consequence of physical, mental or sensory impairment. To the extent that some of these problems may be genetic in origin, advances in genetic research may provide ways to prevent or cure them.

C. THE AIDS EPIDEMIC

Acquired immunodeficiency syndrome (AIDS) and the entire spectrum of diseases associated with human immunodeficiency virus (HIV) infection have rapidly emerged as major global and national public health problems. About 183,000 cases of AIDS had been reported in 152 countries, as of 30 September 1989, but the actual number is estimated to be over three times as high.[8] In addition, there are estimated to be 6 to 8 million who are infected with the virus, but do not yet show major symptoms.[9] The latest estimates show a continuing and even increasing spread of the disease. WHO's projections indicate that the epidemic will continue to grow throughout the next decade, with about 15 million new infections expected in the 1990s. Moreover its geographic scope will be much wider, as the disease is already gaining footholds in previously unaffected regions. In countries where it is already prevalent, it is growing in hitherto lightly affected population groups, including children and rural communities.[10]

As the epidemic has been followed for only about seven years, it is not known what proportion of the people infected with HIV will ultimately develop the symptoms of AIDS. Current estimates are that about 50 per cent will develop AIDS within 10 years, but the percentage that will develop AIDS after 15 or 20 years cannot be predicted at this time, nor can the proportions who will eventually die of the disease. The fatality rate among those who develop symptoms appears to be high, but many essential epidemiological characteristics, including the natural history of asymptomatic infections, have yet to be elucidated. The cumulative total of AIDS cases world-wide is projected by WHO to exceed 1 million by the early 1990s and could exceed 3 million by the late 1990s.[11]

AIDS is a prolonged, physically debilitating illness that often is economically and emotionally devastating for the victims and their families. Most of the people with AIDS are young and middle-aged adults, whose illness and death deprive their countries of a valuable resource. The number of infants born with HIV infections is increasing, particularly in some developing countries, jeopardizing these countries' recent, hard-won gains in infant and child survival. At present there are no very effective medical techniques for the prevention or treatment of AIDS.[12] Consequently, educational campaigns to prevent it from spreading are essential while the search for effective treatment continues. The main lines of defence against AIDS are education to reduce high-risk behaviour and provision of a safe blood supply for transfusions, through screening for HIV antibodies. As with most other infectious diseases, a fairly stable prevalence of HIV infections will eventually be established, but how high or low that prevalence will be will depend on the effectiveness of prevention programmes. (The relationship of AIDS to drug abuse is discussed in Chapter 13.)

The costs of the HIV/AIDS epidemic could prove staggering for both the developed and the developing countries. In the United States, the country with the most reported cases, total federal expenditures on AIDS are projected to exceed $2 billion in fiscal year 1989; the average lifetime costs per AIDS patient in the United States are estimated at $50,000 to $60,000.[13] Treatment with AZT, the most effective drug available so far for HIV/AIDS, has been costing about $8,000 per patient per year, although some selective reductions in price have recently been offered by the manufacturer. Clearly, such costs are beyond the means of the developing countries, where per capita expenditure on health often does not exceed $5 annually. The enormous cost of caring for AIDS patients threatens to divert resources from other health programmes, with adverse consequences for overall health and mortality.

Although the United States has by far the largest number of reported AIDS cases, several developing countries in the Americas and in central and eastern Africa have a higher incidence of infection. The impact of the disease in these countries will go beyond the normal concern of public health authorities. Associated ethical and humanitarian problems will increase, along with human suffering, and these countries' economic and social development may be held back severely unless treatments are found or a vaccine is discovered in the next few years and made widely available. In some countries in Africa, the incidence of infection is 10 per cent and up among the urban adult population, both male and female, especially those between ages 20 and 50. Workers in this age group are essential in the more modern sectors of the economy, notably in the mining industry in certain African countries. The incidence of infection is also increasing rapidly in several Latin American countries, and is beginning to surge in at least one Asian country (Thailand). Policy-makers in countries whose key industries are about to be seriously affected by AIDS, to a point where they might no longer be internationally competitive, may be forced to use the limited means available to retard the impact of the disease on the workforce in these industries. In the case of the mining industry in Africa, the demographic structure and traditions of health care offer some potential for a comparatively good response to a sustained educational effort.

Estimated demographic impact of AIDS in a hypothetical country in Central Africa

While it is not yet possible to project the long-term incidence of HIV infections and AIDS cases with much certainty, WHO has used the available information to estimate the impact of AIDS on mortality and population growth in a hypothetical country. This hypothetical case is instructive because the country has characteristics similar to those in some central African areas, where up to 25 per cent of the population 20 to 40 years of age in some cities were infected with HIV in 1987. In the WHO model, the rate at which infected persons progress to AIDS has been estimated to be 20 to 25 per cent within 5 years and close to 50 per cent within 10 years. The progression rate for adults is projected to be 75 per cent within 15 years and 100 per cent within 20 years. The model assumes that half of the infants born to HIV-infected mothers will be infected, and that 80 per cent of infected children will have progressed to AIDS by their fifth birthday. Because of the high infection rates of sexually active females in some urban areas, about 10 per cent of children under five years old in urban areas are assumed to be infected. Persons with AIDS are assumed to die in the same year in which the disease develops. With a population of 20 million and an average HIV infection prevalence of 2.3 per cent in the country as a whole, there would be 450,000 infected people.

In the absence of AIDS, the population would increase by about 6.5 million between 1987 and 1997. Between 1987 and 1997, there would be 479,000 deaths from AIDS, including 320,000 urban residents (187,000 adults and 133,000 children) and 159,000 rural residents. Although the overall effect of AIDS on population growth would be modest in the 10-year period (population growth would be reduced by about 7 per cent over-all), population growth would be 36 per cent less in urban areas. Among the urban population aged 25 to 59 in 1997 (15 to 49 in 1987), the projected population increase between 1987 and 1997 would be 70 per cent less with AIDS; the under–5 age group in 1997 would have grown 50 per cent less than without AIDS. Projections beyond 1997 would depend on the patterns of spread of the HIV infection. If the virus were to continue to increase in urban areas and to spread extensively in rural areas, population growth could turn negative.[14]

D. NUTRITION, WATER SUPPLY AND SANITATION

Adequate nutrition, safe drinking water and adequate sanitation are vital for the prevention of serious disease and the maintenance

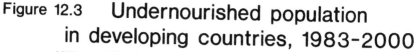

Figure 12.3 Undernourished population in developing countries, 1983-2000

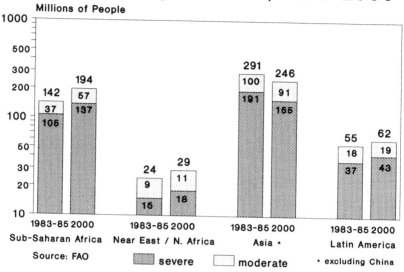

Source: FAO

of good health and high labour productivity. In most parts of the world, nutrition has improved over the past 25 years, as reflected in declining infant and child mortality rates and in declining percentages of the total population suffering from undernutrition. But the improvements in child nutritional status in the 1970s ceased, on average, in the 1980s.[15] Some 100 million children under the age of five show protein energy malnutrition; more than 10 million suffer from the severe form that is normally fatal if not treated.[16] The estimated number of people suffering from severe undernutrition, with calorie intakes providing an energy level less than 1.2 times the basal metabolic rate (BMR), increased from 320 million in 1980 to 348 million by 1984 in 89 developing countries (excluding China). The number below 1.4 BMR increased from 475 to 512 million (figure 12.3). (BMR = 1.0 is the energy needed under resting and fasting conditions. It varies with body weight and sex.) The proportion of the population that is under-nourished fell in the early 1980s in Asia, North Africa, and Central America, but there was no overall improvement in South America. The proportion rose sharply in sub-Saharan Africa, which has suffered long-term declining food availability per capita and increased malnutrition, due to economic stress and severe drought.[17] Within regions, economic stress in the 1980s has been strongly associated with malnutrition, based on a recent survey of 33 countries (16 in Africa, 6 in Asia, and 11 in Latin America and the Caribbean).[18]

Assuming that the recent pattern of income distribution and food consumption relative to per capita income continues, FAO estimates that the total number of people suffering acute malnutrition will increase slightly to 353 million (in 89 developing countries) by the year 2000, and the number below 1.4 BMR will increase to 532 million (figure 12.3). To reduce these numbers significantly, the system of income and food distribution will need improvement in many countries, and food production will need to accelerate.

Adequate nutrition is but one facet of disease prevention and health maintenance. A safe water supply and adequate sanitation are also necessary. Percentages of the population that have access to safe drinking water supply and adequate sanitation increased in many developing countries from 1975 to 1985, although variations in national interpretations of these concepts and changes in the number of countries reporting on them to WHO limit the comparability of the data, both between countries and over time. Of 89 countries surveyed in 1985, 73 per cent of the urban population and 42 per cent of the rural population had safe supplies of drinking water, compared with 74 per cent of the urban population (in 76 countries) and only 19 per cent of the rural population (in 69 countries) in 1975.[19]

Although the percentage served did not increase much in the urban areas, the number of people served increased greatly, along with the total urban population. The percentage of urban populations with adequate sanitation increased from 51 per cent in 60 countries in 1975 to 61 per cent in 65 countries in 1985. In rural areas, adequate sanitation increased from 11 to 15 per cent over the 10-year period.[20]

In 1985, the only groups of countries in which less than 74 per cent of the urban population had safe drinking water were the least developed countries (52 per cent) and Southeast Asia (49 per cent). In contrast, less than 50 per cent of the rural population had safe water in all of the developing regions, except Western Asia and the Mediterranean (table 12.2). The percentage of the urban population with adequate sanitation in 1985 was more diverse, although the only country groups averaging less than 55 per cent were South Asia (34 per cent) and the least developed countries (44 per cent). The rural percentages were mostly between 15 and 35 per cent, but only 3 per cent in South Asia (table 12.3).

With the slowdown in economic growth in many developing countries in the 1980s, it has become apparent that few of them will have reached the ambitious target of 100 per cent water supply and sanitation coverage originally set for the end of 1990, as the goal of the International Drinking Water Supply and Sanitation Decade (1981–1990). Based on the cross-section relation between percentages served and per capita GDP in 1985, and on the baseline projections of GDP growth for 1990 and the year 2000, relatively small increases from 1985 to 1990 and the year 2000 will occur in the percentages of safe water and adequate sanitation in most regions (see tables 12.2 and 12.3). Additional increases of a few percentage points could be expected with higher total investment in a scenario for more rapid economic growth. But large increases in coverage would also require an increase in water supply and sanitation as a share of total investment. It might also require significant reductions in average unit costs, or increased efforts to raise sufficient revenues from taxes and user charges to cover the costs of construction, operation and maintenance.

Meeting the goal of 100 per cent coverage is a serious challenge. Although countries with average tariffs equal to or higher than costs of production have seen significant progress, the poorer regions, including Africa and the least developed countries have not. For most regions the most serious constraints on meeting

the goal have been funding limitations and inadequate cost recovery frameworks, insufficient trained personnel and unsatisfactory operation and maintenance.[21]

If low-cost technologies are used, construction costs for safe
drinking water and adequate sanitation facilities for 100 per cent
of the population by the year 2000 could be less than 1 per cent
of annual GDP during the period from 1986 to the year 2000 in
most of the developing countries. The cost would be higher, 1
to 2 per cent, in sub-Saharan Africa.[22] These low-cost technologies
include public standpipes rather than individual house connections
for water supply, and non-water-borne sanitation (dry-pit privies,
night-soil collection, etc.). Water-borne sewage systems for urban
areas would cost considerably more to construct, but might have
lower costs for operation and maintenance.[23]

E. ACCESS TO HEALTH SERVICES

Access to health services in the developed countries has been
largely complete for many years, and a few developing countries
report 80 to 100 per cent coverage. Maternal and child health
services have increased in most developing countries, but care for
children under five years of age is still very limited. Availability
of essential drugs and treatment for common diseases and injuries
are quite widespread, but lack of resources and poor transportation
and communications are still major obstacles in rural areas.

In all countries, demand for more sophisticated health services
has increased. Overcrowded, costly hospitals in urban areas and
poorly equipped intermediate health facilities cannot satisfy the
demand. Economically sound approaches are needed to clear this
bottleneck in the health-care delivery system. Very few countries
have incorporated health goals into the revised national budgets
that have been compelled by the severe economic problems in the
1980s. These goals can minimize the impact of disease and protect
high-risk groups most vulnerable to adverse effects of recent aus-
terity measures. Increased access to food and primary health care

is needed, especially for women and children, working populations at high risk and the poor and underprivileged.

Projections of life expectancy indicate that current inequalities
in women's health between developed and developing regions will
remain largely unaltered by the year 2000. Policies to improve
female health care in developing countries in childhood and the
reproductive years should remain a priority, especially in rural
areas where maternal mortality rates are highest. Medical examinations and basic medical care should be brought to the village,
the school, the farm, and other places of employment.

In 1977, the Thirtieth World Health Assembly decided that
the main social goal of Governments and WHO in the coming
decades should be worldwide attainment by the year 2000 of a
level of health that would permit all people to lead socially and
economically productive lives.[24] The key to attaining this goal is
availability of primary health care: essential health care made accessible at a cost the country and community can afford, with
methods that are practical, scientifically sound and socially acceptable. Everyone in the community should have access to it and
be involved in it. Primary health care should include community
education on prevalent health problems and methods of preventing or controlling them; the promotion of adequate food supplies,
proper nutrition, sufficient safe water and basic sanitation, and
maternal and child health care, including family planning; the
prevention and control of locally endemic diseases; immunization
against the main infectious diseases; appropriate treatment of common diseases and injuries; and the provision of essential drugs.

In the early 1980s, WHO estimated that primary health care
could be provided in the developing countries for $10 to $15 per
person per year (excluding food, water and sanitation). This
amount is more than most Governments spent for health during
the early 1980s (among the developing countries with data), especially in Africa and South and Southeast Asia (see table 12.4).
Total governmental and private expenditures combined (see table
12.5) would be sufficient to provide primary health care in many
countries, however, if the services were priced and distributed
more equitably than they are now. In the poorest countries—

mainly in South Asia and sub-Saharan Africa—the total expenditures would have to increase by $5 or $10 per capita (roughly 3 to 4 per cent of GDP per capita), along with development of a wider delivery system to reach more of the rural and low-income urban population. But as little as $1 to $5 per capita could significantly reduce child mortality in many low income countries, if allocated to the most cost-effective means of primary health care and delivered by health care workers paid according to national per capita income levels.[25]

The mobilization and management of financial resources for health have been identified by WHO as critical for achieving the long-term goal of "Health for All by the Year 2000" through primary health care. While financial cutbacks present major problems in the short run, the best long-run options are to tap additional and new sources of domestic resources, and to make more efficient use of all available resources. In many countries, national health plans have been found to be too expensive to fund and implement. A greater mobilization of domestic resources is possible: employers and employees could contribute to health insurance plans; employers could provide health services directly; public or private institutions might be created to attract voluntary insurance contributions; other types of community financing might be developed; and consumers might be required to pay direct fees for some of the health services they use. Recent studies suggest that it would be both equitable and efficient to charge middle-income and upper-income groups for curative services, thus preventing excessive consumption of free services and allowing limited government funds to provide health care to more of the low-income population. Even if it is necessary to charge user fees to low-income groups, this can provide better health to more people than systems that rely on inadequate government funds.[26]

Even if health, broadly conceived, is accorded very high priority, national development planners face complex trade-offs. They must try to estimate the relative effectiveness of allocating limited resources among investments and operating expenses for primary health care facilities, high-technology hospitals, modern and traditional medical training, public health education, nutrition programmes, safe water supply and sanitation, shelter, etc.[27] Focusing on specific goals and timetables, such as reducing the infant mortality rate below 50 by the year 2000, helps to mobilize the necessary resources.[28]

The recent rise in concern with cost-containment in many countries is likely to continue throughout the 1990s. Determining the appropriate mix of public and private services, providers and funding sources will call for considerable research and public policy debate. There is substantial room for improvement in the cost-efficient allocation of resources among drugs, surgery and other methods of health care. A strong case can also be made for a reorientation of health services towards primary health care and rural areas.

NOTES

1. *World Population Prospects* 1988, United Nations publication, Sales No. E.88.XIII.7, table 15.

2. WHO, *Maternal Mortality Rates, A Tabulation of Available Information*, second ed., Geneva, 1986.

3. *World Population Trends and Policies: 1989 Monitoring Report*, United Nations, ESA/P/WP.107, 1 February 1989, paras. 447–448. (The final version of the report will be published with the title *World Population Monitoring* 1989, ST/ESA/SER.A/113).

4. WHO, *Evaluation of the Strategy for Health for All by the Year* 2000, *Seventh Report on the World Health Situation*, Geneva, 1987, p. 73.

5. Based on WHO, *Evaluation of the Strategy for Health for All by the Year* 2000, *op. cit,,* pp. 75–85, and other sources as noted.

6. UNICEF, *State of the World's Children* 1990, Fig. 4, p. 17.

7. *The New York Times*, 9 February 1988.

8. World Health Organization, "Update: AIDS Cases Reported to Surveillance, Forecasting and Impact Assessment Unit (SFI), Global Programme on AIDS," 30 September 1989 (mimeo), and Mann, Jonathan M., "Global AIDS into the 1990s,"

address presented at the Fifth International Conference on AIDS, Montreal, Canada, 4 June 1989.

9.   *The New York Times*, 1 December 1989, p. D19

10.   WHO Global Programme on AIDS, October 1989.

11.   *World Population Trends and Policies: 1989 Monitoring Report, op. cit.*, para. 449.

12.   Recently an experimental vaccine has been found quite successful in protecting monkeys against simian AIDS, which is caused by a virus similar to HIV, but it probably will be at least several years before this could lead to a safe, effective vaccine against human AIDS. (*The New York Times*, 8 December 1989, p. A1).

13.   *Ibid.*

14.   *World Population Trends and Policies: 1989 Monitoring Report, op. cit.*, paras. 472–475.

15.   United Nations, ACC Subcommittee on Nutrition, First report on the world nutrition situation, November 1987, p. i.

16.   WHO, *Evaluation of the Strategy for Health for All by the Year* 2000, *op. cit.*, p. 88.

17.   See ACC, *op. cit.*, paras. 56–60.

18.   United Nations, ACC Sub-Committee on Nutrition, "Update on the Nutrition Situation—Recent Trends in Nutrition in 33 countries," January/February 1989, chap. 3.

19.   WHO, *The International Drinking Water Supply and Sanitation Decade,* 1981–1990, CWS Series on Co-operative Action for the Decade, Geneva, September 1987, tables A.3.2.1 and A.3.2.3., pp. 23 and 25, and subsequent revisions in WHO's data bank.

20.   *Ibid.*, tables A.3.2.2. and A.3.2.4., pp. 24 and 26, and subsequent revisions in WHO's data bank.

21.   WHO, *The International Drinking Water Supply and Sanitation Decade, op. cit.*, p. 14.

22.   Based on the baseline scenario of GDP and on country and regional unit costs per capita reported in WHO, *The International Drinking Water Supply and Sanitation Decade, Review of Mid-Decade Progress (as at December* 1985*)*, CWS Series, September 1987.

23. For reviews of alternative systems for water supply and sanitation, see *Global Report on Human Settlements 1986*, published by Oxford University Press for the United Nations Centre for Human Settlements (Habitat), 1987, pp. 148–153, and Mahesh S. Patel, "Eliminating Social Distance between North and South, Cost-effective Goals for the 1990s," UNICEF Staff Working Paper No. 5, October 1989, annex 16.

24. This goal and its accompanying strategy have been endorsed by the United Nations General Assembly in its resolutions 34/58 of 29 November 1979 and 36/43 of 19 November 1981.

25. Patel, *op. cit.*

26. For a more detailed review of these issues, see World Bank, *Financing Health Services in Developing Countries, an Agenda for Reform*, Washington, D.C., 1987. For a review of the effects of user charges, including a case study comparing the fee structures of government and mission health centres in Rwanda, see Donald S. Shepard and Elizabeth R. Benjamin, "User Fees and Health Financing in Developing Countries: Mobilizing Financial Resources for Health," in David E. Bell and Michael R. Reich, eds., *Health, Nutrition, and Economic Crises, Approaches to Policy in the Third World*, Dover, Massachusetts, Auburn House Publishing Co., 1988, pp. 401–424.

27. For further analysis of goals and estimated costs of the WHO Strategy for Health for All by the Year 2000, see Patel, *op. cit.*, and Mahesh Patel, "An Economic Evaluation of 'Health for All'", in *Health Policy and Planning* (Oxford University Press), vol. I, No. 1, 1986, pp. 37–47.

28. See ACC, *op. cit.*, para. 70.

TABLE 12.1 *Number of countries with infant mortality rates or life expectancy not meeting the goals set for 1990 and 2000 in the International Development Strategy for the 1980s*

Country group	Total number of countries in group	Infant mortality rate		Life expectancy below 60 in 2000
		Above 120 in 1990	Above 50 in 2000	
Developing countries				
North Africa	5	0	3	0
Sub-Saharan Africa	45	17	41	36
South and East Asia				
South Asia	7	3	6	4
East Asian newly-industralizing economies	3	0	0	0
Others	9	1	3	3
Western Asia	13	0	3	2
Mediterranean	4	0	0	0
Western hemisphere	28	0	3	1
Total, developing countries	114	21	59	46
Least developed countries	35	17	32	31
China and Asian planned economies	4	0	0	0
Developed countries	33	0	0	0

Source: United Nations Secretariat, Department of International Economic and Social Affairs, based on country data underlying figures 12.1 and 12.2.

TABLE 12.2 *Percentage of population with safe drinking water,*
developing countries, 1985–2000[a]

Country group	Number of countries	1985 population (millions)	1985 Urban	1985 Rural	1985 Total	1990 Total	2000 Total
North Africa	4	98.7	93.0	47.1	68.1	69.0	74.0
Sub-Saharan Africa	39	391.3	74.7	23.0	36.2	34.4	36.3
South and East Asia	15	1,386.0	69.9	46.1	52.4	54.9	61.8
South Asia	5	1,006.6	74.4	46.8	53.5	56.0	63.0
East Asian newly industrializing economies	3	49.1	92.2	49.3	79.4	85.5	96.6
Others	7	330.4	49.2	43.6	45.1	46.9	53.1
Western Asia and Mediterranean	7	131.3	96.6	61.3	80.6	82.6	89.8
Western hemisphere	24	388.2	84.4	46.2	72.7	73.0	74.7
Total	89	2,395.6	78.5	42.4	55.2	56.4	60.6
Least developed countries	27	333.8	52.1	32.3	35.5	36.2	39.9

Source: United Nations Secretariat, Department of International Economic and Social Affairs, based on country data compiled by WHO as of June 1989.

[a] *Country group figures are averages of individual country percentages weighted by urban, rural or total population.*

TABLE 12.3 *Percentage of population with adequate sanitation, developing countries, 1985–2000*[a]

Country group	Number of countries	1985 population (millions)	1985			1990 Total	2000 Total
			Urban	Rural	Total		
North Africa	2	29.0	81.2	34.8	55.8	56.0	59.5
Sub-Saharan Africa	24	140.3	68.7	26.1	36.2	34.9	36.1
South and East Asia	13	1,379.9	44.3	13.3	21.5	24.1	31.9
South Asia	5	1,006.6	33.6	3.1	10.5	13.8	22.7
East Asian newly industralizing economies	2	43.6	99.9	100.0	99.9	100.0	100.0
Others	6	329.7	55.1	40.7	44.6	46.4	53.7
Western Asia and Mediterranean	4	31.7	99.2	30.7	78.9	77.8	83.5
Western hemi-sphere	22	387.6	79.2	15.4	59.5	59.0	59.6
Total	65	1,968.5	61.3	15.0	31.4	33.2	39.0
Least developed countries	20	247.9	44.1	15.2	19.9	22.0	28.6

Source: United Nations Secretariat, Department of International Economic and Social Affairs, based on country data compiled by WHO as of June 1989.

[a] *Country group figures are averages of individual country percentages weighted by urban, rural or total population.*

TABLE 12.4 *Government health expenditures per capita,[a] in 1980 dollars (number of countries)*

Country group	Total outlays			Final consumption expenditure			
	All countries	1980	1985	Number of countries	1970	1980	1985
Developing coun- tries							
North Africa	18.29 (4)	10.15 (2)	12.09 (2)	(2)	9.49	29.77	30.16
Sub-Saharan Africa	5.92 (16)	8.99 (8)	8.33 (8)	(18)	6.41	6.68	6.96
South and East Asia	3.12 (10)	3.05 (9)	4.08 (9)	(9)	1.30	2.27	3.24
South Asia	2.28 (4)	2.28 (4)	3.33 (4)	(4)	1.03	1.61	2.58
East Asian newly-in- dustrializ- ing econ- omies	7.76 (2)	7.76 (2)	10.67 (2)	(1)	0.61	3.11	3.10
Others	5.08 (4)	5.13 (3)	5.88 (3)	(4)	5.48	10.68	12.60
Western Asia	117.93 (2)	117.93 (2)	155.70 (2)	(4)	16.21	48.15	41.37
Mediterranean	175.45 (2)	175.45 (2)	140.62 (2)	(3)	8.80	17.20	17.48
Western hemi- sphere	41.08 (8)	39.34 (3)	37.28 (3)	(8)	21.36	24.13	27.49
Subtotal, develop- ing countries	8.86 (42)	7.49 (26)	7.81 (26)	(44)	3.85	6.84	7.70
Least developed countries	2.07 (13)	2.04 (7)	2.08 (7)	(12)	2.41	1.92	2.08
China	6.70 (1)	..	..		..	..	..
Developed market economies	552.58 (23)	552.58 (23)	569.70 (23)	(15)	154.94	226.24	240.46

Source: United Nations Secretariat, Department of International Economic and Social Affairs, based on country data from United Nations Statistical Office, National Accounts Statistics data bank tables 2.1, 2.3, 2.5; IMF, Government Finance Statistics Yearbook 1987, p. 98, *and World Bank,* Financing Health Services in Developing Countries, Washington, D.C., 1987, table 3, p. 16.

[a] *Country group averages are weighted by population.*

TABLE 12.5 *Government and private 1980 health expenditures per capita, in 1980 dollars[a]*
(Number of countries)

Country group	Government total outlays	Private expenditure[b]
Developing countries		
North Africa	18.29 (4)	10.14 (2)
Sub-Saharan Africa	5.92 (16)	7.71 (16)
South and East Asia	3.12 (10)	8.20 (11)
South Asia	2.28 (4)	3.89 (3)
East Asia newly industrializ-		
ing economies	7.76 (2)	57.37 (3)
Others	5.08 (4)	12.63 (5)
Western Asia	117.93 (2)	51.30 (2)
Mediterranean	175.45 (2)	59.93 (2)
Western hemisphere	41.08 (8)	56.10 (9)
Total, developing countries	8.86 (42)	14.41 (42)
Least developed countries	2.07 (13)	5.34 (10)
China	6.70 (1)	3.16 (1)
Developed market economies	552.58 (23)	519.94 (24)

Source: United Nations Secretariat, Department of International Economic and Social Affairs, based on sources for table 12.4.

[a] *Country group averages are weighted by population.*

[b] *Includes some expenditures by missions and non-governmental organizations, as well as private expenditures on health care, as estimated by the World Bank.*

13.
Social Policy

A. BROADER PARTICIPATION

The fuller participation of all elements of society in defining and achieving the common goals of development, with full respect for fundamental freedoms, is likely to be a major issue for the balance of the century. The principle of broader participation has been adopted at several major conferences held under United Nations auspices in recent years.

Progress towards fuller participation can contribute directly to improving the situation of disadvantaged groups and society as a whole. It also has the potential of influencing economic performance, through its impact on motivation, innovation and productivity. Although this influence is essentially intangible and has mostly defied quantification, it is nonetheless real. Participation may be expected to have a generally positive impact on economic performance through increased motivation, by opening opportunities for groups whose involvement in productive activities tends to be artificially restricted and by making fuller use of underused or latent skills and talents.

Of growing importance and interest are the continuing strength and proliferation of various co-operative, self-help, and community groups and non-governmental organizations and the increasingly organized articulation by various groups of their interests, reflected in their demands for a greater say in decisions affecting them. Numerous initiatives have been taken all over the world to give more people a greater voice in the running of institutions. Such initiatives seek to give workers a greater role in the management of enterprises, to give greater autonomy to public enterprises in countries with centrally planned and mixed economies, to devolve power to local authorities, and to establish new forms of partnership between government and non-governmental organizations. The process of codifying human rights has also gained momentum in a number of global agreements relating to the advancement of women and the situation of specific groups of the population, in particular, youth, the aging, migrant workers and their families, disabled persons, and those in detention or accused of crime.

Of particular significance from the economic point of view are the expansion and diversification of the co-operative and other mutual self-help movements; the experiments to improve motivation and efficiency through greater decision-making autonomy and worker participation; greater participation of clients in the design and administration of more decentralized social services; and the reorientation of welfare services towards mutual self-help, prevention, rehabilitation, and income-generating activities for welfare service recipients, the latter being of special significance in developing countries.

B. ADVANCEMENT OF WOMEN

Progress towards achieving equality between the sexes is one of the most dramatic social changes of this century. The achievement of this equality is a world-wide goal, set in 1975 and reaffirmed in 1985 at the end of the United Nations Decade for Women. The Nairobi Forward-looking Strategies for the Advancement of

Women[1] foresee the achievement of full equality by the year 2000. Although this ambitious target has strong implications for the future global economy and society, projecting its consequences requires particular care. The effect of a progressive elimination of inequalities, on which many social and economic relations are still based, may not be fully visible until well into the next century.

Between 1985 and the year 2000, the number of women in the world is expected to increase by some 635 million, from 2.4 billion to just over 3 billion, with almost 80 per cent of them living in the developing regions. The proportion of women in the total population will fall slightly, from 49.7 per cent to 49.6 per cent, reflecting faster growth in population in the developing regions. With the exception of Africa, these regions will continue to have more men than women, especially in Latin America and South and East Asia, although the trend is towards parity. In South Asia, the projected ratio is 104.9 men to every 100 women by the year 2000. This contrasts with the developed regions, where the ratio of men to women was 94.2 in 1983 and is projected to rise slightly to 95.6 by the year 2000.

A likely effect of increased life expectancy for women in developing countries will be more women entering the formal labour force after their child-bearing years. How the economies of these countries will adjust to the large numbers of women wishing to enter the labour market will be a major issue. If current trends are not modified, projections indicate that the participation of women in the officially measured economically active population will decline. Throughout the world women make an important contribution to the economy, however, even though many of their productive activities are not formally recognized. In addition to their presence in formal employment, women contribute significantly to work on family farms and enterprises and in the informal sector, by providing "free" services that maintain and support current and future workers, services that would otherwise need to be provided by the State, or bought in the market. Increased productivity in all such activities can be a major source of increased well-being and economic growth. The entry of more women into formal and more skilled employment could improve their productivity and thereby national incomes.

An increase in the relative number of female workers is unlikely to influence male unemployment adversely. There is no evidence that greater female participation has in the past been at the expense of male employment; employment trends for both sexes have tended to move in the same direction. In the coming years, when the informal sector is expected to increase in importance, women are likely to be hired in jobs that men do not want, based on current preferences, because working hours are limited, or because the job offers a less secure link to the employing enterprise.

At the micro-economic and micro-social levels, women's participation in the economy is often the only way to protect the family in times of difficult economic conditions. Women's employment and the income derived from it maintains, and sometimes ensures by itself, the standard of living of the family.

The number of women who are their family's main economic earners has been increasing in recent years, and this evolution is likely to continue. The trend whereby women work in order to compensate for an otherwise declining standard of living can be expected to continue in the 1990s, especially in those developing countries where no significant increase in per capita income is anticipated. Women's participation is necessary for the economic survival of the family in the early stages of a country's development; in economies characterized by family-based employment, women have higher rates of participation than in economies based on wage labour. Thus, as the development process modifies the structure of employment, women's participation appears as an important adjustment factor within the economy and the family. Even in developed economies, the role of women as secondary wage earners may be essential for the family, and this characteristic is likely to increase by the year 2000. In some countries, such as the United States, studies indicate that women's participation may be inversely related to husbands' wages. Thus, the wife takes a job in order to compensate for an insufficient or declining family income. Studies in other countries suggest that wives of men earning either very low or very high incomes had higher participation rates than wives of men earning middle incomes. These two interpretations of the relationship between female economic participation and the family's, or the husband's income indicate that, in cases of economic difficulties, women are likely to increase their participation in the economy.

The participation of women in the economy is affected by relationships between education, health, and fertility, all of which influence the incentive for a firm to hire a female worker and her strategy in the labour market. These relationships are usually part of a vicious cycle contributing to the exclusion of women from the formal economy. But a policy that targets each aspect of these relationships may generate a virtuous circle promoting better use of women's talents and energies. Specific policies are necessary to promote equal access by women to education, since current trends indicate that full equality in access to education will not be achieved by the year 2000. Policies to promote equal access to education are to be complemented by training policies targeting older age groups. (The need to supplement formal education with training for women, not just men, is also evident). Women who have received little or no schooling should benefit from special training programmes to enable them to function effectively in a modern economy.

Women's reproductive role should not be an obstacle to full economic participation. The development of better support systems in the 1990s could influence the environment in which women determine their strategy in the labour market and the terms on which women reconcile their responsibilities in the household as parents and as workers. In most of the world, women work within family enterprises, where social support and economic roles can be combined. Urbanization has reduced the significance of this type of socio-economic structure in many countries, as the work-force in the formal sector increases. This trend can be expected to continue, and is one of the factors underlying the projected reduction in women's share in the global work-force. In order to overcome this effect in economic sectors where family enterprises do not exist, efforts can be made to create an environment in which parental and work responsibilities can be combined, by providing such services as day-care and parental leave. The incentives for an employer to hire a woman should not be lowered by measures that, though intended to favour women workers, may raise the costs they represent for a firm. Thus, parental leave is to be preferred to maternal leave, for example. The question of reconciling parental and work responsibilities can be addressed most easily in the context of more flexible attitudes to career patterns, which make allowances for further study, as well as family responsibilities, for both spouses.

To overcome past conditions, special programmes need to be organized to ensure that women who are in low-skill jobs, unemployed, or who stopped work in order to have children can get special training. Women returnees, in particular, can be an asset to an employer, as they have acquired maturity and certain skills. Their previous education represents an important investment by the society and needs to be used. If a woman decides to go back to work, support should therefore be available to her.

Policies in these areas will have a major bearing on the nature of the contribution that women will make to the economy and its overall impact in the future.

C. TRENDS IN SOCIAL WELFARE POLICY

The scope, complexity, and costs of publicly sponsored social security and social welfare services and programmes have increased significantly in many parts of the world, although their scope and coverage remain limited in most developing countries. Social welfare concepts and practices have also been the object of considerable debate and rethinking in recent years.

Spending on a broadly defined category of social welfare programmes, including social security, has increased steadily in real terms since the late 1960s, typically at rates faster than economic growth or total government expenditure. By the mid-1980s, social welfare spending by central and local government together was the equivalent of about 14 per cent of total output in developed countries and about 6 per cent in a small sample of the developing countries, although only 3 per cent and 1.5 per cent for Africa and South and East Asia, respectively.

In the developed countries, social security and welfare services are recognized as essential elements in the social advances that have been made. However, their rapidly rising costs have been a cause of concern and, despite the resources they absorb, some have come under scrutiny for their alleged inefficiencies and failure to provide for those most in need. Expansion and increased costs are built into most systems, although budgets are likely to continue to be restricted by slow economic growth. Administrative complexity pushes up delivery costs. Services are labour-intensive, and increased professionalism and training escalate unit costs. Increasing numbers of middle-class people use services, especially in a period of slow growth in personal income. Changing age structures, in particular the aging of the population, add a new element, which will be progressively more significant. While the increased costs associated with an aging population may be offset by savings in maternity, child, and youth services, this change will nonetheless require a major redirection of resources and re-training of personnel. Partly inspired by the drive to greater economy, but reflecting also changes in professional views as of appropriate forms in which to provide care, institutionalization of people who cannot support themselves is being de-emphasized in favour of community-based and family-based support. Perhaps the most significant trend is greater prominence for prevention and rehabilitation, to enhance people's capacity to function independently, effectively, and productively.

In many developing countries, the need for social welfare services is increasing with the spread of urbanization, migration, changing family and kinship support systems, and greater female participation in the modern economy. But as recession and economic decline in some areas are placing greater demands on the typically limited capacity of existing public systems, Governments are seeking ways to maintain existing family support systems. Social welfare programmes are increasingly taking on a developmental character, with an emphasis on creating income-earning opportunities for the poor, vulnerable, dependent, or disabled. Even limited resources can have significant economic benefits if used for prevention, maternal and infant care, immunization against childhood diseases, and supplementary feeding for preschool and school-children, as well as some rural community services. To replicate such programmes in large numbers would require a redirection of resources from urban, often middle-class-oriented services, with all that this implies.

D. THE FAMILY

The family as a basic social unit has undergone profound change, but with no uniform pattern. From an economic perspective, the most important changes are those related to family formation and fertility, the family as a system of support, and the supporting services that families increasingly need in order to function effectively in a changing environment. In developing countries, the role of the family as a production unit and source of employment continues to be of major, though diminishing, importance.

The extent to which the family, nuclear or extended, has been eroded as an effective social support system is the subject of considerable debate. Lack of precise information on the actual support rendered for family members to each other tends to make the discussion conjectural. It is probably safe to say that, in the developed countries, the family as a support institution has not been eroded as much as is commonly supposed, whereas in developing countries, the stereotype of the self-sufficient family is no longer an entirely accurate reflection of reality. In the areas of education and health, families are probably making a greater contribution than at any previous time, although family members receive a greater proportion of their total education and health services outside the family.

Recent trends suggest that pressure will continue for families to rely more on external support, much of it provided by public authorities in the form of specialized services and care, in particular in developed countries. In developing countries, too, where parents are less able to prepare their children for a world outside their realm of experience, families may need outside support, especially in finding suitable employment for the next generation. In many countries, demands are growing for additional services and support that would better enable parents, especially mothers, to reconcile parental, household, and work responsibilities. These demands will be a major issue in developed countries and will become increasingly relevant in developing countries as fewer women will earn a living from home-based employment. At the same time, however, restraints on the financial and administrative resources of Governments, and on the availability of adequately trained child-care workers, will limit the ability of Governments to provide adequate child-care for all young children. New arrangements, including participation by employers, primary schools, and other existing institutions, will be needed. In some cases, it may be more efficient and socially beneficial for Governments to provide direct income supplements to enable parents to spend more time caring for their children in their own homes or in various co-operative arrangements with neighbours or relatives.

In both developed and developing countries, in a period of budgetary constraints, Governments have looked with renewed interest at the family as a system of support that could bear a larger share of the burden of looking after the sick, the disabled, and the aged. The professional view supports such arrangements as being in many cases preferable to institutionalization and recommends public support and assistance to encourage families to provide more such support. However, the burden of care now tends to fall disproportionately on women. There is thus a potential conflict between this trend and the goal of widening opportunities for women, especially in education and employment.

E. SPECIFIC POPULATION GROUPS

The coming decade will witness an acceleration of population aging, as discussed earlier. The global population aged 60 and above will total 485 million in 1990 and increase to approximately 610 million in the year 2000 (and to 755 million in 2010; to 1,170 million in 2025). The growth of the population aged 80 and above will be even more rapid, and women will comprise the majority of this group. Worldwide, most of the elderly will be living in urban areas. In developing countries, however, the majority of the elderly will still be residing in rural areas. The roles of the private and public sectors in caring for the elderly, traditionally performed by the family and the local community, will probably have to increase. This support will be particularly needed in rural areas of developing countries due to the rural-to-urban exodus of the young and the consequent "aging" of these areas. Rural development strategies aimed at providing employment opportunities for aging men and women and at strengthening family and community support for the aging, could help to secure the well-being of this large segment of the world's elderly population.

Social expenditures incurred by the aging of populations are high and rising in many industrialized countries. Income security and health care provisions will pose a challenge to public and private sectors well into the next century. Mitigating actions could include efforts to raise national saving and investment rates, collection of higher social welfare contributions from workers and employers, reduction of benefits, and introduction of complementary public and private pension systems.[2] Flexibility of retirement age may also be considered, but early retirement as a means of opening up employment opportunities for the young—a trend observed in several countries—may aggravate the financial and social problems of the elderly. The provision of more genuine choices for older workers, which is especially needed in some of the developed countries, could help ensure participation of able elderly in the economic and social life of their countries.[3]

The elderly are occupying an increasing proportion of general hospital beds, with wide variations between quality of care and length of stay from country to country and within countries. Unnecessarily long periods and high costs of hospitalization could be reduced by more effective management and the establishment of broader-based community support. Geriatric training and institutions that provide long-term care for the frail, dependent elderly are inadequate in most countries and urgently need to be improved in anticipation of the rapid expansion of this population group. To contain health care costs and ensure that providing care for the frail elderly is not left unduly to any one sector or group, a broader system of geriatric care is required. Geriatric care should incorporate provisions for acute and chronic illnesses, training, community support, and service delivery. National and local governments, professional and voluntary organizations, the family, and the elderly themselves can collaborate in supporting and delivering the care.

Like the elderly, the young also have special needs. The ages of 15 to 24 are critical, when young people become integrated in their communities as adults. In times of rapid social and economic change, family bonds weaken as traditional values of parents seem less relevant to problems of the young. Employment opportunities are critical for the absorption of the next generation. Where generations of young men and women come to maturity without opportunities to work and make reasonable lives for themselves, a seething pool of discontent invariably forms among energetic and talented young people. A particularly daunting prospect is that the majority of the youth facing limited employment opportunities today will be parents in the year 2000, with only a tenuous hold on the economic ladder.

High unemployment of youth in most developing countries can be tackled effectively only in a context of more vigorous economic growth. At the same time, public and private programmes can be geared towards making youth employable. Suitable training, in and out of school, and provision of initial employment opportunities are essential. In many countries, the past 10 years have been especially difficult for youth employment, as a growing youth cohort coincided with recession, slow economic growth and economic restructuring. Although the youth cohort is already declining and will be considerably smaller in the 1990s, thereby reducing the likely levels of youth unemployment, youth with low skills will have increasing difficulty finding entry-level jobs. In most developing countries, many young people find only a series of casual jobs, often in the informal sector. There is in many countries a serious mismatch between the skills acquired in school and the needs of employers: young people without skills face particularly bleak futures, especially in urban areas.

The most critical needs are faced by rural youth. A general lack of basic amenities in rural areas is combined with few organizations specifically for young people, contradictions between aspirations and traditional values and systems, and often limited access to land. Efforts directed at improving rural conditions in general, with special emphasis on rural youth, can be an important element in slowing down migration to urban areas and providing greater opportunities for youth in general.

Yet another special population is the disabled. The economic as well as human costs of disability are very large. While no single, precise estimate of the number of disabled persons exists, a conservative estimate puts the global number of people in the world suffering from all types of disability at over 500 million. Even relatively minor types of disability are closely associated with the incidence of poverty in many developing countries. Prevention and rehabilitation can yield potentially widespread social and economic benefits.

Despite strained economic circumstances, Governments are making increasing political commitments to the prevention of disability and to rehabilitation and equalization of opportunities for disabled people. These commitments frequently are contained in legislative measures or constitutional clauses. Disability can affect all aspects of life. Policies at all levels aimed at dealing with disability issues should, therefore, be an integral part of the larger efforts aimed at promoting a better life for all. These policies should form an integral part of each country's development efforts and should enhance a society's overall productive capacity.

Financial limitations and the need for trained human resources in dealing with a disability have been identified as the two major obstacles in implementing goals of the World Programme of Action Concerning Disabled Persons (see General Assembly resolution 37/52 of 3 December 1982). With lack of expertise identified as the next greatest obstacle in implementing disability programmes, training and education have been identified by a large proportion of developing and least developed countries as a priority in future technical assistance programmes.

Mental disabilities have a uniquely unfortunate impact on society. In both the developed and developing world, mental illness has reportedly been increasing. Since the mentally ill and mentally retarded are among those receiving the least coverage in vocational training schemes and rehabilitation services, especially in the least developed countries, concerted research efforts, as well as increased provisions of treatment, are urgently called for.

The World Programme of Action Concerning Disabled Persons recommends the integration of mentally retarded and other severely disabled children into the general school system. Special attention needs to be drawn to this challenge in the light of the discovery that over 70 per cent of countries at all stages of development in all regions report that school authorities have the discretion to exclude some categories of disabled children from the school system.

The vast majority of the world's disabled persons live under conditions of deprivation, without access to social assistance, especially where infrastructural conditions are rudimentary. The extension of social security on a universal basis would be an important step towards alleviating the problems of disabled persons since, today, such coverage is largely concentrated among developed countries.

Effective community-based rehabilitation requires a network of community services, as well as specialized referral services. Concerted efforts appear to be essential in this area, if a strategy of community-based rehabilitation is to be successful in offering the services required by many disabled people. The integration of disabled people within the community also requires access to public buildings and transportation. While living conditions in largely rural countries may not immediately demand the same measures to improve accessibility required by more urbanized countries, it is nonetheless important that appropriate legislation evolve in view of anticipated needs.

Research capacity on disability is distributed unevenly among countries. Many countries have expressed a need to enhance such research capacity. Accelerating research and saving resources as well may be possible, if increases in national research capacity were accompanied by co-operation through regionally-based disability research institutes.

F. CRIME

Direct and indirect costs of crime in terms of human, social and economic losses seriously distort development priorities and goals. Expenditures on the maintenance of law and order divert funds urgently needed in other sectors and are a heavy burden on national budgets. Problems encountered include the emergence of sophisticated forms of crime new to many countries lacking the experience and resources to respond adequately.

Although attempts have been made to put a "price" on traditional types of crime, none has been acceptable. The really important costs of crime are damage to the quality of life, incapacitated and frightened victims, restriction of movement, and so on, but these costs cannot be linked directly to a country's economic situation. The remedy that has gained much support in recent years is that of victim-support. The cost of such schemes is small compared with other costs of crime and crime control.

The relationship between the advance of technology and other aspects of economic development, and the rate and type of criminal activity can be measured somewhat more precisely, but still leaves a lot to guesswork. Many criminal justice officials and research criminologists believe that the link between "organized crime" and legitimate business is growing stronger. Telecommunications makes it possible, even easy, to carry out fraud and embezzlement over a wider geographical area and on a much grander scale.

National economies are likely to suffer increasingly from costs and effects of conventional crime, growth of organized crime, including the use of legitimate or quasi-legitimate organizational techniques and structures for illegal economic grain and from costs of attempts to control crime. Based on findings of the first and second United Nations Surveys of Crime Trends, Operation of Criminal Justice Systems and Crime Preservation Strategies, projections of recent trends suggest that criminal justice systems are a major growth industry. For every 100 recorded crimes in 1975, there would be 160 in the year 2000; for every 100 police officers there would be over 170; and for every 100 adults in prison, there would be over 200.

Economic growth might bring some increase in some types of crime, while others will decrease. However, types likely to increase are those that are most likely to be reported, so that an increase in recorded criminality could possibly accompany a decrease in unrecorded traditional criminality. However, unrecorded crime, specifically in respect to economic crime, is likely to continue to grow rather than decrease . The broad category of different techniques involving technology for the non-violent but illegal acquisition and use of money seem likely to grow considerably; it will directly affect the economy of some, perhaps many, countries. Many criminal justice practitioners and policy-makers believe that the most effective tool for prevention and control of such activities is the forfeiture or freezing of assets. To ensure wide practice, the banking industry's co-operation is needed, including less secrecy.

The preceding are projections and not forecasts. However, they do show that a huge increase in demands made upon the national economy by the criminal justice system is, at least, highly likely, and perhaps inevitable in many countries. Because prison is a very expensive institution in any country, an even more alarming feature is the fast-rising number of adults in prison. If that number continues to rise at the 1975–1980 rate, the cost of prison service alone will make criminal justice a major component in the budget of every country's public sector. On the one hand, more police officers are being recruited, leading to more arrests; and on the other, there is evidence that courts in many countries are handing down longer sentences because they perceive themselves faced with a rising crime wave. The self-amplifying nature of this phenomenon is particularly worrying, in that the larger police force "creates" the impression of a larger crime problem by arresting more suspects. It is thus extremely difficult to determine how much of the increase is genuine and how much is the result of policies adopted in the different criminal justice agencies. However, in this context, the even more important issue is that the impact on the national budget will continue to increase. One response for a national administration is to allow the continued strengthening of the "intake" end of the system, the police, but not to expand the capacity for disposal after trial. That results in overcrowded prisons, however, which both offend generally accepted standards of human rights and are widely thought to be themselves criminogenic.

In summary, the rising levels of recorded crime and of State responses to it can be expected to have a significant and deleterious effect on many national economies by the year 2000. The harm done to individual victims may not be easily quantifiable in economic terms, but organized crime—and with it a threat to legitimate business practices—seems likely to grow. Finally, the rising cost of criminal justice will compel the diversion of resources from more popular and desirable components of the public sector.

G. DRUG ABUSE

Problems stemming from drug abuse and illicit trafficking have been growing at an alarming rate over the past 20 years. During this period, the abuse of narcotic drugs and psychotropic substances has increasingly spread throughout the world, primarily among the young, crossing all social, economic, political, and national boundaries. While the extent of drug abuse varies from country to country and from one population group to another within the same country, abuse has spread to countries and population groups that had not previously been involved, and has increased further in those population groups where it already existed. The spread reflects expanded illicit production and distribution. These trends are most likely to continue and, given the known consequences of drug abuse, to have significant adverse effects on public health and general social and economic conditions throughout the 1990s.

Drug abuse severely affects normal social functioning, intelligent and responsible behaviour, and the ability and motivation to engage in the complex tasks required in modern societies. Heavy drug abusers show very pronounced tendencies toward inactivity, apathy and self-neglect. Loss of interest in conventional goals and lethargy lead to decreased productivity at school and at work. In addition to the costs of drug-related crimes and incarcerations, heavy costs are inflicted on national economies by disabilities, absenteeism, accidents, and deaths due to drug abuse.[4]

Forms of drug abuse are becoming increasingly complex: abuse involving two or more substances is widespread and has become the predominant pattern in a number of countries. The age of first drug use is falling from adolescence to preadolescence and even earlier in some countries. In the 1980s, there has been an alarming increase in the spread of AIDS and certain other viral infections among abusers who inject drugs and, subsequently, from abusers to the general population through such modes as sexual intercourse. Societies most likely will be faced with increasing demands for resources to cope with problems related to AIDS, including more effective programmes designed to prevent the transmission of the virus through drug abuse. This demand will require more intensive search for effective methods of prevention and treatment of drug abuse, as well as broader implementation of such measures. At present, methadone maintenance has, in some instances, shown useful results in the process of treatment for opiate-addicted persons. The usefulness of alternative programmes, such as free distribution of sterilized needles and syringes, is being explored. In addition, educational and other preventive programmes, designed to meet the needs of various target groups, should be provided in all social settings.

To cope effectively with drug abuse problems in the years to come, traditional and novel prevention and treatment forms will be required. In addition to promoting traditional services, societies will make increasing efforts to provide these new approaches:

(a) Broadly-based educational programmes, in natural social settings, to help individuals at risk to acquire necessary knowledge and confidence to resist the temptation to use illicit drugs, and to increase their ability to cope with day-to-day problems of living;

(b) After-care and social reintegration, especially with a view to reducing relapse rates after completion of treatment and rehabilitation. Involving the family, the local community and other appropriate forms of social support will reduce relapse rates;

(c) Positive community response to drug-related problems and community involvement in providing readily available preventive and treatment services at as low a cost as possible;

(d) Participation of youth in preventive programmes and encourage the creation of conditions in which young people can find scope for their capacities for social integration and receive due recognition and support for their activities.

The illicit supply of and trafficking in drugs have also increased at an alarming rate in most parts of the world over the past 20 years. The forbidden cultivation of narcotic plants has grown to enormous proportions in certain areas. Narcotic drugs and psy-

chotropic substances are increasingly produced by illegal laboratories. Diversion from legal sources into other channels adds considerably to the problem of illicit supply of drugs. While strong
law enforcement and advanced technology may greatly improve
a nation's ability to destroy these crops, production in some areas
is likely to continue unless reasonable economic alternatives are
offered to those involved. Reducing the economic incentive to
grow the crops, as part of a long-term goal of eradicating illicit
production, has increased in strategic importance over the past
decade. Future efforts will require increased technical and financial
resources for this purpose.

Drug trafficking has become very sophisticated and complex,
involving organized crime in a variety of illegal activities, including conspiracy, bribery, intimidation and corruption of public
servants, tax evasion, banking law violations, racketeering, illegal
money transfers, import/export violations, smuggling of weapons, crimes of violence and terrorism. Drug-related problems thus
directly affect social stability and public safety and are associated
with social disintegration.

Increasing the efficiency of the criminal justice system in arresting, prosecuting, and sentencing traffickers will effectively
supplement the activities of police and customs authorities. This
process includes strengthening legal tools to ensure appropriate
penalties. Depriving individuals involved in drug trafficking of
their profits has proven to be an effective countermeasure in various parts of the world.

A number of Governments have initiated vigorous and innovative methods for disrupting drug-trafficking networks. These
methods and experience in using them can be shared with other
Governments. In many cases of drug trafficking, it is necessary
to look for evidence in countries or territories other than that
where the accused individual has been brought to trial. Therefore
a international co-operation is essential to ensure the effective
prosecution of these individuals and the removal of their illegally
gained profits. An important action being taken by the international community in this regard has been the adoption in 1988 of
a new United Nations Convention against Illicit Traffic in Nar-

cotic Drugs and Psychotropic Substances, which deals with those aspects of the problem not covered in existing international drug control treaties. The international drug control system will thus be strengthened to cope more effectively with the drug-abuse challenge in the year 2000.

The commitment of the international community to strive for universal accession to international drug control treaties and their strict implementation will intensify co-operation through the United Nations to strengthen each nation's handling of drug abuse and associated problems. The Comprehensive Multidisciplinary Outline of Future Activities in Drug Abuse Control, adopted at the 1987 International Conference on Drug Abuse and Illicit Trafficking,[5] provides a basis for strengthening the international co-operation by the year 2000.

To summarize, fuller participation of all elements of society in defining and achieving the common goals of development has the potential to stimulate motivation, innovation, and productivity. There is great potential in further use of co-operative, self-help and community groups, non-governmental organizations, and workers' participation in the management of enterprises. Economic and social development can benefit from greater autonomy for public enterprises, devolution of power to local authorities, and new forms of partnership between governmental and non-governmental organizations. The reorientation of welfare services towards mutual self-help, prevention, rehabilitation, and income-generating activities is especially significant in developing countries. Rapidly rising costs of social welfare programmes have been a cause of concern in the developed countries, as have their alleged inefficiencies and failure to provide for those most in need. Institutionalization is being de-emphasized in favour of community-based and family-based support, prevention, and rehabilitation.

Progress towards equality has wide implications for the future global economy and society. Women make essential contributions to economic and social life although many of their activities are not formally recognized, especially their work in households, family farms and enterprises, and in the informal sector. Greater productivity in such activities could be a major source of increased well-being and economic growth. With increasing life expectancy and other changes in the developing countries, many more women are likely to enter the formal labour force.

In many developing countries the need for social services is growing, but with recession and economic decline in some areas, Governments are seeking to maintain existing family support systems. Social welfare programmes emphasize creating more income-earning opportunities. National economies will suffer from the effects of crime, including the use of legitimate or quasi-legitimate organizational techniques and structures for illegal economic gain. The use of new techniques for non-violent but illegal acquisition and use of money will grow and significantly affect the economy in many countries.

Drug abuse and illicit trafficking have spread throughout the world and are likely to continue. Drug abuse, primarily among the young, crosses all social, economic, and political boundaries. Its spread reflects expanded illicit demand and production as well as the traffic in drugs, which has become sophisticated and complex, involving organized crime. The cultivation of narcotic plants has grown to enormous proportions in certain areas of the world. While strong law enforcement and advanced technology may improve a nation's ability to destroy illicit crops, production in some areas is likely to continue unless reasonable economic alternatives are offered to those involved.

NOTES

1. See *Report of the World Conference to Review and Appraise the Achievements of the United Nations Decade for Women: Equality, Development and Peace* Nairobi, 15–26 July 1985 (United Nations publication, Sales No. E.85.IV.10) chapter I, sect. A.

2. "Aging and Social Expenditure in the Major Industrial Countries, 1988–2025," by Peter S. Heller, Richard Hemming and Peter W. Kohnert, International Monetary Fund, Washington, D.C. (Occasional Paper No. 47), September 1986.

3. "Labour flexibility and older worker marginalisation: the need for a new strategy," Guy Standing, International Labour Review, vol. 125, No. 3, May-June 1986.

4.   For detailed information, see "Measures to assess drug abuse and the health, social and economic consequences of such abuse: summary of information from 21 countries," *Bulletin on Narcotics* (United Nations publication), vol. 35, No. 3, July-September 1983, pp. 26–31.

5.   Report of the International Conference on Drug Abuse and Illicit Trafficking, Vienna, 17–26 June 1987 (United Nations publication, Sales No. E.87.I.18).

14.
Concluding
Observations

ALL ATTEMPTS to look into the future run into fundamental problems. First, what will happen depends greatly on human decisions. If the trends indicated by present evidence are not acceptable, Governments and individuals will try to change them. The purpose of perspective studies is not so much that of forecasting as that of changing the future in directions that are considered necessary or desirable.

Secondly, as happened in the 1970s and 1980s, unforeseeable developments are quite likely to put their stamp on the world economy in the 1990s, for better or for worse.

Thirdly, the impact of many of the most important processes of change currently under way in the world economy is difficult or impossible to incorporate into a quantitative assessment of the future of the world economy. The changes will modify significantly many of the traditional relationships and linkages on which models of the world economy are based, but the timing and magnitude of such effects are difficult to capture even in alternative scenarios. Some of them have been referred to above, but others have not. This overview of the socio-economic perspectives would not be complete without a summary of some of the most important ones:

(a) A greater measure of financial and monetary stability in the world economy would reduce the uncertainty that presently discourages much investment or directs it into undesirable channels. For many countries in Latin America and Africa, whether their paralyzing debt problems are alleviated at an early or a late stage in the 1990s will make a decisive difference;

(b) Should genuine progress on disarmament result from a lessening of political tensions, extensive resources could be released for civilian uses. Military expenditures account for 5 to 6 per cent of the output in the world as a whole. But this understates their economic impact. The development of new weapons systems absorbs a large share of the highly skilled manpower in research and puts great strains on government resources. In view of the fiscal constraints facing countries at all stages of development and the climate of hope arising from progress in negotiations on nuclear arms reductions, the share of output devoted to military expenditure in the most powerful countries is more likely to decline than to increase. Debt problems and other economic difficulties have already made for slower growth of military spending in developing countries. Such spending is often out of all proportion to development programmes, but substantial reductions will depend on progress in finding political solutions to perceived security problems;

(c) The international trading system is liable to undergo important changes in the medium term. It cannot yet be predicted what progress will be made in the Uruguay Round on such major issues as roll-backs of protectionist measures, trade in services, and the dismantling of agricultural subsidies, but the outcome will affect the world economy in the next decade. Significant progress towards the realization of an internal market in the European Community can be expected by 1992, augmented by closer ties with Eastern Europe and the USSR. The implementation of the free trade agreement between the United States and Canada will also affect global prospects. These developments raise apprehensions among non-participants, but if protectionism in world-wide trade is contained or reversed they will be of benefit to all. Economic reforms under way in the Soviet Union and Eastern Europe aim not only at major domestic reform but also at new patterns of international economic relations. Trade between centrally planned economies and market economies has always fallen far short of potential. If these trading relations are gradually opened up in the years to come, gains from trade and from an improved international division of labour would accelerate world growth;

(d) The reform of fiscal systems is on the agenda all over the world, chiefly because they have grown too complex to remain workable. In an increasingly internationalized world economy, there is also a need for international harmony if unanticipated distortions in investment flows are to be avoided;

(e) Technological change in a broad sense is the mainspring of economic growth. Its impact is not smooth and gradual; breakthroughs that take a long time to absorb occur occasionally. So it has been with the electronics revolution currently transforming the world system of production, communication, finance, and transportation. This revolution may have displaced more jobs than it created for some time. In what seems like a paradox, it has coincided with the recent retardation of economic growth. But the historical experience of similar breakthroughs suggests that this will be reversed when the new technology has been absorbed and its contributions to productivity have been reflected in overall growth. The 1990s may become therefore a decade of considerably faster growth than presently expected. Similarly, apprehensions about the impact of new technology on developing countries should be balanced against the opportunities that it holds out to them;

(f) The internationalization of the world economy has been going on for a very long time, but it is only in recent years that technological advances in communication and transportation have created a global community not even dreamed of when the United Nations was born. The full implications of the pressure from an increasingly global conception of major investments and economic operations are yet to be seen. It is difficult at this stage to assess its impact on growth and development in the next decade;

(g) Development does not occur in a social and political vacuum. Profound social change accompanies any transformation in the way that people acquire their livelihood, and change is frequently disruptive. The role of the family as a core unit of social organization is strained, and traditional values are challenged. Cultural and religious factors that hinder modernization reassert themselves sometimes with great force. The status of women is in a state of unprecedented global review. The continued increase in the large numbers living in poverty and those in need of adequate food, shelter, education and health services generates pressures for more rapid social progress. The immediacy of world-wide information about national events has created a new dimension of politics. The violation of human rights is no longer seen as a purely domestic affair. Political systems are in transition: a trend towards decentralization and wider popular participation is tempered by concerns about political stability. The outlook for the 1990s depends not only on economic but also on political and social progress;

(h) The implications of the need for sustainable development may become clearer in the course of the next decade. Environmental concerns facing the world community so far stem mostly from alarming evidence that past and present methods of production inflict serious and sometimes irreparable damage on the ecological system and the biosphere on which the human community depends for its survival. Far less is known about how to guide economic and social progress through channels that will reduce such damage and make it possible to leave the world with better prospects for the future in 2000 than in 1990.

These examples clearly imply that the outlook for the next decade depends vitally on the progress made both in national policy-making and in international co-operation. It is impossible to look forward to the 1990s without the impression that the confrontation between the forces making for an internationalization of the world economy and those seeking to retain a measure of national and local autonomy will be intensified and have to find new solutions and compromises. The future of the world economy has not been decided, and no study can reveal it. There are limits to the possible, but they are wide. At one extreme, there is the spectre of stagnation and environmental disaster. At the other extreme, there are opportunities for relieving poverty, improving the quality of life, safeguarding the environment for future generations, stabilizing the world economy, and moving towards a global community. Neither perspective can be dismissed as impossible. The world's actual course in the vast gulf between them will be decided by how individual people, countries, and the international community meet these challenges.

EXPLANATORY
NOTES

The designations employed and the presentation of the materials in this publication do not imply the expression of any opinion whatsoever on the part of the United Nations Secretariat concerning the legal status of any country, territory, city or area or of its authorities, or concerning the delimitation of its frontiers or boundaries.

The term "country" as used in the text of this report also refers, as appropriate, to territories or areas.

For analytical purposes, countries have been classified into the following groups:

Eastern Europe and the Soviet Union:	Union of Soviet Socialist Republics, Bulgaria, Czechoslovakia, German Democratic Republic, Hungary, Poland, Romania;
Asian centrally planned economies:	China, Democratic People's Republic of Korea, Mongolia, Viet Nam;
Developed market economies:	North America, southern and western Europe (excluding Cyprus, Malta and Yugoslavia), Australia, Israel, Japan, New Zealand, South Africa;
Developing countries:	Latin America and the Caribbean, Africa (other than South Africa), Asia (excluding China and the centrally planned economies of Asia, Israel

and Japan), Oceania (excluding Australia and
New Zealand), Cyprus, Malta, Yugoslavia.

For particular analyses, the developing countries for which
relevant data are available have been subdivided into the following
groups:

By geographic region

North Africa:	Algeria, Egypt, Libyan Arab Jamahiriya, Morocco, Tunisia;
Sub-Saharan Africa:	Developing countries in Africa, except North Africa;
Latin America and the Caribbean:	Developing countries in the western hemisphere;
Mediterranean:	Cyprus, Malta, Turkey, Yugoslavia;
Western Asia:	Bahrain,[a] Democratic Yemen,[a] Iran (Islamic Republic of), Iraq, Jordan, Kuwait, Lebanon,[a] Oman,[a] Qatar,[a] Saudi Arabia, Syrian Arab Republic, United Arab Emirates,[a] Yemen;[a]
South and East Asia:	Afghanistan,[a] Bangladesh, Bhutan,[a] Democratic Kampuchea,[a] Fiji, Hong Kong, India, Indonesia, Lao People's Democratic Republic,[a] Malaysia, Myanmar, Nepal, Pakistan, Papua New Guinea, Philippines, Republic of Korea, Singapore, Sri Lanka, Taiwan, Province of China, Thailand;

By income level

High-income oil exporters (countries above $11,000 per capita in 1980):	Bahrain,[a] Brunei,[a] Kuwait, Libyan Arab Jamahiriya, Qatar,[a] Saudi Arabia, United Arab Emirates;[a]
Other high-income countries and subregions (between $2,000 and $11,000 per capita in 1980):	Algeria, Argentina, Chile, Cyprus, Gabon, Hong Kong, Iran (Islamic Republic of), Iraq, Malta, Mexico, Singapore, Taiwan, Province of China, Turkey, Uruguay, Venezuela, Western Asian oil importers (Jordan and Syria Arab Republic), Yugoslavia;
Middle-income countries and subregions (between $700 and $2000 per capita in 1980):	Bolivia, Brazil, Central America and the Caribbean, Colombia, Ecuador, Malaysia, Morocco, Nigeria, Paraguay, Peru, Philippines, Republic of Korea, Thailand, Tunisia;
Low-income countries and subregions (below $700 per capita in 1980):	Developing Africa and South and East Asia (except those included in the three preceding income groups); Haiti, Pakistan

By export orientation

Oil-exporting countries:	Angola, Algeria, Bahrain,[a] Brunei,[a] Cameroon, Congo, Ecuador, Egypt, Gabon, Indonesia, Iran (Islamic Republic of), Iraq, Kuwait, Libyan Arab Jamahiriya, Nigeria, Oman,[a] Qatar,[a] Saudi Arabia, Syrian Arab Republic, Trinidad and Tobago, United Arab Emirates,[a] Venezuela;
Major exporters of manufactures:	Brazil, Hong Kong, India, Republic of Korea, Singapore, Taiwan, Province of China, Yugoslavia;
Other manufacturing-oriented countries:	Argentina, Chile, Colombia, Costa Rica, Côte d'Ivoire, Cuba,[a] Cyprus, El Salvador, Guatemala, Malaysia, Malta, Mexico, Morocco, Nicaragua, Pakistan, Paraguay, Peru, Philippines, Sri Lanka, Swaziland, Thailand, Turkey, Uruguay, Zambia, Zimbabwe;
Primary commodity and services exporters (other than the least developed countries):	Bolivia, the Caribbean and Central America, (except those included in the three preceding export groups), Democratic Kampuchea,[a] Fiji, Ghana, Guyana, Jordan, Kenya, Lebanon, Liberia, Madagascar, Mauritius, Mozambique, Namibia, Papua New Guinea, Reunion, Senegal, Seychelles, Solomon Islands, Suriname, Tunisia, Zaire;
Least developed countries:	Afghanistan,[a] Bangladesh, Benin, Bhutan,[a] Botswana, Burkina Faso, Burundi, Cape Verde, Central African Republic, Chad, Comoros, Democratic Yemen,[a] Djibouti, Ethiopia, Equatorial Guinea, Gambia, Guinea, Guinea-Bissau, Haiti, Kiribati,[a] Lao People's Democratic Republic,[a] Lesotho, Malawi, Maldives,[a] Mali, Mauritania, Myanmar, Nepal, Niger, Rwanda, Samoa,[a] Sao Tome and Principe, Sierra Leone, Samolia, Sudan, Togo, Tuvalu,[a] Uganda, United Republic of Tanzania, Vanuatu,[a] Yemen;[a]

Other analytical levels

Highly indebted developing countries:	Argentina, Bolivia, Brazil, Chile, Colombia, Costa Rica, Côte d'Ivoire, Ecuador, Jamaica, Mexico, Morocco, Nigeria, Peru, Philippines, Uruguay, Venezuela, Yugoslavia.

The following tables show the relative share of one grouping in another in terms of gross domestic product (GDP) for the year 1985. For example, from table A it follows that two thirds of the

least developed economies consist of sub-Saharan African countries and one third of South and East Asian countries. Sub-Saharan
Africa consists of countries with different export orientations; oil-
exporting countries account for more than 40 per cent of this
regions's GDP and the least developed countries account for about
a quarter of this region's GDP (table D).

ª Some indicators are not available for these countries and grouping averages are
therefore based on approximations.

TABLE A. *Shares of geographic regions in developing countries grouping
by income level
(in percentages)*

	North Africa	Sub-Saharan Africa	Latin America and the Caribbean	Mediterranean	South and East Asia	Western Asia
High income	7.8	0.4	41.0	14.3	0.1	26.4
Middle income	4.6	9.0	56.7	—	29.8	—
Low income	6.0	23.1	0.3	—	70.6	—
Least developed	—	63.6	1.7	—	34.8	—

TABLE B. *Shares of groupings by income level, in geographic regions
(In percentages)*

	High income	Middle income	Low income
North Africa	56.3	21.2	22.5
Sub-Saharan Africa	2.2	31.8	66.0
Latin America	52.9	47.1	—
Mediterranean	100.0	—	—
South and East Asia	15.3	29.1	55.6
Western Asia	100.0	—	—

TABLE C. *Shares of geographic regions in grouping by export orientation (In percentages)*

	North Africa	Sub-Saharan Africa	Latin America and the Caribbean	Mediterranean	South and East Asia	Western Asia
Oil-exporting	18.2	13.3	11.1	—	14.0	43.3
Major manufacturing exporters	—	—	34.6	10.0	55.5	—
Other manufacturing exporters	2.8	3.1	62.7	10.3	21.2	—
Primary commodities and services exporters	14.1	44.5	30.6	—	5.3	5.4

TABLE D. *Shares of country groupings by export orientation, in geographical regions (In percentages)*

	Oil-exporting	Major manufacturing exporters	Other manufacturing exporters	Primary commodities and services exporters	Least developed countries
North Africa	78.8	—	13.9	7.4	—
Sub-Saharan Africa	43.8	—	11.7	17.7	26.8
Latin America and the Caribbean	8.6	32.0	56.4	2.9	0.2
Mediterranean	—	49.8	50.2	—	—
South and East Asia	12.7	60.3	22.4	0.6	4.0
Western Asia	98.5	—	—	1.5	—

TABLE E. *Shares of country groupings by income level, by export orientation*
(In percentages)

	Low income	Middle income	High income
Oil-exporting	22.1	12.5	65.4
Major manufacturing exporters	29.3	46.6	24.1
Other manufacturing exporters	9.1	28.8	62.1
Primary commodities and services exporters	49.9	44.7	5.4

TABLE F. *Shares of country groupings by export orientation, in groupings by income level*
(In percentages)

	Oil-exporting	Major manufacturing exporters	Other manufacturing exporters	Primary commodities and services exporters	Least developed countries
High income	39.1	17.3	43.2	0.4	—
Middle income	11.7	52.0	31.3	5.0	—
Low income	25.5	40.5	12.2	7.0	14.8

In chapter II, developing countries have been further subdivided in the following groups:

By export orientation

Agricultural exporting economies:	Argentina, Barbados, Colombia, Costa Rica, Côte d'Ivoire, Dominican Republic, El Salvador, Fiji, Ghana, Guatemala, Guyana, Honduras, Kenya, Madagascar, Malaysia, Mauritius, Mozambique, Nicaragua, Panama, Paraguay, Philippines, Reunion, Senegal, Seychelles, Sri Lanka, Swaziland, Thailand, Turkey, Uruguay;
Mineral exporting economies:	Bolivia, Chile, Jamaica Jordan, Liberia, Morocco, Namibia, Papua New Guinea, Peru, Suriname, Tunisia, Zaire, Zambia, Zimbabwe.

Another grouping of developing countries has also been used in chapter II:

By income groups

Countries with per capita income greater than $700 in 1980:	Algeria, Argentina, Barbados, Bolivia, Botswana, Brazil, Chile, Colombia, Congo, Costa Rica, Côte D'Ivoire, Cyprus, Djibouti, Dominican Republic, Ecuador, El Salvador, Fiji, Gabon, Guatemala, Hong Kong, Iran (Islamic Republic of), Iraq, Jamaica, Jordan, Kuwait, Libyan Arab Jamahiriya, Malaysia, Malta, Mauritius, Mexico, Morocco, Namibia, Nicaragua, Nigeria, Panama, Papua New Guinea, Paraguay, Peru, Philippines, Republic of Korea, Reunion, Saudi Arabia, Seychelles, Singapore, Suriname, Swaziland, Syrian Arab Republic, Taiwan, Province of China, Thailand, Trinidad and Tobago, Turkey, Tunisia, Urganda, Uruguay, Venezuela, Yugoslavia, Zimbabwe;
Countries with per capita income greater than $300 but less than $700 in 1980:	Angola, Benin, Cameroon, Cape Verde, Central Africa Republic, Comoros, Egypt, Gambia, Ghana, Guyana, Honduras, Indonesia, Kenya, Liberia, Madagascar, Mauritania, Niger, Pakistan, Sao Tome and Principe, Senegal, Sierra Leone, Somalia, Sudan, Togo, Zambia;
Countries with per capita income less than $300 in 1980:	Bangladesh, Burkina Faso, Burundi, Chad, Ethiopia, Equatorial Guinea, Guinea, Guinea-Bissau, Haiti, India, Lesotho, Malawi, Mali, Mozambique, Myanmar, Nepal, Rwanda, Sri Lanka, United Republic of Tanzania, Zaire.

The term "newly" industrializing economies" refers to Hong Kong, the Republic of Korea, Singapore and Taiwan, Province of China.

The term "dollars" ($) refers to United States dollars unless otherwise indicated.

The term "tons" refers to metric tons unless otherwise indicated.

For more information about United Nations Publications and for a copy of our free catalogue write to:

United Nations Publications
Room DC2-853, Dept. 600
United Nations
New York, N.Y. 10017
Fax No. (212) 963-4116

or

United Nations Publications
Sales Section
Palais des Nations
1211 Geneva 10
Switzerland

Notes

93166—March 1993—2.5M